The Books of Moses Revisited

# The Books of Moses Revisited

PAUL LAWRENCE

WIPF & STOCK · Eugene, Oregon

THE BOOKS OF MOSES REVISITED

Copyright © 2011 Paul Lawrence. All rights reserved. Except for brief quotations in critical publications or reviews, no part of this book may be reproduced in any manner without prior written permission from the publisher. Write: Permissions, Wipf & Stock 199 W. 8th Ave., Suite 3, Eugene, OR 97401.

Wipf & Stock
An Imprint of Wipf and Stock Publishers
199 W. 8th Ave., Suite 3
Eugene, OR 97401

www.wipfandstock.com

ISBN: 978-1-61097-417-2

Manufactured in the U.S.A.

# Contents

*List of Maps* / vi
*List of Tables* / vii
*Acknowledgments* / ix
*List of Abbreviations* / x
*Introduction* / xv

**Chapter 1** Moses and the Pentateuch / 1
**Chapter 2** The World of Moses / 18
**Chapter 3** Genesis / 29
**Chapter 4** Patterns in the Pentateuchal Covenants and the Late Second Millennium Hittite Treaties / 47
**Chapter 5** Detail, Detail: The Heart of the Matter / 65
**Chapter 6** The Rest of the Pentateuch / 95
**Chapter 7** On Kidnapping, Oxen, and Fruit Trees: A Few Specific Laws / 102
**Chapter 8** Wider Horizons: A Comparison with Epic Poems of the Ancient World / 107
**Chapter 9** Conclusion / 120

**Appendix 1** Chronology / 129
**Appendix 2** List of Ancient Law Collections and Treaties / 132
**Appendix 3** A Possible Outline of the Pentateuch / 137

*Bibliography* / 147
*Index of Ancient Sources* / 153
*Index of Scripture* / 155
*Index of Subjects* / 159

# Maps

1. The World of Moses
2. Hittite Treaty Partners 1380–1180 BC
3. Find Spots of Treaties
4. Find Spots of Law Collections

# Tables

1. The English names of the books of the Pentateuch
2. The Hebrew names of the books of the Pentateuch
3. The books of the Pentateuch in the Dead Sea Scrolls
4. Summary: History of the Pentateuch text
5. A summary of the Documentary Hypothesis
6. The Flood story divided between sources P and J
7. The dates of the Patriarchs
8. "These are the generations of" formulae as markers of documents
9. The Table of the Nations and the List of the Rulers of Edom within the Genesis documents
10. Genesis divided by the Table of the Nations and the List of the Rulers of Edom
11. Egyptian loan-words in Gen 41
12. Treaties in Genesis
13. The treaty between Abraham and Abimelech Gen 21
14. The treaty between Zimri-Lim of Mari and Atamrum of Andarig
15. The covenant between the LORD and Abraham
16. The treaty between Abba-An of Aleppo and Yarim-Lim of Alalakh
17. Deuteronomy as a covenant document
18. Exodus/Leviticus as a covenant document (with extra material)
19. Exodus/Leviticus as a covenant document (without extra material)
20. Exodus/Leviticus and Deuteronomy as covenant documents
21. Treaty of Shattiwaza of Mitanni and the Hittite king Suppiluliuma I
22. Deuteronomy as a covenant document
23. The Succession Treaty of Esarhaddon, 672 BC
24. Comparison between Deuteronomy and the Succession Treaty of Esarhaddon, 672 BC
25. The Laws of Lipit-Ishtar (1934–1924 BC)

26. The Laws of Hammurabi (1792–1750 BC)
27. The Laws of Hammurabi compared with the Treaty of Shamshi-Adad V
28. The number of Stipulations in ancient Near Eastern Law Collections
29. A comparison between the curses in Deut 28 and the Succession Treaty of Esarhaddon, 672 BC
30. A comparison between the curses in Deut 28 and the Laws of Hammurabi
31. Egyptian loan-words in Exod 2:3
32. Egyptian loan-words in the high priest's breastpiece (Exod 28:17–20)
33. Akkadian loan-words in the high priest's breastpiece (Exod 28:17–20)
34. Textual transmission of the Story of Sinuhe
35. Textual transmission of the *Epic of Gilgamesh*
36. The *Epic of Gilgamesh*
37. Textual transmission of the *Iliad*
38. Additions to the *Iliad*
39. The similarity of the transmission of Homer's *Iliad* and the Pentateuch
40. Evidence for a Second Millennium date for the Pentateuch
41. Evidence for subsequent updating of Pentateuch
42. Genesis according to the JEDP Hypothesis and the Eleven Document Hypothesis

# Acknowledgments

SPECIAL THANKS ARE DUE to Professors K. A. Kitchen and A. R. Millard for their invaluable comments and constructive criticisms and also to Hugh Hollinghurst for his helpful insights into the Homeric Epics. I would also like to thank David Back, Kevin Bidwell, Eric Corcoran, James Dannenberg, Wolfgang Ertl, Lindsay Ferguson, Mark Higginbotham, Daniel Hill, Jonathan Jarvis, my wife Jane Lawrence, Geoffrey Lewis, Sean Logan, Nicholas Lunn, Richard and Gillian Midmer, John Roberts, Simon Rock, Graham Slattery, Tony Taylor, Paul Watts and Richard Worsley for reading the manuscript and making many useful comments. Thanks too are due to Jon Robinson for his help with computer problems. Any errors that remain are entirely the fault of the author. I would also like to thank the Institute of Aegean Prehistory for financing me to assist Professor Kitchen in writing *Treaty, Law and Covenant in the Ancient Near East*. This material has made the biggest contribution to this book.

# Abbreviations

| | |
|---|---|
| *AB* | Anchor Bible (commentary series). New York: Doubleday, 1964ff. |
| *ABD* | *The Anchor Bible Dictionary.* 6 vols. Edited by David Noel Freedman. New York: Doubleday, 1992. |
| *ANET* | *Ancient Near Eastern Texts relating to the Old Testament.* 2nd ed. Edited by J. B. Pritchard. Princeton UP, 1955. |
| *AnSt* | *Anatolian Studies.* |
| *ARAB* | *Ancient Records of Assyria and Babylonia.* Chicago UP, 1926. |
| *ARI* | *Assyrian Royal Inscriptions.* Wiesbaden: Harrassowitz, 1976. |
| *BA* | *Biblical Archaeologist.* |
| *BEAWNP* | *Brill's Encyclopaedia of the Ancient World.* Leiden: New Pauly, Brill, 2002. |
| *BT* | *The Bible Translator.* |
| C | Century. |
| *CAD* | *Chicago Assyrian Dictionary*, edited by A. L. Oppenheim et al. Chicago Oriental Institute (and latterly several other publishers), 1956ff. |
| *CAH* | *Cambridge Ancient History.* Cambridge UP. |

| | |
|---|---|
| CoS | *The Context of Scripture*. 3 vols. Edited by W. W. Hallo and K. L. Younger. Leiden/Boston/Cologne: Brill, 1997, 2000, 2002. |
| D | The Deuteronomist source. |
| DOTP | *Dictionary of the Old Testament: Pentateuch*. Downer's Grove: IVP, 2003. |
| E | Elohist source. |
| Eg. | Egyptian. |
| ESV | English Standard Version, 2001. |
| GNT | Good News Translation (Today's English Version), 1976. |
| HALOT | *The Hebrew and Aramaic Lexicon of the Old Testament*. Edited by L. Koehler and W. Baumgartner, translated by M. E. J. Richardson. Leiden/Boston/Cologne: Brill, 2001. |
| ICC | *International Critical Commentary*. |
| IDB | *The Interpreter's Dictionary of the Bible*. 4 vols. Edited by George Arthur Buttrick. Nashville: Abingdon, 1962. |
| IDBSup | *The Interpreter's Dictionary of the Bible. Supplementary Volume*. Edited by Keith Crim. Nashville: Abingdon, 1976. |
| Il. | The *Iliad*. |
| IllBD | *Illustrated Bible Dictionary*. Leicester: IVP, 1980. |
| J | Jahwist source. |
| JANES | *Journal of the Ancient Near Eastern Society of Columbia University*. |
| JBL | *Journal of Biblical Literature*. |
| JETS | *Journal of the Evangelical Theological Society*. |
| M | Millennium. |
| NASB | New American Standard Bible, 1971. |

| | | |
|---|---|---|
| *NCB* | | New Century Bible (commentary series). |
| NEB | | New English Bible, 1970. |
| *NICOT* | | *New International Commentary on the Old Testament.* |
| NIV | | New International Version, 1978. |
| *NIV Study Bible* | | New International Version Study Bible. London: Hodder and Stoughton, 1987. |
| NJPS | | *Tanakh the Holy Scriptures: The New JPS Translation According to the Traditional Hebrew Text.* Philadelphia/New York: Jewish Publication Society, 1988. |
| NRSV | | New Revised Standard Version, 1989. |
| Obv. | | The front face of a cuneiform tablet. |
| *Od.* | | The *Odyssey.* |
| OLA | | Orientalia Lovaniensia Analecta. Leuven (Louvain). |
| *OROT* | | *On the Reliability of the Old Testament.* Grand Rapids: Eerdmans, 2003. |
| *OTL* | | Old Testament Library (commentary series). |
| OTS | | *Oudtestamentische Studien.* |
| P | | The Priestly Writer. |
| *PEQ* | | *Palestine Exploration Quarterly.* |
| REB | | Revised English Bible, 1989. |
| Rev. | | The back face of a cuneiform tablet. |
| *RITA* | | *Ramesside Inscriptions Translated and Annotated, Translations.* Oxford: Blackwell, 1998ff. |
| *RLA* | | *Reallexikon der Assyriologie.* Berlin: de Gruyter, 1928ff. |
| RSV | | Revised Standard Version, 1952. |
| *SPCK* | | Society for Promoting Christian Knowledge (commentary series). |

| | |
|---|---|
| *TC* | Tyndale Commentary. |
| *TLC* | *Treaty Law and Covenant in the Ancient Near East*. K. A. Kitchen and P. J. N. Lawrence. Three volumes (unpublished). |
| TNIV | Today's New International Version, 2004. |
| UP | University Press. |
| *WBC* | Word Biblical Commentary. |
| ZA | *Zeitschrift für Assyriologie*. |

# Introduction

THE FIRST FIVE BOOKS of the Bible, often called Genesis, Exodus, Leviticus, Numbers, and Deuteronomy, are foundational texts to both Judaism and Christianity. Islam also makes reference to many incidents recorded in these books. Traditionally the authorship of these books has been ascribed to Moses, who is the leader credited with rescuing Israel from slavery in Egypt sometime in the second half of the second millennium BC. This book attempts to revisit the "Books of Moses," focusing on the question "Who is the author?"

After examining the question in Jewish tradition and the New Testament we shall look at the development of a commonly held view, called the "Documentary Hypothesis" (or the "JEDP Hypothesis"), which holds that these books are a pastiche of sources compiled hundreds of years after Moses is supposed to have lived. By looking in particular at treaties of the late Second Millennium BC made between the Hittites (of what is now Turkey) and the surrounding states, it shall be shown that there is much evidence to support a late second millennium BC date for the "Books of Moses" and that therefore the "Documentary Hypothesis" is an inadequate explanation of their origin.

# Chapter 1

## Moses and the Pentateuch

### MOSES

A THREE-MONTH-OLD BABY BOY lies in a basket among some reeds growing along the bank of the Nile. The baby is a Hebrew baby. The king of Egypt has ordered that all Hebrew baby boys be thrown into the Nile. This baby, however, is discovered by none other than Pharaoh's daughter, who adopts him, while allowing the baby's own mother to bring him up. The baby is called Moses,[1] which sounds like the Hebrew for "to draw out."[2]

Moses grew up at the court of Pharaoh. Doubtless he received a good education, but at the age of forty he had to flee to Midian, the northeastern part of Arabia, east of the Red Sea,[3] where he spent the next forty years.[4]

Then one day the LORD[5] appears to Moses in a burning bush and commissions him to rescue his people from slavery in Egypt.[6] So Moses

---

1. Hebrew Mōše (Moshe).

2. *HALOT*, 642b. The commonly advanced identification with the Egyptian name *mś(w)* meaning "child" cannot be defended linguistically; see further Muchiki, *Egyptian Proper Names*, 216–17; Kitchen, *OROT*, 297. For these events see Exod 2:1–10.

3. For map, see *IllBD*, 998a.

4. That Moses was forty years old at the time of his flight to Midian is recorded in Stephen's speech in Acts 7:23. The question has to be asked if the division of Moses' life into three forty-year periods represents some kind of literary convention, hitherto not fully understood, rather than exact chronological information.

5. For further, see p. 14 n 53.

6. Exod 2:11—4:17. For Old Testament references the English system is adopted,

returns to Egypt, aged eighty.[7] The LORD sends ten dramatic plagues and Moses leads his people out of Egypt, but the Egyptian army follows the Israelites in hot pursuit.[8]

The LORD opens up a path for Israel across the Reed Sea,[9] but the Egyptian army is drowned as the returning waters overwhelm it.[10] The Exodus of the Israelites from Egypt is arguably the most significant event in Old Testament history and the one that constituted Israel into a people and affirmed Moses as its leader.

Moses then leads the Israelites through the Sinai desert for nearly forty years before he dies on Mount Nebo[11] overlooking the Promised Land.[12]

The book of Deuteronomy closes with this epitaph for Moses:

> *Since then, no prophet has arisen in Israel like Moses, whom the LORD knew face to face, who did all those miraculous signs and wonders the LORD sent him to do in Egypt—to Pharaoh and to all his officials and to his whole land. For no one has ever shown the mighty power or performed the awesome deeds that Moses did in the sight of all Israel.* (Deut 34:10–12 (NIV[13] slightly modified)

---

rather than the system used in the Hebrew Bible that at times is different.

7. Exod 7:7. See p. 1 n 4.

8. Exod 7:14–14:4.

9. This is simply a literal translation of the Hebrew *yam sūp̄*, rendered *Erythra Thalassa* "Red Sea" by the Septuagint (Greek Old Testament) and the New Testament (Acts 7:36; Heb 11:29); this in turn suggests a location of one of the shallow lakes to the north of the Gulf of Suez, where salt-tolerating reeds and rushes (halophytes) are known to grow. See further Hoffmeier, *Israel in Egypt*, 199–222; Lawrence, *Atlas of Bible History*, 35.

10. Exod 14:5–15:21.

11. Perhaps Mount Nebo is to be identified with Jebel en-Neba (835m) in modern Jordan some sixteen km east from the northern end of the Dead Sea. It commands extensive views from the glistening white peak of Mount Hermon in Lebanon/Syria to the southern end of the Dead Sea shimmering away over a thousand meters below.

12. Deut 34:1–5. Moses' age at death is given as 120 in Deut 5:7, see p. 1 n 4.

13. The NIV is the Bible version commonly cited in this work, unless a more literal version is required, in which case the ESV is quoted. The slight modification is "risen" to "arisen."

## THE BIBLICAL TEXTS AS TEXTS TRANSMITTED IN MANUSCRIPT

Traditionally Christians and Jews have assigned to Moses the authorship[14] of the first five books of the Bible, now commonly known by their largely Greek names of Genesis, Exodus, Leviticus, Numbers, and Deuteronomy thus:

Table 1. The English names of the books of the Pentateuch

| Greek name | English name | Meaning |
|---|---|---|
| Genesis | Genesis | "origin," "source," "birth," "generation" |
| Exodos | Exodus | "going out" |
| Leuitikon | Leviticus | "relating to the (priestly tribe) of Levi"[A] |
| Arithmoi | Numbers | "numbers"[B] |
| Deuteronomion | Deuteronomy | "reiteration of the (original) law (for the next generation)" |

A. Leviticus may mean "priestly" in general. Levine "Leviticus," 312a.
B. Numbers, Greek (*Arithmoi*), is literally translated into English, though "census" would be a more accurate name.

In the Hebrew Bible the books are known by the opening words of each book thus:[15]

---

14. The terms "authorship" and "author" in this work are not to be understood (in the modern sense) of someone responsible for the writing of every word in a given text. Cases will be adduced of where the "author" appears to have used existing sources (pp. 30–32) and where redactors (editors) may have updated the text (pp. 32–33, 99), but it should not be assumed that redactors totally subsumed the work of earlier authors. The "author," as a prophet (Exod 7:1), may have dictated his words in the first person ("I, Moses") to a scribe who transcribed his words in the third person ("Moses ... he ... "), hence the predominance of the third person in the Pentateuch, (and the rest of the Old Testament). The third person encourages authorial invisibility and anonymity, as Ska has noted in *Our Fathers Have Told Us*, 45, "In the Bible, most of the time ... the narrator remains invisible and undramatised."

15. This was a convention also adopted in ancient Mesopotamia, where the *Epic of Gilgamesh* was called *ša naqba īmuru* "He who saw the deep" and the Creation Epic *enuma eliš* "When on high."

Table 2. The Hebrew names of the books of the Pentateuch

| Hebrew name | English translation | Traditional English name |
|---|---|---|
| $b^e$-rēšît | In the beginning | Genesis |
| $w^e$-ēlle š$^e$môt | And these are the names | Exodus |
| way-yiqrā | And he called | Leviticus |
| bam-mi$\underline{d}$bār | In the wilderness[c] | Numbers |
| ēlle had-d$^e$$\underline{b}$ārîm | These are the words | Deuteronomy |

c. This is not the opening word in Hebrew, but a phrase taken from the first verse.

In some traditions[16] these books are called "the Books of Moses." Genesis is even called 1. Moses, Exodus, 2. Moses, and so on. Collectively they are sometimes called the "Pentateuch," a Greek word meaning "five-volumed."[17]

Although there are no extant originals of the Pentateuch, manuscripts of this important text have been transmitted for many centuries. The text of the Priestly Blessing of Numbers 6:24–26, is quoted among other material on two tiny silver amulets from Ketef Hinnom on the outskirts of Jerusalem. These amulets are dated by archaeological context to the late seventh century BC, and are thus the earliest attested citation of any pentateuchal text.[18] All five books of the Pentateuch are partially attested among the collection of biblical texts[19] and other religious literature[20] commonly known as the "Dead Sea Scrolls." This collection was found in caves near the western shore of the Dead Sea. Its oldest text is probably the Leviticus scroll dating from the third century BC. Some argue that the Dead Sea Scrolls were deposited in the caves near the Dead Sea as early as the mid first century BC, as the non-biblical texts make no allusions to events after that time.[21] Others citing paleographic

---

16. E.g., German 1 Mose, 2 Mose, etc.
17. Liddell and Scott, *English-Greek Lexicon*, 1175b.
18. Schneidewind, *How the Bible Became a Book*, 105; Picture in Lawrence, *Atlas of Bible History*, 12.
19. Conveniently presented in Abegg et al., *Dead Sea Scrolls Bible*.
20. For which see Vermes, *Complete Dead Sea Scrolls in English*.
21. Young, *Gilgameš and the World of Assyria*, 175. There is thus no reason to suppose that the scrolls were written in the first century, certainly not as late as AD 68 when the Roman army destroyed the nearby settlement of Qumran.

(handwriting style) evidence date at least one of the pentateuchal scrolls to the early years of the first century AD.[22]

It should be emphasized that even though all five books of the Pentateuch are found among the Dead Sea Scrolls, the collection only provides us with a partial text of them thus:

Table 3. The books of the Pentateuch in the Dead Sea Scrolls

| Book | Number of manuscripts | % of text covered by DSS |
|---|---|---|
| Genesis | 24 | 21 |
| Exodus | 18 | 64 |
| Leviticus | 16 | 58 |
| Numbers | 11 | 41 |
| Deuteronomy | 33 | 71 |

The so-called "Nash Papyrus" from Egypt should also be mentioned, in passing. This is a liturgical or devotional version of the Ten Commandments (Exod 20:2–17 and Deut 5:6–21), dated to second or first century BC.[23]

In the fifth and sixth centuries AD a group of Jewish scholars became alarmed at the diminishing use and understanding of Hebrew, so they added a series of vowel points under the consonants, so as not to break up the consonantal text, which they regarded as sacred. These scholars were called Masoretes (from the Hebrew "*masōrā*"—"tradition") and the text they produced is called the "Masoretic Text." This text, exemplified by its three principal manuscripts,[24] still remains the base text for the Pentateuch. A consonantal text virtually identical to the Masoretic Text can be traced back to some (but by no means all) of the Dead Sea Scrolls in the second century BC. It was the text used for the commentaries found among the Dead Sea Scrolls, which suggests it had already been accorded canonical status.

---

22. Cross, *Encyclopaedia of the Dead Sea Scrolls*, 631a, dates the 11Q1 Leviticus scroll to AD 1–50.

23. Würtwein, *Text of the Old Testament*, 33, 132.

24. In chronological order (1) The British Library Pentateuch, Or.4445, late ninth century AD; (2) The Aleppo Codex 96.85/221A, ca. AD 930, but for the Pentateuch only Deut 28:17—34:12 is preserved; (3) The St. Petersburg Codex, B19A, dated by five separate colophons (scribal notes about the writing of the text) [see p. 30 n 3] variously AD 1008–1010. The latter forms the basis of the standard critical edition of the Hebrew Bible the *Biblia Hebraica Stuttgartensia*.

The Pentateuch was probably the first part of the Old Testament to be translated into Greek. The commissioning of the so-called Septuagint translation is traditionally[25] ascribed to the Egyptian king Ptolemy II (285–246 BC) who wanted every piece of world literature to grace his newly established library at Alexandria.[26]

So in summary:

Table 4. Summary: History of the Pentateuch text

| | |
|---|---|
| Earliest citation of a portion of text in the archaeological record | Ketef Hinnom amulets late 7th C BC |
| Earliest extant scroll | 3rd C BC |
| First translation | Septuagint—early 3rd C BC |
| Creation of standard edition | Masoretic Text 5th–6th C AD, but it can be traced back to Dead Sea Scrolls 250 BC–mid 1st C BC |
| Earliest extant standard text | Late 9th C AD |

## WHEN DID MOSES LIVE?

When did Moses live? The issue is one that has perplexed and divided Bible scholars. Essentially there are two schools of thought:

1. Those who take the Pentateuch itself as their primary evidence give primacy to Exod 1:11, which states that the Israelites, while slaves in Egypt, built the store cities of Pithom and Rameses. The reference to Rameses suggests that it was the famous Egyptian pharaoh Ramesses II (1279–1213 BC)[27] who commissioned these

---

25. According to the *Letter of Aristeas* (first century BC or earlier).

26. We should note in passing the curious matter of a scroll of Deuteronomy that a certain Moses Wilhelm Shapira claimed to have discovered in 1883 in a cave near the Dead Sea. Shapira, known to have been involved in faking a number of artifacts, claimed a ninth-century BC date for his scroll, but well-known scholars of the time, Clermont-Ganneau and Ginsberg declared it a forgery. The manuscript is now apparently lost, though some scholars think it was a genuine ancient text, but not as old as Shapira claimed. Christensen, *WBC Deuteronomy* (lxii).

27. This work uses Rameses for the name of the city and Ramesses for the king. It follows the conventional chronology for Egypt of Kitchen, *Synchronisation of Civilisations*, 39–51. It should be pointed out that the evidence presented in this work relating to the historical development of treaties does not support proposed chronological revisions such as those of Rohl, *A Test of Time*, and James, *Centuries of Darkness* (among others).

cities.²⁸ The exodus is thus placed in his reign, commonly at ca. 1270 BC and the conquest of Canaan forty years later in ca. 1230 BC. The approximately 120 year life of Moses, attributed to him by the Pentateuch itself, is thus placed ca. 1350–1230 BC.²⁹ This is the position adopted in this book.³⁰

2. Those who take several chronological statements made by Bible writers at face value, (but who are perhaps unaware of ancient methods of chronological computation), argue for a date of the exodus in 1447 BC.³¹ Moses is thus placed ca. 1527–1407 BC.

Although, as I shall argue, the balance of evidence cited in this book relating to the treaty-covenant pattern also supports a thirteenth-century BC exodus, this book is not primarily concerned with the date of the exodus. Its primary conclusion that the Pentateuch is a Second Millennium BC document, not a First Millennium BC document, is not affected by either placement.³²

## LATER TRADITIONS

That Moses was regarded as the author of parts if not all of the Pentateuch was a view advanced by the writers of the New Testament and Jewish

---

28. Ramesses I can probably be ruled out as he only reigned for one year 1295–1294 BC.

29. This is based on Moses being eighty at the time of the exodus (Exod 7:7) and thirty-eight years of wandering in the wilderness (Deut 2:14).

30. The ten-generation genealogy from Aaron to Zadok given in 1Chr 6:3–8 also suggests only some 300 years from Moses to Solomon.

31. 1 Kgs 6:1 *"In the 480th year after the Israelites came out of Egypt, in the fourth year of Solomon's reign . . . he began to build the temple of the LORD"* is often quoted. The fourth year of the reign of Solomon is known to have been 967 BC, thus giving 1447 BC for the date of the exodus. However, some argue that the 480 (actually only 479) years need not be taken literally, being seen either as representing twelve generations, calculated at forty years each, which in reality were significantly shorter or which overlapped or as the total length of the periods of Israelite rule recorded in the book of Judges, which are known to have been partly overlapping. See Table 28 in Kitchen, *OROT*, 309. Other chronological statements such as Judg 11:26 and Acts 13:20 are also sometimes cited.

32. Adherents to an early exodus, ca. 1447 BC, are urged not to dismiss this work simply because it does not endorse their beliefs.

tradition, as exemplified by the Apocrypha,[33] the Mishnah,[34] and the historian Flavius Josephus.

### The View of the New Testament

In the New Testament Jesus regarded Moses as the author of the Ten Commandments:

> For Moses said, "Honor your father and your mother," and, "Anyone who curses his father or mother must be put to death." Mark 7:10 (NIV) quoting Exod 20:12 and Deut 5:16

Similarly both Peter and Paul regarded Moses as the author of the book of Deuteronomy. Thus Peter:

> For Moses said, "The Lord your God will raise up for you a prophet like me from among your own people; you must listen to everything he tells you. Anyone who does not listen to him will be completely cut off from among his people." Acts 3:22–23 (NIV) quoting Deut 18:15,18,19

And Paul:

> For it is written in the Law of Moses: "Do not muzzle an ox while it is treading out the grain." 1 Cor 9:9 (NIV) quoting Deut 25:4

### The View of the Apocrypha

In the Apocryphal Book of Ecclesiasticus (also known as the Wisdom of Jesus, son of Sirach) 24:23, Moses' authorship of the Book of the Covenant[35] (Exod 20:1—23:19) is clearly affirmed thus:

> All this is the book of the covenant of God Most High, the law laid on us by Moses. (REB)

---

33. The Apocrypha is a collection of Jewish writings, now preserved in Greek, written in the period between the Old and New Testaments.

34. The Mishnah is a codification of Jewish oral law.

35. The word "covenant" represents the Hebrew bᵉrît, an agreement made between God and his people.

### The View of the Mishnah

The Mishnah similarly affirms that it was Moses who received the Law on Mount Sinai and who handed it down to Joshua: So the third century work the "Sayings of the Fathers" (*Pirqê Abōt*) begins:

> Moses received the Law from Sinai and handed it down to Joshua, and Joshua to the elders, and the elders to the prophets and the prophets handed it down to the men of the great synagogue. (*Pirqê Abōt* 1.1)

### The View of Flavius Josephus

The first-century historian Flavius Josephus (AD 37/38—ca. 100) in *Antiquities of the Jews* 1.29 ascribes the beginning of Genesis to Moses:

> This then should be the first day, but Moses spoke of it as [day] one. (Referring to Gen 1:5)

## THROUGHOUT THE CENTURIES

Throughout the centuries several have pointed out passages in the Pentateuch that they believed were interpolations and thus added later than Moses. The classic case is Deuteronomy 34,[36] the account of Moses' own death. However, the belief that Moses was the author of the Pentateuch was not seriously questioned until the eighteenth century.

## PENTATEUCHAL CRITICISM BEFORE WELLHAUSEN

Modern pentateuchal criticism[37] can be traced back to a Frenchman, Jean Astruc. He was private physician to Louis XV (1715–74) and Professor of Medicine in Paris.[38] In 1753 Astruc published a book in which he argued there were two distinct sources in the book of Genesis based on the two main names of God in the book. These eventually became known as the J or (Jahwist) and the E or (Elohist) sources. Astruc maintained that Moses

---

36. The writer says, "*but to this day no one knows where his grave is*" (34:6), but this gives no clue as to date.

37. Summarized in Ska, *Introduction to Reading the Pentateuch*, 98–126.

38. For further biographical information on Jean Astruc, see Smend, *From Astruc to Zimmerli*, 1–14.

was the author of Genesis. According to Astruc, Moses simply combined two main sources, later termed J and E.[39]

In 1798 Karl David Ilgen posited a second E or Elohist source. This was first called the Younger Elohist, but it later became known as P for "the Priestly Writer" (following Abraham Kuenen in 1869).[40]

In 1805 another source was proposed by Wilhelm Martin Leberecht de Wette.[41] This was the so-called D (or Deuteronomist) source.

The Book of the Law found by Judah's king Josiah in the Temple in 621 BC was the book known as Deuteronomy. However, the essence of de Wette's contention was that this book had not been written by Moses,[42] but by the priests in the years immediately before 621 BC. It was this suggestion of a late D source that significantly altered the landscape of pentateuchal criticism. He was thus suggesting that part of the Pentateuch was written some 600 years after the period in which it is argued Moses lived.

## JULIUS WELLHAUSEN

The final stage in the formulation of the Documentary Hypothesis, as it came to be known, comes from the work of the German professor Julius Wellhausen.[43] Between 1876 and 1883[44] Wellhausen proposed that the detail and genealogy-loving Priestly Writer (often called P) lived after the Babylonian exile, perhaps a contemporary of Ezra and Nehemiah in the mid fifth century BC. Now it was being suggested that part of the Pentateuch was written some 800 years after the period in which it is argued Moses lived. Finally the various sources were put together by a redactor (i.e., an editor), who also occasionally left his mark on the text. It is disputed whether there was one redactor or two and when they might have done their work, but such refinements need not concern us. In formulating his views Wellhausen was governed by his own view of the development of Israelite religion in which the prophets came first, then the law with its emphasis on ritual and priesthood.

39. Astruc, *Conjectures*, 1753.
40. Ilgen, *Die Urkunden*, 1798.
41. de Wette, *Dissertatio* and *Beiträge*. For further biographical information on Wilhelm de Wette, see Smend, *From Astruc to Zimmerli*, 43–56.
42. So 2 Chr 34:14.
43. For further biographical information on Julius Wellhausen, see ibid., 91–102.
44. Wellhausen, *Die Composition*; *Prologomena*; *Geschichte Israels*.

## THE DOCUMENTARY HYPOTHESIS

In summary, according to the classic Documentary Hypothesis, the Pentateuch was composed of four distinct sources: the Jahwist (or J) source, written about 850 BC; the Elohist (or E) source, written about 750 BC; the Deuteronomist (or D) source, written just before 621 BC; and the Priestly (or P) source, written in the mid fifth century BC. This can be further summarized in table form thus:

Table 5. A summary of the Documentary Hypothesis

| |
|---|
| J ca. 850 BC |
| E ca. 750 BC |
| D just before 621 BC |
| P fifth century BC |

The Documentary Hypothesis is sometimes called the "JEDP Hypothesis" after the order in which the documents are supposed to have been written. In modern formulations of the JEDP Hypothesis the use of different divine names is less significant, supposed vocabulary and stylistic preferences are given more weight. Where similar accounts of similar incidents exist, for example Abraham passing off Sarah as his sister to Pharaoh in Gen 12:11–19 and to Abimelech, king of Gerar, in Gen 20:2–5, these are assigned to different sources.

## OTHER LINES OF ENQUIRY NOT PURSUED IN DETAIL

The focus of this work is thus to compare the Pentateuch with *external* material rather than look at supposed vocabulary and stylistic preferences allegedly discernible within the text, since this kind of reasoning is often circular. Stylistic criteria such as supposed vocabulary preferences are used to assign passages to J, E, D or P. Thus D is supposedly characterized by exhortations to obedience; P is dry, precise, and full of detail.[45] The Hebrew words *berît* and *qāhāl*, "covenant" and "assembly" respectively, are assigned to D, whereas P has *ʿēdut* and *ʿēdā* for the above. Mount

---

45. Style is notoriously difficult to evaluate objectively, but most texts have considerable stylistic variation, simply to avoid monotony. Furthermore, these styles are not unique to Israel. A Deuteronomic style is found in second millennium texts from Ugarit in Syria and in Assyrian inscriptions of Tukulti-Ninurta I (1244–1208 BC) and Tiglath-pileser I (1115–1077 BC) (see further Niehaus, "Joshua and Ancient warfare," 45–50) and Priestly style writing can be traced within Egyptian and Urartian (from E Anatolia) texts. Kitchen, *Ancient Orient and Old Testament*, 125.

Horeb (for Mount Sinai) is regarded as a peculiarity of D. The pronoun *ānōkî* "I" is seen as a characteristic of J, E, and D, whereas *ᵃnî* (also "I") is a characteristic of P.[46] It is also beyond the remit of this work to attempt to date the vocabulary of the Pentateuch.[47] Neither does this work address the issue of verbal allusions to the Pentateuch in other Old Testament books. In the story of the Levite seeking hospitality in a town of Benjamin, told in Judges 19:22–23, there are many resonances, some overtly verbal, to the coming of the angels to Sodom in Genesis 19:4–8. This strongly suggests that the Genesis story was known to the writer of Judges.[48]

## THREE EXAMPLES OF THE DOCUMENTARY HYPOTHESIS

It is helpful to see how the Documentary Hypothesis is commonly applied. Here are three examples from the book of Genesis:

### Gen 37:1–5

Here all three suggested sources, J, E, and P are combined thus:

P  *Jacob lived in the land where his father had stayed, the land of Canaan. This is the account of Jacob. Joseph, a young man of seventeen,*

J  *was tending the flocks with his brothers, the sons of Bilhah and the sons of Zilpah, his father's wives, and he brought their father a bad report about them. Now Israel loved Joseph more than any of his other sons, because he had been born to him in his old age; and he made a richly ornamented robe for him. When his brothers saw that their father loved him more than any of them, they hated him and could not speak a kind word to him.*

E  *Joseph had a dream, and when he told it to his brothers, they hated him all the more.*

---

46. However, both these forms are intermixed in Ugaritic texts from the fourteenth century BC. Walker, *A tribute to Gleason Archer*, 36.

47. The latter issue is one that Kitchen and this author hope to address at a future date. Preliminary results from a consideration of the vocabulary of Deuteronomy, show that 699 of the 1,285 individual words identifiable in the book can be found in non-Hebrew texts from the third and second millennia (54.4 per cent of the whole), whereas only 97 words can be found exclusively in first millennium non-Hebrew texts (7.5 percent). 454 examples (35.4 per cent) of the vocabulary of Deuteronomy have no parallels outside of the Hebrew material and 35 (2.7 percent) require further investigation.

48. I am grateful to Lunn for pointing this out to me. See further Burney, *Book of Judges*, 443–44.

## Gen 6:9—9:19

According to the Documentary hypothesis the Flood Story of Gen 6:9—9:19 alternates between the P source and the J source thus:

Table 6. The Flood story divided between sources P and J

| Sections assigned to P | Sections assigned to J |
|---|---|
| 6:9–22 | 7:1–5 |
| 7:6–11 | 7:12 |
| 7:13–16a | 7:16b–17 |
| 7:18–21 | 7:22–23 |
| 7:24—28:2a | 8:2b–3a |
| 8:3b–5 | 8:6–12 |
| 8:13a | 8:13b |
| 8:14–19 | 8:20–22 |
| 9:1–17 | 9:18–19 |

However, division of the text into multiple sources obscures the literary pattern that is present in the text. B. W. Anderson[49] argues that the same passage Gen 6:1—9:19 (The account of the Flood) is structured as a large chiasm[50] thus:

Transitional introduction (6:9-10)
    Violence in creation (6:11–12)
        First divine speech: resolve to destroy (6:13–22)
            Second divine speech: "enter ark" (7:1–10)
                Beginning of the flood (7:11–16)
                      The rising flood (7:17–24)
                          FOCUS God remembers Noah (8:1a)
                      The receding flood (8:1b–5)
                Drying of the earth (8:6–14)
            Third divine speech: "leave ark" (8:15–19)
        God's resolve to preserve order (8:20–22)
    Fourth divine speech: covenant (9:1–17)
Transitional conclusion (9:18–19)

---

49. Anderson, "From Analysis to Synthesis," 38.

50. A chiasm is a figure of speech named after the Greek letter X in which elements are picked up in inverted order. Note the focus of the chiasm is *"God remembered Noah"* (8:1a).

# 14 THE BOOKS OF MOSES REVISITED

## The Whole of Genesis

For how "Documentary Hypothesis" looks when applied to the whole of Genesis see Table 42 (pp. 125-26).

### CRITICS OF THE DOCUMENTARY HYPOTHESIS

It has to be acknowledged that the Documentary Hypothesis is the dominant explanation for the origin of the Pentateuch in modern biblical scholarship. Its tenets are reproduced, often without critical appraisal in numerous books and commentaries,[51] but over the decades it has always had its critics.[52] Umberto Cassuto paid particular attention to the variation in divine names. He argued that it is not accidental, but by deliberate design. God's personal name YHWH (the LORD)[53] is employed when God is presented in his personal character and in direct relationship to his covenant-people or nature. $^e$lōhîm (God) is used when the deity is alluded to as a transcendent being who exists outside the physical universe[54] and

---

51. For example the following commentaries on Genesis: Skinner, *ICC*, xxxiv-xvii; von Rad, *OTL*, 24–28; Speiser, *AB*, xx–xliii; and Wenham, *WBC*, xxviii–xxxv.

52. For example, Manley, *Book of the Law*; Cassuto, *Documentary Hypothesis*; Wiseman, *Clues to Creation in Genesis*, 75–94; Kitchen, *Ancient Orient and Old Testament*, 112–29; *Bible in its World*, 56–73; *Reliability of the Old Testament*, 241–312. See further Baker, "Source Criticism," 804a.

53. I see no reason to change the convention traditionally adopted by English Bibles, following the Septuagint (Greek Old Testament) and the New Testament of rendering the Hebrew YHWH by "the LORD." Its earliest attested occurrence is on the Moabite Stone (line 18) from Dibon in Jordan ca. 830 BC and it occurs frequently in the Dead Sea Scrolls (250 BC – mid first century BC), but no vowels were written, hence its pronunciation is uncertain. In the earliest surviving examples of the Masoretic Text (late ninth century AD and onwards), YHWH is written Yahwa, with the first and last vowels of Adonay "Lord" substituted for the original vowels. In Jewish tradition this is read Adonay "Lord" or "*haš-šēm*" (the Name). The traditional pronunciation "Jehovah" is thus a hybrid form, first attested at the start of the twelfth century AD, with all the vowels of Adonay "Lord" substituted for the original vowels. The commonly advanced modern pronunciation "Yahweh," is based on citations in three Church Fathers (1) Clement of Alexandria (ca. 150 – ca. 215), *Stromata (Miscellanies)*, 5.6.76 Iaou (Migne, *Patrologia Graeca*, 9,60; Wilson, *Writings of Clement of Alexandria*, 2, 241; (2) Iave in a note (on Exod 6:3) of the scholiast (commentator) to the Hexapla of Origen (185–254) (Field, *Origenis Hexaplorum*, I, 90a); and (3) Iave in Theodoret of Cyrrhus (ca. 393–466), *Questions on Exodus*, 15, (although here is he is citing Samaritan usage) (Migne, *Patrologia Graeca*, 80, 244) and its use on Egyptian magical papyri from the end of the third century *IBD* II, 409b.

54. Cassuto, *Documentary Hypothesis*, 71.

when those outside the covenant-community are addressed. Taking several specific examples from the early chapters of Genesis Cassuto pointed out the following:

1. In the first account of creation in Gen 1:1—2:3 *ᵉlōhîm* "God" is used throughout, but in the second account 2:4b–25 the words used are the compound *YHWH ᵉlōhîm* (LORD God). It is clear that the writer wanted to tie the personal name YHWH (traditionally LORD) directly to God, simply to have said YHWH would doubtless have sown the thought of there being two different deities. However, since the writer shifts the focus from the creation of the universe culminating in humankind in the first account, to the specific creation of man and woman in the second account, the introduction of YHWH is entirely appropriate there.
2. The statement of Gen 5:1 should be noted: "*When God created man, he made him in the likeness of God.*" It would have been irreverent to have written "*likeness of YHWH.*"
3. In Gen 6:2, 4 the writer has "*sons of God*" to denote the line that intermarried with the daughters of men. Again it would have been unthinkable to have used YHWH with "*sons.*" However, when the deity intervenes in judgment he is twice called "*the LORD*" (Gen 6:3, 5).
4. In Gen 9:26 Noah says: "*Blessed be the LORD, the God of Shem,*" but in Gen 9:27 he says: "*May God extend the territory of Japheth.*" It was Shem's descendants who would preserve the knowledge of the LORD, so the use of "*the LORD*" in connection with Shem is entirely appropriate.[55]

## CONCLUSION

We have briefly looked at the Pentateuch's own account of the life of Moses. We have examined how the text of the Pentateuch has been transmitted to us, looked at the main evidence regarding when Moses could have lived and reflected upon the claims in the New Testament, the Apocrypha, and Jewish tradition that Moses is the author of the Pentateuch. We have traced the development of the so-called "Documentary Hypothesis," concisely stated its basic tenets and mentioned some of its main critics. This

---

55. Ibid., 16, 35, 36, 74.

is a subject to which we will return,⁵⁶ but the only firm conclusion I can offer in this chapter is:

1. Rather than marking different source documents, the use of the differing divine names *ᵉlōhîm* "God" and YHWH "LORD" is not arbitrary, but a deliberate choice based on clear theological intent.

## THE AIM OF THIS BOOK

The aim of this book is to evaluate the claims of the Documentary or JEDP Hypothesis in the light of a wealth of material that has emerged from what is commonly called the ancient Near East over the past hundred years or so. I am greatly indebted to Professor Kenneth Kitchen for his vision and determination for well over fifty years in assembling a collection of all the published treaties and Law Collections from the ancient Near East.⁵⁷ This has formed the basis of our joint publication that Professor Kitchen has very graciously allowed me to use to write this book.⁵⁸ This material covers some 2,500 years from Eannatum, ruler of the Sumerian city of Lagash, down to the Roman period. It is material that has been translated from a wide variety of ancient languages: Sumerian, Elamite, Eblaite, Akkadian (Babylonian and Assyrian), Egyptian, Hittite, Ugaritic, Aramaic, and Greek, not to mention the Hebrew Pentateuch itself.⁵⁹ It is material that has been found in a diverse group of modern countries—Iraq, Syria, Turkey, Egypt, and Iran.

Some may question whether such material should be used to shed light on or even to defend what is regarded as the sacred text of the Pentateuch. For those who espouse the rallying cry of the Protestant Reformation "*Sola scriptura*" [only scripture], the use of extra-biblical material may be seen to detract from the uniqueness of the Pentateuch. However, I would counter by saying that whatever we may believe about the divine origin, inspiration or sacredness of the Pentateuch, it is surely also the product of the time when it was written, and that only by

---

56. See pp. 123–27.

57. This material, excluding the nine biblical texts, comes to ninety-seven texts, of which nearly seventy are mentioned in this work, but it represents only a tiny fragment of what has survived from antiquity; there are some 600,000 cuneiform tablets for example.

58. Kitchen and Lawrence, *TLC*.

59. With the exception of the biblical texts I have kept the numbers used by Kitchen and Lawrence, *TLC*. These appear in italic enclosed in a bracket thus *[94]*.

examining all the evidence set forth in this book, may we arrive at a fair assessment as to when the Pentateuch was written. Using contemporary material derived from other ancient texts also frees us from the circular reasoning of having to appeal to the Bible or tradition to validate our claims. The use of other ancient texts may also help to answer the question whether the Pentateuch was written as a whole or in parts that were subsequently combined.

## WHERE THIS BOOK IS GOING

In the next chapter we will consider the world in which Moses lived. This in turn will lead us to a brief consideration of the world-changing events that took place at the beginning of the twelfth century BC, well after Moses' death.

In the subsequent chapters 3–5 we will look at the book of Genesis and the covenants contained in Exodus/Leviticus and Deuteronomy. These covenants will be compared with contemporary treaties made between the Hittites of Anatolia[60] and their neighbors. A very different treaty pattern was to emerge in the First Millennium BC that we will sketch in graphic contrast. In chapter 6 we will consider material from the rest of the Pentateuch, most notably the book of Numbers. A brief look at the laws of the Pentateuch forms the focus of chapter 7, while chapter 8 makes some general comparisons (primarily in the area of the transmission of the texts) between the Pentateuch and the great epic poems of antiquity—the Mesopotamian *Epic of Gilgamesh* and Homer's *Iliad* and *Odyssey*.

The book ends with the conclusion found in chapter 9. Here I shall argue that the detailed comparisons with the late Second Millennium Hittite treaties support a late Second Millennium date for the Pentateuch. I would like to draw the attention of the reader to the chronological chart, the list of ancient texts used in this volume and the maps that close this volume.

60. See p. 20 n 3.

# Chapter 2

# The World of Moses

IN THE PREVIOUS CHAPTER we briefly traced the life of Moses from his birth near the banks of the Nile to his death on Mount Nebo overlooking the Promised Land. In this chapter we will consider Egypt in the time of Moses, before looking at what kind of education would have been available to Moses as an Egyptian prince. We shall then cast our gaze further afield to consider what Moses may have known of the wider world around him, look at his possible knowledge of languages and conclude by outlining some of the world-changing events that happened after Moses' death.

## EGYPT IN THE TIME OF MOSES

According to Exod 12:40 Moses' people, the Israelites, had lived in Egypt for 430 years. There they were enslaved, put to work building the store cities of Pithom[1] and Rameses[2] (Exod 1:11). Both these cities were in the eastern part of the Nile Delta, doubtless within the confines of the fertile land of Goshen, the land that had been allotted to Joseph's brothers and their descendants (Gen 45:10). It was thus in the flat, swampy, but abundantly fertile eastern Nile delta that Moses grew up.

---

1. Identified as Tell el-Retaba, Kitchen, *OROT*, 258.

2. The Egyptian Pi-Ramesse (Domain of Ramesses), now the huge site of Qantir (6 km long by over 3 km wide), the Delta capital of Ramesses II, was largely abandoned in ca. 1130 BC. Its stones were later plundered to build the city of Tanis, the Zoan of the Old Testament (now San el-Hagar) some twenty km to the north. See further Kitchen, *OROT*, 255.

In the previous chapter it was argued that the life of Moses is to be placed ca. 1350–1230 BC. In terms of Egyptian history Moses lived during the so-called New Kingdom, which lasted from 1540 BC to 1070 BC. In this period Egypt was ruled by three dynasties, the Eighteenth (1540–1295 BC), the Nineteenth (1295–1186 BC) and the Twentieth (1186–1070 BC).

It is beyond the remit of this book to summarize Egyptian history for that period. History cannot be viewed simply as the achievements of kings or the ruling classes; nevertheless the achievements of four New Kingdom pharaohs are worthy of mention here.

Tuthmosis III (1479–1425 BC) conducted seventeen campaigns in Syria between the twenty-third and forty-second years of his reign 1458–1438 BC. His enemy there was a state called Mitanni (a kingdom to the northwest of Assyria in what is now eastern Turkey and northern Syria). Huge temples were built such as the huge memorial temple of Tuthmosis' co-regent Queen Hatshepsut (1479–1457 BC) fronting the cliffs at Deir-el-Bahri in Western Thebes.

Amenophis IV (1353–1357 BC), also called Akhenaten, has aroused much interest for his new monotheistic faith, symbolized by the worship of the sun-disc, Aten. He also established a new capital Akhetaten ("Horizon of Aten"), called today Tell el-Amarna, whose art is characterized by realism as the old conventions were laid aside. After his death, however, Amarna and the cult of Aten were abandoned and the traditional gods were restored.

Kings of the New Kingdom were buried in the Valley of the Kings, situated in hills to the west of Thebes on the west bank of the Nile. The tomb of the comparatively minor pharaoh Tutankhamun (1336–1327 BC) was found intact by the English archaeologist Howard Carter in 1922. It contained a fabulous assemblage of chests, chariots, statues, funerary beds, vases, jewelry, a gold dagger, a bow, a trumpet, and three gaming boards. Arguably the most spectacular were a wooden shrine overlaid with gold, the solid gold coffin, and the gold funeral mask of the deceased king himself, inlaid with blue glass and semi-precious stones.

The Nineteenth Dynasty was dominated by Ramesses II (1279–1213 BC). He campaigned in Syria against the Hittites of central Anatolia (modern Asiatic Turkey)[3] for twenty years, including his inconclusive battle at Qadesh (Tell Nebi Mend) with the Hittite king Muwatallis II in 1275 BC. This was eventually followed by a formal peace treaty with the Hittite king Hattusil III in 1259 BC, which exists both in an Akkadian version from the Hittite capital of Hattusas and in two Egyptian copies[4] from Thebes in Egypt *[71A,71B]*.[5] The treaty was later sealed by a marriage between Ramesses and the daughter of the Hittite king.

Ramesses' huge memorial temple at Thebes, popularly known as the Ramesseum, and his hypostyle hall bear eloquent witness to the magnificence of his building projects. At Abu Simbel, 280 km south of Aswan, Ramesses II had four huge stone statues, each more than 20 meters high, carved out of the solid rock. Behind them a memorial temple with a complex of halls and chambers was also carved out of the rock.

## MOSES' EDUCATION

The book of Exodus says very little about Moses' life in the court of Pharaoh, but as the adopted son of Pharaoh's daughter (Exod 2:10) he doubtless received an education worthy of his status as a royal prince. Royal princes were tutored in writing, grammar, literature, simple arithmetic, and algebra.[6] Great store was set on memory, not much on originality, logic or critical thought. Writing would have involved learning the complexities of the hieroglyphic writing system, which was used for monuments. In its classic form, Middle Egyptian (ca. 2200–1600 BC), had some 700 signs. This script had also spawned a more cursive (free-flowing, joined-up) version known as hieratic, which was used in administration, literature, and correspondence. Beginners copied cen-

---

3. The term Anatolia is derived from the Greek *anatōlē* meaning "east." By the tenth century AD it was used for the land east of Constantinople (modern Istanbul) namely Asiatic Turkey. "Turkey" cannot be used to describe the land in antiquity since the Turks were not living there then. The Turks (Tourkoi) do not occur in Byzantine records until AD 568.

4. From (a) near the Great Hypostyle Hall of Temple of Amun in Karnak (Eastern Thebes) and (b) the Ramesseum, the memorial temple of Ramesses II in Western Thebes.

5. It should be noted that these two events tie Hittite chronology to that of Egypt.

6. E.g., the famous Rhind Mathematical Papyrus of ca. 1660 BC (based on an earlier Twelfth Dynasty work) solves equations with one "unknown."

turies old Middle Egyptian texts, before moving on to learn to write the Late Egyptian script and language of their own day. Material used to train would-be scribes included old correspondence, specially crafted "Instructions" and long lists of words in specific categories.

Royal princes enjoyed shooting with the bow at targets while riding two-wheeled chariots. Swimming in specially constructed pools and running were also practiced.

As well as joining the army on campaign, royalty were expected to join in the hunting of game. Tuthmosis III (1479–1425 BC) claims to have bagged one hundred and twenty Syrian elephants, seventy-five ostriches, and seven lions, not to mention a rhinoceros in Nubia (Sudan). The Eighteenth Dynasty pharaoh Amenophis III (1391–1353 BC) boasts of having slain a hundred and two lions during the first ten years of his reign. He also claims to have killed ninety-six wild bulls. Ramesses III (1184–1153 BC) is shown on reliefs from his temple at Medinet Habu in Western Thebes hunting wild cattle, lions, wild oxen, and ostriches.

Not all expeditions were military. Maybe royal princes like Moses would have joined expeditions to bring stone, minerals, timber, and other materials. Lebanon was exploited for cedar and other coniferous woods, Nubia (Sudan) for gold, the Sinai Peninsula for malachite and turquoise, and the Eastern Desert for amethyst, agate, and other minerals. If indeed the young Moses did join either a military or a hunting expedition or an expedition to exploit natural resources it would have given him first hand experience of lands outside of the land of his birth.[7]

Another function performed by royal princes was the supervision, or at least the regular visiting, of construction projects. As well as the construction of giant temples and the preparation of royal tombs, New Kingdom public works would also have included the construction and repair of dykes, the excavation and clearance of canals and the development of mines and quarries. It should not be forgotten that by far the greatest part of Egypt's population was engaged in agriculture. In an earlier age Moses' compatriot Joseph, had supervised agricultural production throughout the land (Gen 47:11–26), but Egyptian hostility towards the Israelites in Moses' own time would probably have prevented Moses being given a similar role.

---

7. One wonders if the writer's knowledge of the now extinct aurochs or wild ox *Bos primigenius* (Deut 33:17) and of the precious stones used in the High Priest's breastpiece (Exod 28:17–20) (see pp. 97–98) can be seen in this light.

One final area in which royal princes would have participated is religion and the temple cults. Whether Moses participated in this area is of course unknown, but it is unlikely that given the divine status accorded to the pharaoh, he could have opted out altogether. The book of Exodus makes it clear that it was Moses' personal encounter with the LORD at the burning bush (Exod 3:1—4:17) that renewed, even transformed his relationship with the God of his fathers. Extremely reluctantly at first, Moses accepted the LORD's call to rescue his people from slavery in Egypt.

## THE WORLD OF THE TIME OF MOSES

It is mistaken to suppose that Moses' horizons would have been confined merely to the land of his birth. One of the most remarkable archaeological discoveries relating to the New Kingdom period was made in 1887 at Tell el-Amarna, short-lived capital of the "heretic pharaoh"[8] Akhenaten, otherwise known as Amenophis IV (1353–1337 BC). Three hundred and eighty-two clay tablets from the reigns of Amenophis III (1391–1353 BC), Amenophis IV (1353–1337 BC) and Tutankhamun (1336–1327 BC) have been discovered.[9] These, however, were not written in an Egyptian script or language, but rather in the cuneiform, or wedge-shaped writing system that originated in Mesopotamia (modern Iraq). Three hundred and fifty of the tablets were letters, written in Akkadian, the language of Mesopotamia, or more specifically in a Babylonian dialect. One tablet was written in the Assyrian dialect of Akkadian, one in Hurrian,[10] two in Hittite, and twenty-eight in a Hurro-Akkadian dialect. Within the tablets the largest group was of 307 letters from Canaan. They were also written in Babylonian Akkadian, but in a form of the language heavily impregnated with Canaanite, the language spoken in Palestine at that time.[11]

---

8. See p. 19. An earlier example is a fragment of a cuneiform tablet from a sealed well at Avaris in the Delta and dating to the Hyksos period ca. 1648–1540 BC. See further *TLC* III, 287; van Koppen and Radner *Der Hyksospalast* 108 fig. 22, 115–19.

9. Synchronisms are provided by letters of the Babylonian king Burnaburiash II (1359–1333 BC) to all of the above and of the Assyrian king Ashur-uballit I (1363–1328 BC) who wrote to Amenophis IV and Tutankhamun. The chronology of the kings of Babylon and Assyria follows that of Brinkman in Oppenheim, *Ancient Mesopotamia*, 335–48.

10. A non Indo-European language spoken during the Second Millennium BC in Upper Mesopotamia and Syria, the forerunner of Urartian, with some similarities to some languages of the Caucasus.

11. Albright, "The Amarna Letters from Palestine," 98. For the text of the letters see Moran, *Amarna Letters*.

The "Amarna Letters," as they are called, give us detailed insight into Egyptian control over Palestine at that time. Of the Israelites there is no explicit trace, fuelling support for an Israelite conquest of Canaan after this time,[12] but the letters clearly show that the Egyptians had contacts further afield. Amenophis IV exchanges correspondence with his "brother" the Kassite king of Babylon Burnaburiash II (1359–1333 BC). Relations were further cemented when Amenophis IV married one of Burnaburiash's daughters. Other senders include the kings of Assyria, the kings of the Hittites from central Anatolia (now Turkey), and the rulers of Mitanni,[13] Arzawa (western Anatolia), and Alasia (Cyprus).[14] Since this single archive reminds us of the interrelationships that existed between Egypt and its neighbors, let us now briefly look in turn at each of the states with which New Kingdom Egypt had relations.

Much of southern Mesopotamia was ruled by Babylon. In the early eighteenth century BC Hammurabi (1792–1750 BC)[15] had defeated the kings of all the neighboring states to unite Mesopotamia under Babylonian rule. Towards the end of his reign Hammurabi drew up a collection of laws, the most famous copy of which, a 2.7-meter-high stela of polished basalt, was found in Susa in southwest Iran in 1901 and is now exhibited in the Louvre Museum, Paris *[14]*. In 1595 BC Babylon fell to a surprise attack from the Hittite king Mursil I from central Anatolia (Turkey). The main beneficiaries of this attack were a group called the Kassites who ruled Babylonia until ca. 1158 BC, when Babylon was conquered by Shutruk-nahhunte of Elam in southwest Iran. It was he who took Hammurabi's stela to Susa.

---

12. The Apiru who occur frequently in the letters are sometimes identified with the Hebrews ('*ibrîm*). The Apiru appear to be bands of displaced peoples, maybe some Hebrews were included among them, but a simple equation of the Apiru with the Hebrews is not possible.

13. For location see p. 19.

14. See further *TLC* II, 67. See The World of Moses, map 1, p. 142.

15. The so-called "Middle Chronology" for Babylonian history is followed. This was originally based on an astronomical observation tablet listing observations of the planet Venus for twenty-one years of the reign of an unidentified king. Since the eighth year bears a year name that is the same as that of the eighth year of the Old Babylonian king Ammisaduqa it is clear that the observations relate to his reign. It is known that Venus disappeared along with the moon in the sixth year of his reign, a phenomenon that only occurs in fifty-six-year cycles, so in theory dates fifty-six years later or earlier (the so-called Low and High Chronologies) are also possible.

The central part of Anatolia (modern Turkey) was occupied by a people called the Hittites. The Hittites were an Indo-European people, speaking a language that is part of the extensive Indo-European language family that includes English, French, German, Greek, Portuguese, Spanish, Persian, Hindi, and Sanskrit (the language of ancient India). Clay tablets from the Assyrian colony at Kanesh (Kültepe), near Kayseri in central Anatolia, attest the presence of Indo-Europeans there before the destruction of the site in ca. 1780 BC. The Hittites were to establish a powerful state in Central Anatolia around their windswept upland capital of Hattusas (modern Boğazköy). It was a state that was to make its influence felt far and wide, even as far as Egypt,[16] until its eventual collapse in ca. 1177 BC.

In the fifteenth and early fourteenth centuries BC northern Mesopotamia was dominated by a state to the northwest of Assyria in what is now eastern Turkey and northern Syria named Mitanni. It was ruled over by an Indo-European speaking aristocracy. Its capital, Washukkanni, is probably to be located at Tell Fekheriyeh in northern Syria.[17]

By taking advantage of a civil war in Mitanni, Assyria under its king Ashur-uballit I (1363–1328 BC)[18] was to assert control over Mitanni. The other main beneficiary of the collapse of Mitanni was the Hittite king Suppiluliuma I who extended Hittite influence over much of Syria and installed a certain Shattiwaza[19] on the throne of Mitanni.[20]

Egypt had contact too with the Aegean world. The Egyptian place-names Keftiu and Alasia are to be identified with the islands of Crete and Cyprus respectively. Several places in Crete are mentioned on a statue base from the memorial temple of Amenophis III (1391–1353 BC) in Western Thebes, among which are Knossos, its port Amnisos, Lyktos, and Phaestos. Mention is made too of the island of Kythera, and of Nauplia, Mycenae, and (Greek) Thebes[21] on the Greek mainland.[22]

---

16. As has been shown on p. 23.

17. However, neutron activation analysis of trace elements found in clay tablets of Tushratta, king of Mitanni, suggests a different location some eighty km further north, perhaps near the Turkish town of Mardin. Dobel, Asaro and Michael, "Neutron Activation Analysis," 375–82.

18. Assyrian chronology is based on the Assyrian King List, but one king Ninurta-apil-ekur, however, is credited with either a thirteen- or a three-year reign in different versions of the list; a thirteen-year reign is assumed here.

19. Also called Mattiwaza or Kurtiwaza in older scholarly literature.

20. For the treaties between Suppiluliuma and Shattiwaza [55A, 55B, 56A, 56B] see pp. 71–72, 74–75.

21. Or possibly Tegea.

22. Kitchen, "Theban Topographical Lists," 34, 6; *Arty-crafty Kaphtorim*; TLC II, 55;

New Kingdom Egypt ruled the Nile Valley down to the Fourth Cataract of the Nile, near Gebel Barkal in modern Sudan. Queen Hatshepsut (1479–1457 BC) sent a trading expedition to Punt (eastern Sudan to the Red Sea and parts of Eritrea). Painted reliefs on her funerary temple at Deir el-Bahri record the physique and dress of its African inhabitants, whose houses are shown as being built on piles. The reliefs clearly show the fauna and flora of the region; a giraffe, rhinoceros, baboons, doum palms, and the object of the expedition—frankincense and myrrh. It is the first known anthropological study of an alien culture.[23]

Finally, New Kingdom Egypt exploited the minerals of the Sinai peninsula, turquoise at Serabit el-Khadim and copper at Timna to the north of the Gulf of Aqaba. New Kingdom Egypt's contacts and influence were clearly wide-ranging. Any prince growing up in New Kingdom Egypt should have been aware (albeit hazily) of a world that stretched from the windswept uplands of Anatolia (Turkey) to the tropical African villages of Punt, from the rocky Aegean islands to the flat, fertile Tigris and Euphrates river valleys of Mesopotamia.[24]

## MOSES' KNOWLEDGE OF LANGUAGES

Since Moses grew up in Egypt it can be assumed that he was fluent in Egyptian. New Kingdom Egypt spoke a form of the language that is termed "Late Egyptian." As a Hebrew he would also seem to have been conversant in an early form of Hebrew (or perhaps more correctly early West Semitic); certainly he gives his son Gershom a Hebrew name (Exod 2:22). The presence of the Amarna cuneiform tablets in Egypt shows that there must have been some, albeit perhaps a very small number, who could read them. So it is possible that Moses was acquainted with the cuneiform script and the Akkadian language.

Since both Egyptian scripts—hieroglyphics and hieratic—and Mesopotamian cuneiform are highly complex pictographic writing systems; they remained the monopoly of a scribal elite. However, it is interesting that it is Egypt that has produced the earliest example of an

---

Latacz, *Troy and Homer*, 130–31. See The World of Moses, map 1, p. 142.

23. Aldred, *Egyptians*, 151.

24. See The World of Moses, map 1, p. 142. This can be further illustrated to some extent from the "Satirical letter" of Papyrus Anastasi I (end of thirteenth century BC) in which one scribe taunts another about his knowledge of Canaan. See further Wilson, "An Egyptian Letter," 475–79, especially 477.

alphabetic writing system. In 1999 archaeologists found what may be the earliest alphabetic inscriptions in Wadi el-Hol in Upper Egypt. They were apparently the work of Semitic speaking mercenaries or migrant labor miners, and are generally dated to the nineteenth century BC.[25] These Semites used pictographs to record single sounds, all of them consonants. Other examples of an early alphabet come from Egyptian turquoise mines of Serabit el-Khadim (perhaps the Dophkah of Num 33:13) in the Sinai peninsula. These were again done by Semite miners and date to ca. 1700 BC. At least twenty-three separate characters were used, nearly half of which were clearly borrowed from Egyptian. It is thus possible that Moses would have used the early Semitic alphabet to record his own Semitic language.[26]

## THE END OF AN ERA

The world so familiar to Moses and other inhabitants of New Kingdom Egypt was to change dramatically at the beginning of the twelfth century BC. Although Egypt was to survive relatively unscathed, the political entities of western Asia were to be changed irrevocably. That all was not well with the Hittites of Anatolia can be deduced from remarks by the Egyptian king Merenptah (1213–1203 BC) who records in his fifth year (1209 BC) that he sent grain ships *"to keep alive the land of Hatti."* The famine in Hatti is also mentioned in records from the Syrian port-city of Ugarit, which was asked to send 2,000 kors of grain[27] from Mukish in Syria to Ura (Silifke) on the southern coast of Anatolia *"to alleviate the famine there."* Hittite texts also speak of plague. In his fifth year (1209 BC) Merenptah repels a group of invaders, whom his scribes collectively call the "Sea Peoples." These were a loose confederation of peoples, largely of Aegean origin, whose ranks include the Lukku, Aqawasha, and Sheklesh.[28]

There were other pressures on the Hittites. Arzawa (western Anatolia) threw off Hittite control. Internal friction between the last Hittite king Suppiluliuma II and the southern internal satellite kingdoms[29]

---

25. Some date these to the seventeenth century BC. Kitchen, *OROT*, 371.

26. What exactly that language was remains uncertain; it could be termed "proto-Hebrew," but it has to be faced that there is no contemporary evidence for it.

27. Some 450 tonnes.

28. Kitchen, *RITA* IV, 7,18.

29. These internal satellite kingdoms were ruled by a "king," related to, but subordinate

of Tarhuntassa[30] and Carchemish must have eroded the political unity and the total loyalty that the Hittite Empire used to enjoy.

Meanwhile in Egypt Ramesses III (1184–1153 BC) records three battles—in Years 5 and 11 (1180 and 1174 BC) in Libya, and in Year 8 (1177 BC) a land and sea battle on the coasts of the northeast Delta. Ramesses III's exploits there in defeating the Sea Peoples were recorded on carved reliefs on the walls of his memorial temple at Medinet Habu, in Western Thebes. They show the "Sea Peoples" arriving in Egypt by wagon and ship with their families and belongings. Among the Sea Peoples is a group called Peleset, who are depicted wearing head-dresses of reeds rising vertically from a horizontal band. These are commonly believed to be the Philistines of the Old Testament.[31]

Ramesses III wrote in his eighth year (1177 BC):

> *The foreign countries made a conspiracy in their islands. All at once the lands were removed or scattered in the fray. No land could stand before their arms. Hatti* [The Hittites], *Kode* [Cilicia], *Carchemish, Arzawa* [W Anatolia] *and Alasia* [Cyprus] *were destroyed at one time . . . They desolated the people, and the land was like that which has never come into being. They were coming towards Egypt, while the flame was prepared before them. Their confederation was the Peleset, Tjekker, Sheklesh, Denyen, and Weshwesh lands united.*[32]

A later text (the Great Harris Papyrus of Ramesses IV [1153–1147 BC]) states:

> *I extended all the frontiers of Egypt and overthrew those who attacked from their lands. I slew the Denyen in their islands while the Tjekker and the Peleset were made ashes. The Sherden and the Weshwesh of the Sea were made non existent, captured all together, and brought in captivity to Egypt like the sands of the shore.*[33]

---

to, the central Hittite monarchy.

30. Tarhuntassa is to be located in S Anatolia. For location see *TLC* II, 62.

31. Note, however, also the reservations expressed on pp. 33–34.

32. Wilson, "Egyptian Historical Texts," 262b (fourth sentence slightly modified); see also: Breasted, *Ancient Records of Egypt*, 37§ 64; Wood, *In Search of the Trojan War*, 220; Sandars, *Sea Peoples*, 119.

33. Wilson, "Egyptian Historical Texts," 262a (with slight modification of geographical names); see also Breasted, *Ancient Records of Egypt*, 201§ 403; Sandars, *Sea Peoples*, 133; Peden, *Egyptian Historical Inscriptions*, 215.

The origins of the Sea Peoples cannot be explored in detail here, but suffice it to say that the names of some of the names that the Sea Peoples were eventually to help to identify some of the Sea Peoples, e.g., Lukku = Lycia in SW Anatolia, Sheklesh = Sicily, Sherden = Sardinia. The Aqawasha are sometimes equated with the Achaeans, the name given to the Mycenaean Greeks in the writings of the Greek Epic poet Homer.[34]

The Sea Peoples are often blamed for the collapse of the Hittite Empire, but the reality was probably more complex. The unruly Kaskeans in the mountains behind the Black Sea coast may have been more instrumental than Sea Peoples in bringing down the Hittite Empire. It could well have been the case, that after the chaos caused by the invasion of so-called "Sea Peoples" at the beginning of the twelfth century BC, many other peoples took advantage of the Hittites' weakness.[35]

Drought-related crop failures may have further contributed to the collapse of the Hittite Empire. What is clear, however, is that the Hittite Empire and its capital Hattusas were destroyed. This destruction is to be dated to year 8 of the reign of Ramesses III, 1177 BC. Other states were to collapse around the same time. In Syria many cities were destroyed, including the port city of Ugarit. The vacuum created in Syria by the collapse of the Hittite Empire encouraged the Aramaeans to invade from the Syrian desert. The Mycenaean civilization of Greece succumbed to an invasion of Dorian Greeks in ca. 1200 BC. Iran too had its own Indo-European emigrants, who were later to emerge as the Medes and the Persians. Egypt emerged virtually unscathed, though it is perhaps significant that Egypt did not mount another campaign in Asia for nearly 250 years.[36] The world familiar to Moses was never to be the same again.

---

34. See further pp. 111–17. Probably the Achaeans are to be equated with the Hittite Ahhiyawa, identified by Mountjoy "The East Aegean – West Anatolian Interface," 49 as a maritime kingdom stretching down from Miletus to Rhodes, including coastal Anatolia and the offshore islands. This is precisely the area for which the evidence for Mycenaean cultural evidence is steadily accumulating.

35. The Greek Historian Herodotus' tale (*Histories* 7.73) of the Briges or Phrygians crossing into Anatolia from southeastern Europe may be an example. Studies in climate patterns through tree rings and level changes in peat bogs and lake levels suggest there was a crisis in the climate of the European and Aegean worlds in ca. 1200 BC that could have triggered the migrations (Wood, *In Search of the Trojan War*, 221).

36. 1 Kgs 9:14 records that an unidentified pharaoh, perhaps Siamun (979–960 BC) captured the Canaanite town of Gezer, giving it as a wedding gift to his daughter who had become Solomon's (970–930 BC) wife. Shoshenq I (945–924 BC) (Shishak) attacked Palestine in the fifth year of Rehoboam, king of Judah, 926 BC (1 Kgs 14:25).

# Chapter 3

# Genesis

HAVING LOOKED AT THE world of Moses, we now turn our attention to the first of the books that are traditionally attributed to Moses—the book of Genesis. We shall see how the formula *"these are the generations of"* or its like divides up the book into a series of possible source documents. We shall look at the writer's acquaintance with Egypt and consider evidence for updating the source documents and for editing after the time of Moses. Two sections—"The Table of Nations" and "The List of the Rulers of Edom"—will be considered in more detail. Finally we shall look the covenants preserved in the book of Genesis and consider how far they mirror the treaties of the early Second Millennium.

## THE BOOK OF GENESIS

The first book of the Pentateuch is commonly called Genesis. This title is derived from a Greek word meaning "origin," "source," "birth" or "generation."[1] In the Hebrew Bible it is simply called $b^e$-$r\bar{e}\check{s}\hat{\imath}t$ "in the beginning" after its opening word. Genesis details the primeval history of the world, then traces God's dealings with the Patriarchs Abraham, Isaac, Jacob, and Joseph. Many consider it unwise to assign firm dates to the events of primeval history, but the Patriarchs can be approximately dated. The following scheme is based on a ca. 1270 BC Exodus and takes state

---

1. Liddell and Scott, *Greek-English Lexicon*, 304b.

ments made by the compiler of the book of Genesis concerning their ages at face value,[2] thus:

Table 7. The dates of the Patriarchs

| Abraham | ca. 1990–1815 BC |
|---|---|
| Isaac | ca. 1890–1710 BC |
| Jacob | ca. 1830–1683 BC |
| Joseph | ca. 1730–1620 BC |

## MARKERS IN THE TEXT: A PATTERN IN GENESIS

One of the most oft-repeated phrases in the book of Genesis is the phrase *"These are the generations of"* that occurs eleven times throughout the book thus:

2:4a  *These are the generations of the heavens and the earth when they were created.*

5:1  *This is the book of the generations of Adam.*

6:9a  *These are the generations of Noah.*

10:1  *These are the generations of the sons of Noah, Shem, Ham, and Japheth.*

11:10a  *These are the generations of Shem.*

11:27a  *These are the generations of Terah.*

25:12  *These are the generations of Ishmael, Abraham's son, whom Hagar the Egyptian, Sarah's servant bore to Abraham.*

25:19a  *These are the generations of Isaac, Abraham's son.*

36:1  *These are the generations of Esau (that is Edom).*

36:9  *These are the generations of Esau the father of the Edomites in the hill country of Seir.*

37:2a  *These are the generations of Jacob.* (ESV)

The eleven *"These are the generations of"* phrases divide up the text of the book of Genesis into twelve sections thus:[3]

---

2. Abraham 175 years (Gen 25:7); Isaac 180 years (Gen 36:28); Jacob 130 years when he went to Egypt (47:9); Joseph 110 years (Gen 50:22).

3. Wiseman, *Clues to Creation*, argued that the *"these are the generations of"* formulae functioned as colophons—a feature found in clay tablets from Assyria and Babylonia that is a note appended to a text by a scribe detailing its contents, or a statement about the tablet and the persons connected with its production. Viewed this way the formulae were considered to look back, and suggest that Ishmael was primarily responsible for preserving the story of Abraham, that Isaac was responsible for Ishmael's history, that Esau preserved Jacob's history. This seems unlikely. With the possible exception of 5:1 all

Here is this information schematized: the figure in brackets is the number of verses.

Table 8. "These are the generations of" formulae as markers of documents

| |
|---|
| Document 1 1:1—2:3 (34) |
| 2:4a These are the generations of the heavens and the earth when they were created.[A] |
| Document 2 2:4b—4:26 (51) |
| 5:1a This is the book of the generations of Adam. |
| Document 3 5:1b—6:8 (39) |
| 6:9a These are the generations of Noah. |
| Document 4 6:9b—9:29 (88) |
| 10:1 These are the generations of the sons of Noah, Shem, Ham, and Japheth. |
| Document 5 10:2—11:9 (40) |
| 11:10a These are the generations of Shem. |
| Document 6 11:10b-11:26 (17) |
| 11:27a These are the generations of Terah. |
| Document 7 11:27—25:11 (377) |
| 25:12 These are the generations of Ishmael, Abraham's son, whom Hagar the Egyptian, Sarah's servant bore to Abraham. |
| Document 8 25:13-18 (6) |
| 25:19a These are the generations of Isaac, Abraham's son. |
| Document 9 25:19b—35:29 (362) |
| 36:1 These are the generations of Esau (that is Edom). |
| Document 10a 36:2-8 (7) |
| 36:9 These are the generations of Esau the father of the Edomites in the hill country of Seir. |
| Document 10b 36:10—37:1 (34) |
| 37:2a These are the generations of Jacob. |
| Document 11 37:2b-50:26 (425) |
| A. However, as Kitchen, *OROT*, 428, notes the division of this verse destroys its literary structure (a chiasm—for which see p. 13 n 50). |

The seventh document is very large, 377 verses, the eighth very short, just six verses. The ninth, again, is very large, 362 verses. The tenth documents, 10a and 10b, can be combined, since they both deal with the generations of Esau. The eleventh and final document, the story of Joseph, is the largest of all, 425 verses.

---

the formulae seem to look forward and it would thus seem better to view the formulae as titles (following Egyptian usage) introducing the next document. The famous words of Gen 1:1 "*In the beginning God created the heavens and the earth*" are thus seen as a title for the first document or perhaps for the book as a whole.

It is clear that no section overshoots the lifetime of the person named[4] and it may be that the "*These are the generations of*" formulae mark out documents used in the compilation of Genesis.

## THE WRITER'S ACQUAINTANCE WITH EGYPT

In Gen 13:10 the writer describes the plain of the Jordan before the destruction of Sodom and Gomorrah and compares it to Egypt, which he seems to know well. "*Lot looked up and saw that the whole plain of the Jordan was well watered, like the garden of the LORD, like the land of Egypt, toward Zoar.*" This fits Moses' personal acquaintance with Egypt.

## UPDATING THE TEXT

There are cases where place names appear to have been brought up to date in the text.[5] These could be the work of Moses updating his source documents. Thus:

| | |
|---|---|
| 14:2,8 | *the king of Bela (that is, Zoar)* |
| 14:3 | *the valley of Siddim (the Salt Sea)* |
| 14:7 | *En Mishpat (that is, Kadesh)* |
| 14:17 | *the Valley of Shaveh (that is the King's Valley)* |
| 16:14 | *Beer Lahai Roi; it is still there* [Heb. hinnē "behold"] *between Kadesh and Bered* |
| 23:2 | *Kiriath-Arba (that is, Hebron) in the land of Canaan* |
| 23:19 | *Mamre (that is at Hebron) in the land of Canaan* |

The last two examples are particularly interesting. A later writer or editor would not need to state where Hebron was. This is because all the Israelites living in the land of Canaan would have known that Hebron was in Canaan, but Moses writing before the Israelites conquered Canaan could well have had to explain where it was.

---

4. Kidner, *TC Genesis*, 23; Wiseman, *Clues to Creation*, 42.

5. It is possible that such explanatory notes were part of the original text. As Millard has noted (private communication) there are two virtually identical explanatory notes in two versions of the Annals of the Assyrian King Shalmaneser III (858–824 BC) Grayson, *Royal Inscriptions*, 19, ii 35b–36a and 51, i 40b–43a "*which the people of the (land of) Hatti call (the city of) Pitru.*" In cuneiform texts, written on stone or clay, such notes are clearly comments of the "author," not updatings of a later editor.

Gen 47:11 says: *"So Joseph settled his father and his brothers in Egypt and gave them property in the best part of the land, the district of Rameses, as Pharaoh directed"*—Rameses would seem to be a clear reference to the great Egyptian pharaoh Ramesses II (1279–1213 BC). So it would seem that a mention of Ramesses in the time of Joseph is not possible. If, as was argued above,[6] Moses were contemporary with Ramesses II, then Moses could have updated this reference.

## EDITING AFTER THE TIME OF MOSES?

The following can be advanced as evidence of the text being edited after the time of Moses:

1. Gen 14:14 says: *"When Abram heard that his relative had been taken captive, he called out the 318 trained men born in his household and went in pursuit as far as Dan."* Judges 18:29 records that the Danites *"Named it Dan after their forefather Dan, who was born to Israel—though the city used to be called Laish."*[7] In the light of Judg 18:29 it would seem that the original name of the city was Laish. It would thus seem that this detail of Gen 14:14 was updated in the period of the Judges or later.

2. The phrase *"Ur of the Chaldeans"* occurs three times in Genesis (11:28, 31; 15:7). Assyrian royal inscriptions first attest the presence of the Chaldeans in what is now southern Iraq in the ninth century BC.[8] So it would seem that the words *"of the Chaldeans"* were added later, perhaps to distinguish Abraham's birthplace in southern Mesopotamia (Iraq) from other places of the same or similar names.[9]

3. In the book of Genesis we encounter the Philistines seven times[10] (21:32, 34; 26:1, 8, 14, 15, 18). The Philistines, as later known, were part of the so-called "Sea Peoples" defeated by the Egyptian king, Ramesses III, in a naval battle in his eighth year—1177 BC.[11] This battle probably took place at the mouth of the Nile and is shown in carved reliefs on the walls of Ramesses III's memorial

---

6. See pp. 6–7.
7. See also Josh 19:47.
8. Oppenheim, "Chaldeans," 550a.
9. Kitchen, *OROT*, 316.
10. This does not include their appearance in the "Table of the Nations" Gen 10:14.
11. See p. 27.

temple at Medinet Habu, in Western Thebes. Some argue that the book of Genesis may provide a case of the text being brought up to date, with the term "Philistine" being used to describe earlier Aegean settlers in Palestine. However, it should be noted that the term "Philistine" occurs in the Mycenaean Greek Linear B tablets dating from the fifteenth century BC from Knossos in Crete and Pylos on the Greek mainland. This suggests that there may have been Philistines present at the time of the events recorded in the book of Genesis and that later updating does not have to be supposed.[12]

4. The phrase "*to this day*" occurs four times in the book. The writer seems to be giving information that was known in his day, but which he suspects was not known in the time he is writing about thus:

   a. Gen 22:14
   *So Abraham called that place "The LORD Will Provide." And to this day it is said, "On the mountain of the LORD it will be provided."* (NIV)

   b. Gen 26:33
   *He called it Shibah, and to this day the name of the town has been Beersheba.* (NIV)

   c. Gen 32:32
   *Therefore to this day the Israelites do not eat the tendon attached to the socket of the hip, because the socket of Jacob's hip was touched near the tendon.* (NIV)

   d. Gen 35:20
   *Over her tomb Jacob set up a pillar, and to this day that pillar marks Rachel's tomb.* (NIV)

Thus it can be concluded that there is some evidence for updating the text. It cannot be said with certainty when this updating took place. The stability provided by the reigns of David and Solomon (1010–930 BC) may have provided such an opportunity.[13]

---

12. Knossos U 0478 and Pylos Vn 1191, see further Kitchen, *Arty-crafty Kaphtorim*.

13. The text may also have undergone some kind of linguistic updating at the same time, since it cannot be denied that the present language of the Pentateuch is not thirteenth century BC, but essentially Classical biblical Hebrew. All the books from Genesis to Kings form one coherent narrative, so it is suggested that the final form of this long text dates from the Babylonian exile when the text of Kings was completed. The final event

## THE LIST OF THE RULERS OF EDOM IN GEN 36:31-43

Gen 36:31 says: *"These were the kings who reigned in Edom before any Israelite king reigned."* It would seem that here is a clue to the date of "the List of the Rulers of Edom." Saul, the first Israelite king, is to be dated to the end of the eleventh century BC, so it seems that this list (at least in its present form) was added to the text of Genesis at the time of the early Israelite monarchy, certainly well after the time of Moses.[14]

## THE TABLE OF THE NATIONS IN GEN 10:1-32

Gen 10:1-32 is commonly called the "Table of the Nations." Nations within the worldview of the writer are listed as descendants of Noah's three sons, Shem, Ham, and Japheth. It should be noted that not all the nations can be identified with equal certainty. A comprehensive survey of all the nations mentioned in the table will not be attempted, but the geographical range is large; from Elam (22) in modern Iran to Caphtor (14) (Crete), from Meshech and Tubal (2) in Anatolia (modern Turkey) to Sheba (28) (Yemen).[15] Certain nations like Misraim (13)—Egypt, and Asshur (22)—Assyria have pivotal roles in Near Eastern history from distant antiquity.

Some of the names in the Table of Nations have a hoary antiquity. Three examples will suffice:

1. Togarmah (3), perhaps a place in central Anatolia now called Gürün, is attested in Old Assyrian texts from their colony at Kanesh in central Anatolia, which was destroyed in about 1780 BC.
2. The Caphtorites (14) are from Crete, which is known as Kaptara in the eighteenth-century Mari archive (destroyed in 1759 BC) from Syria and as Keftiu in Egyptian Middle Kingdom (2023-1795 BC) texts.[16]

---

recorded in Kings (2 Kgs 25:27-30) is the release from prison in Babylon, of Judah's king Jehoiachin, in the first year of the Neo-Babylonian king, Evil-Merodach (Awel-Marduk), 561 BC. So it is suggested that Jehoiachin was responsible for the final writing of this long text. See further Schneidewind, *How the Bible Became a Book*, 149-64; Albright, *Stone Age*, 78-79.

14. Or it may be that it is only the phrase *"before any Israelite king reigned"* that dates from the time of the Hebrew Monarchy.

15. For further treatment see von Rad, *OTL*, 139-43; Westermann, *SPCK Genesis*, 495-530; Wenham, *WBC*, 210-32; Hamilton, *NICOT*, 330-48; Kitchen, *OROT*, 430-37; Osborne, "Table of the Nations," 595.

16. See p. 24. These would appear to be the Minoans of Classical archaeology. See

3. Elisha (4) is perhaps Alasia, a name used for Cyprus in the Amarna Letters[17] from Egypt (mid fourteenth century BC) and texts from Ugarit on the coast of Syria, destroyed in ca. 1180 BC.[18]

Certain peoples make a dateable appearance on the stage of world history after the time of Moses.

For example, Meshech (2) are the Mushki, an Anatolian tribe first mentioned in 1115 BC in the Annals of the Assyrian king Tiglath-pileser I.[19]

The Madai (2) are the Medes from Iran, first attested in Assyrian records in 836 BC.[20]

These later-dated names suggest that the "Table of Nations" was brought up to date after the time of Moses, perhaps as late as the ninth century. However, the place names with attestation before Moses show that the basis of the document could easily date from the time of Moses.

## "THE LIST OF THE RULERS OF EDOM" AND "THE TABLE OF NATIONS" AS MARKERS IN THE TEXT

As we have seen, there is evidence for "The List of the Rulers of Edom" and "The Table of the Nations" being (at least in their final form) later than Moses' time. It is significant that both the List and the Table are not placed in the middle of the proposed source documents, delineated by the phrases *"these are the generations of."* "The Table of the Nations" forms the first part of Document 5. It is introduced by the phrase *"These are the generations of the sons of Noah, Shem, Ham, and Japheth."* "The List of the Rulers of Edom" is placed at the end of Document 10. It is followed by the statement of 37:1. *"Jacob lived in the land where his father had stayed, the land of Canaan,"* and then by the phrase: *"These are the generations of Jacob"* (37:2a).

This can be seen from the following diagram (the number of verses is given in brackets):

---

further Wachsmann, *Aegeans in the Theban Tombs*; Kitchen, *Arty-crafty Kaphtorim*.

17. See pp. 22–23.
18. Cf. the treaty made with the rulers of Alasia *[80]* p. 75.
19. The Annals of Tiglath-pileser I 1.62, Grayson, *ARI* 2, 6.
20. The Black Obelisk of Shalmaneser III, Luckenbill, *ARAB* 1, 206 § 581.

Table 9. The Table of the Nations and the List of the Rulers of Edom within the Genesis documents

| |
|---|
| Document 1 1:1—2:3 (34) |
| Document 2 2:4b—4:26 (51) |
| Document 3 5:1—6:8 (39) |
| Document 4 6:9b—9:29 (88) |
| *The Table of the Nations* 10:1-32 |
| *End of Document 5* 11:1-9 (9) |
| Document 6 11:10b—11:26 (17) |
| Document 7 11:27—25:11 (377) |
| Document 8 25:13-18 (6) |
| Document 9 25:19b—35:29 (362) |
| *Beginning of Document 10* 36:2-30 (29) |
| *The List of the Rulers of Edom* 36:31-43 |
| Document 11 37:2b—50:26 (425) |

Whoever updated "The Table of the Nations" and "The List of the Rulers of Edom" or placed them in the narrative in the first place seems to have understood the structure of the book of Genesis. It would seem that this compiler placed these two sections deliberately to create a "mirror image." The "Table of the Nations" is at the beginning of its document, "The List of the Rulers of Edom" is at the end of its document. It can be argued that they act as a kind of frame for Document 6 and for the big Documents 7 and 9 at the center of the book. Another function of "The Table of the Nations" and "The List of the Rulers of Edom" may be to divide the text of Genesis into three. Interestingly Part One (1:1—9:29) deals with the primeval world, Part Two (11:1—36:30) primarily focuses on events set in Canaan (Palestine)[21] and Part Three (37:1—50:26) is largely centered on events in Egypt.[22]

Thus:

Table 10. Genesis divided by the Table of the Nations and the List of the Rulers of Edom

| |
|---|
| The Primeval World (1:1—9:29) |
| *The Table of the Nations* |
| Canaan (11:1—36:30) |
| *The List of the Rulers of Edom* |
| Egypt (37:1—50:26) |

21. The Tower of Babel, the call of Abram and his journey to Egypt (Gen 11:1—12:20) are exceptions.

22. The story of Judah and Tamar (Gen 38:1-30) is also an exception.

## AN ANCIENT WORD USED CORRECTLY

In the account of Abram's rescue of Lot in Gen 14:14 the word *ḥānîk*, meaning a "trained man" occurs. It is used nowhere else in the Old Testament, but is known to occur in the Egyptian execration (curse) texts of the early second millennium BC,[23] where it is used for the "trained men" of Palestinian chieftains. It was also used some four centuries later by an Egyptian official named Rawose(r) in a clay tablet from Taanach in northern Palestine. Its use in Genesis 14 is worthy of note, it accurately describes the "trained men" in Abraham's force, and would seem to still have the same meaning when the account was included in the book of Genesis.

## CLUSTERS OF LOAN-WORDS

The story of Joseph that occupies thirteen out of the final fourteen chapters of the book of Genesis is largely set in Egypt. It is noticeable that there are more words borrowed from Egyptian in this story than elsewhere in the book. Even just looking at chapter 41, five Egyptian loan-words are to be found. All of them are known to be of considerable antiquity thus:[24]

Table 11. Gen 41

| Reference | Hebrew word | Egyptian word | Meaning |
|---|---|---|---|
| 41:1 | yᵉʾōr | yrw | "Nile" |
| 41:2 | āḥū | 'ḥ(w) | "reed" |
| 41:8 | hartom | hry-tp | "magician" |
| 41:42 | tabaʿat | db'.t | "signet ring" Eg. "seal" |
| 41:42 | šēš | šś | "fine linen" |

Furthermore, the proper names Zaphenath-Paneah, Asenath, and Potiphera (Gen 41:45) are also all Egyptian,[25] and are thus an indication

---

23. The hieratic reading has been disputed by some, but defended by others (Kitchen private communication).

24. All these loan words are known from before the Middle Kingdom (2023–1795 BC) in Egyptian (Kitchen, private communication). They apparently became part of the Hebrew lexicon as they are all used in other Old Testament books. *aḇrēk* in 43 (NIV "make way!") is not included here, as its etymology is uncertain.

25. See further Kitchen, "Egypt, Egyptians," 209b; *OROT* 345–47. The first two names are both good Middle Kingdom (early second millennium BC) examples. Potiphera is a later New Kingdom form (late second millennium BC) modernized from a Middle

that the writer knew the cultural setting that he was writing about, not making it up in another land centuries after the event. The presence of an odd loan-word may just be accidental, but when there is a cluster of loan-words from the same language all in the same story it surely carries greater weight.

## TREATIES IN GENESIS

Within the book of Genesis there are four reports of treaties made between the patriarchs and local rulers.

---

Kingdom form *Didi-re.

Table 12. Treaties in Genesis

| Treaty | Element | Reference | Text |
|---|---|---|---|
| (1) Abraham and Abimelech I 21:23–24 | Oath I | 21:23a | Now swear to me here |
| | Divine witness | 23b | before God |
| | Stipulations | 23c | that you will not deal falsely with me or my children or my descendants. Show to me and the country where you are living as an alien the same kindness I have shown to you. |
| | Oath II | 24 | Abraham said, "I swear it." |
| (2) Abraham and Abimelech II 21:29–33 | Witnesses | 21:29–30a | Abimelech asked Abraham, "What is the meaning of these seven ewe lambs you have set apart by themselves?" He replied, "Accept these seven lambs from my hand as a witness |
| | Stipulation | 30b | that I dug this well." |
| | Insert | 31a | So that place was called Beersheba, |
| | Oath | 31b–32 | because the two men swore an oath there. They made a treaty at Beersheba. . . . |
| | Ceremony | 33 | Abraham planted a tamarisk tree in Beersheba, and there he called upon the name of the LORD, the Eternal God. |
| (3) Abimelech and Isaac 26:28–31 | Oath I | 26:28 | They answered, "We saw clearly that the LORD was with you; so we said, "There ought to be a sworn agreement between us—between us and you. Let us make a treaty with you |
| | Stipulation | 29 | that you will do us no harm, just as we did not molest you but always treated you well and sent you away in peace. And now you are blessed by the LORD." |
| | Solemn Ceremony | 30 | Isaac then made a feast for them, and they ate and drank. |

| | | | |
|---|---|---|---|
| (4) Laban and Jacob 31:44–54 | Oath II | 31 | Early the next morning the men swore an oath to each other. Then Isaac sent them on their way, and they left him in peace. |
| | Witness | 31: 44–46a | "Come now, let's make a covenant, you and I, and let it serve as a witness between us." So Jacob took a stone and set it up as a pillar. He said to his relatives, "Gather some stones." So they took stones and piled them in a heap. |
| | Ceremony and witness | 46b–48a | and they ate there by the heap. Laban called it Jegar Sahadutha[A] and Jacob called it Galeed.[B] Laban said, "This heap is a witness between you and me today." |
| | Insert | 48b–49a | That is why it was called Galeed. It was also called Mizpah,[C] because he said, |
| | Implied curse | 49b | "May the LORD keep watch between you and me when we are away from each other. |
| | Stipulations I + witnesses | 50–51 | If you mistreat my daughters or if you take any wives besides my daughters, even though no one is with us, remember that God is a witness between you and me." Laban also said to Jacob, "Here is this heap, and here is this pillar I have set up between you and me. |
| | Stipulations II + witness | 52 | This heap is a witness, and this pillar is a witness, that I will not go past this heap to your side to harm you and that you will not go past this heap and pillar to my side to harm me. |
| | Implied curses | 53a | May the God of Abraham and the God of Nahor, the God of their father, judge between us." |
| | Oath | 53b | So Jacob took an oath in the name of the Fear of his father Isaac. |
| | Solemn ceremony | 54 | Jacob offered a sacrifice there in the hill country and invited his relatives to a meal. After they had eaten, they spent the night there. |

A. The Aramaic Jegar Sahadutha means "witness heap."
B. The Hebrew Galeed also means "witness heap."
C. Mizpah means "watchtower."

## TREATIES OF THE EARLY SECOND MILLENNIUM

The elements found in the treaties preserved in Genesis—Oath, Witnesses, Stipulations, Ceremony, and Implied Curse—are those found in the treaties of the early Second Millennium from Kanesh (in central Anatolia), Mari, and Tell Leilan (both in Syria). Thus:

From Kanesh: The treaty of an unidentified ruler of Kanesh with Old Assyrian merchants *[16]*; the treaty of Assur with Hahhum *[17]*;

From Mari: Zimri-Lim (1779–1761 BC) of Mari with Ibal-pi-el of Eshnunna *[20]*, with Hammurabi (1792–1750 BC) of Babylon *[21]*, with Atamrum of Andarig *[22]*, and with an unidentified ruler of Kurda *[23]*;

From Tell Leilan (Shubat-Enlil): Till-Abnu of Apum with the City of Assur *[24]* and with Yamsi-Hadnu of Kahat *[25]*

The specific sequence of oath/witnesses + stipulations found in (1) Abraham and Abimelech I *[30]* Gen 21:23–24 is identical to that found in the early Second Millennium treaties listed above (and in no other period).

Thus compare:

Table 13. The treaty between Abraham and Abimelech I Gen 21

| |
|---|
| Oath 23a |
| Witnesses 23b |
| Stipulations 23c |

with:

Table 14. The treaty between Zimri-Lim of Mari and Atamrum of Andarig

| |
|---|
| Witness Obv.1 |
| Oath Obv.2–3 |
| Stipulations Obv.4–Rev.13 |

Furthermore there are reports of Covenants made between the LORD and Noah (Gen 9:8–17) and the LORD and Abraham (Gen 15:7–21). The latter is worthy of note.

*Preamble and Response 7–8*

> He also said to him, "I am the LORD, who brought you out of Ur of the Chaldeans to give you this land to take possession of it." But

*Abram said, "O Sovereign LORD, how can I know that I will gain possession of it?"*

### Solemn Ceremony 9–17

*So the LORD said to him, "Bring me a heifer, a goat and a ram, each three years old, along with a dove and a young pigeon." Abram brought all these to him, cut them in two and arranged the halves opposite each other; the birds, however, he did not cut in half. Then birds of prey came down on the carcasses, but Abram drove them away. As the sun was setting, Abram fell into a deep sleep, and a thick and dreadful darkness came over him. Then the LORD said to him, "Know for certain that your descendants will be strangers in a country not their own, and they will be enslaved and mistreated four hundred years. But I will punish the nation they serve as slaves, and afterward they will come out with great possessions. You, however, will go to your fathers in peace and be buried at a good old age. In the fourth generation your descendants will come back here, for the sin of the Amorites has not yet reached its full measure." When the sun had set and darkness had fallen, a smoking brazier with a blazing torch appeared and passed between the pieces.*

### Stipulation/Promise 18–21

*On that day the LORD made a covenant with Abram and said, "To your descendants I give this land, from the river of Egypt to the great river, the Euphrates— the land of the Kenites, Kenizzites, Kadmonites, Hittites, Perizzites, Rephaites, Amorites, Canaanites, Girgashites, and Jebusites."* (NIV)

The basic pattern of Preamble (with a prologue-like historical allusion), Solemn Ceremony, and Stipulation has affinities with an early Second Millennium Treaty between Abba-An of Aleppo in Syria and Yarim-Lim of Alalakh *[29]*, which has a Historical Prologue, Ceremony, Stipulations, and Witnesses.

Thus compare:

Table 15. The covenant between the LORD and Abraham Gen 15:17–21

| Preamble 7–8 |
|---|
| Solemn Ceremony 9–17 |
| Stipulations 18–21 |

with:

Table 16. The treaty between Abba-An of Aleppo and Yarim-Lim of Alalakh [29]

| Historical Prologue Obv.1–39a |
|---|
| Oath and Ceremony 39b–42 |
| Stipulations 43–67 |
| Witnesses 68–76 |

It can thus be concluded that the treaties preserved in the book of Genesis have several parallels with treaties of the early Second Millennium. These particular groupings of parallels are not observable in any other period.

## THE PRICE OF A SLAVE

In Gen 37:28 Joseph's brothers[26] sell him to the passing Midianite/Ishmaelite merchants for twenty shekels of silver.[27] This price of a slave (expressed as ⅓ of a mina) is the same in the Old Babylonian Law Collection of Hammurabi (1792–1750 BC) [14] 26:49 ($116); 41:43 ($214) and 44:67 ($252). This is the exact price recorded for transactions at contemporary Mari in Syria. In other Old Babylonian documents the average is twenty-two shekels.[28] In subsequent centuries inflation took hold, so by the time of the fifteenth-century documents from Nuzi (in the mountains east of Mesopotamia) and the fourteenth-century documents from the Syrian port city of Ugarit, the price was thirty shekels, as it is in Exod 21:32.[29] Thus the price of Joseph's sale into slavery fits well with contemporary evidence. At the very least this is evidence for the authenticity of that element in the Joseph story.

26. For the approximate date of Joseph see p. 30.

27. Approximately 200 grams.

28. Kitchen, *OROT*, 344; his figure 43 "The Rising Price of Slaves through 2000 years" on page 639 is worthy of further study.

29. Kitchen, *OROT*, 345.

## CONCLUSIONS

By way of conclusion, I offer the following:

1. The eleven phrases *"These are the generations of"* function as a marker in the text. It would seem that the book of Genesis is a compilation of twelve documents (reduced by us to eleven by combining two documents with very similar titles), delineated by these eleven phrases.
2. The updating of geographical names in the sources that were no longer in use in the author's own time and the author's personal acquaintance with Egypt in 13:10 are evidence that point to Moses being the compiler of Genesis.
3. The name "Rameses" (47:11) could well be an addition made by Moses himself.
4. There is also some evidence that points to some editing after the time of Moses. For example the name "Dan" (14:14), the addition of "of the Chaldeans" to the name Ur (11:28, 31; 15:7), the use of the phrase "to this day" (22:14; 26:33; 32:32; 35:20) and maybe the use of the term "Philistine" (21:32, 34; 26:1, 8, 14, 15, 18, 21).
5. There is evidence for some additions to two larger sections, "The Table of the Nations" (perhaps ninth century) and "The List of the Rulers of Edom" (perhaps end of eleventh century).
6. In both cases these sections are not added in the middle of a source document, but are inserted at the beginning and end of a source document respectively. This suggests that they were deliberately placed to give structure to the whole book.
7. It could be said that "The Table of the Nations" and "The List of the Rulers of Edom" serve as a frame for the big documents in the center of the book. Perhaps, more simply, it can be said that they serve to divide the whole text into three, each with its own geographical focus.
8. The use of the word *ḥānîk* "trained man" in Gen 14:14 fits with its known use in the early second millennium BC (and some four centuries later).
9. The clustering of Egyptian loan-words in the Joseph Story suggests that the writer knew the cultural setting that he was writing about, and that he was not making it up in another land centuries

after the event.

10. The treaties and covenants preserved in the book of Genesis have several parallels with treaties of the early Second Millennium. These parallels are not observable in any other period.
11. The sale of Joseph into slavery for twenty shekels of silver (Gen 37:28) fits well with the price of a slave in the eighteenth century BC. Later inflation increased the price, so this shows this particular feature of the Joseph story reflects that period accurately.

# Chapter 4

# Patterns in the Pentateuchal Covenants and the Late Second Millennium Hittite Treaties

WE NOW TURN FROM looking at the book of Genesis to consider the two large covenants at the heart of the Pentateuch—Exodus/Leviticus and Deuteronomy. Because Deuteronomy has a covenant pattern that is more easily discernible, it shall first command our attention, before we turn to the covenant preserved in Exodus and Leviticus. Then our attention will shift to looking at the treaties (thirty-four in number) made between the Hittites of Anatolia and their neighbors in the late Second Millennium BC. Many similarities between these treaties and the pentateuchal covenants will become evident. These similarities will provide strong evidence for the Pentateuch also being a late Second Millennium document.

## DEUTERONOMY

Within the book of Deuteronomy the framework of a covenant document can be discerned. It is the covenant between the LORD and his people, Israel, as they were about to go into the Promised Land. It is a reiteration of the earlier covenant that the LORD made with Israel at Mount Sinai nearly forty years earlier. Thus (brackets refer to the total number of verses):

Table 17. Deuteronomy as a covenant document

| |
|---|
| Title/Preamble 1:1–5 (5) |
| Historical Prologue 1:6—3:29 (93) |
| Stipulations 4:1—26:19 (581) |
| Solemn Ceremony 27:1-26 (incl. Witnesses 2–8) (26) |
| Blessings 28:1–14 (14) |
| Curses 28:15–68 (53) |
| Epilogue 29:1—31:8 (incl. Oath 29:9–14) (57) |
| Deposit and Public Reading 31:9–13 (5) |
| Witnesses 31:14—32:43 (incl. Deposit 31:26) (59) |

However, the book of Deuteronomy does not end there. It closes with an injunction from Moses for the people to take to heart what he has declared to them (Deut 32:44-47). The LORD then tells Moses that he is not to die in the Promised Land, but on Mount Nebo (Deut 32:48-52). The book ends with Moses' blessing of the twelve tribes (Deut 33:1–29) and with an account of Moses' own death (Deut 34:1–12), clearly written posthumously by another author. For some, the presence of this extra material at the end of the book invalidates the arguments for the unity of Deuteronomy, its parallels with ancient treaties and Deuteronomy's origin at the time of Moses.[1] However, the presence of some non-covenantal material in the book of Deuteronomy, does not mean that the book does not contain a covenant. So to formulate views on the fact that Deuteronomy is not wholly covenantal is unjustified.[2]

## EXODUS/LEVITICUS

Having seen the covenant document at the heart of Deuteronomy, the next question is "Is there another covenant in the Pentateuch?" The answer has to be "yes," because Deuteronomy is only the reiteration of the original covenant made between the LORD and his people on Mount Sinai. If we look at the covenant that begins in Exodus 20 with the Ten Commandments we see that the Ten Commandments are introduced by a title: "*And God spoke all these words*": (1) and a Historical Prologue "*I am the LORD your God, who brought you out of Egypt, out of the land

---

1. E.g., Mayes, *NCB Deuteronomy*, 34.
2. As, for example, Weinfeld, *Deuteronomy*, 146-57.

*of slavery.*" (2). After the Ten Commandments there are detailed stipulations, sometimes called the "Book of the Covenant" Exod 20:18—23:19. After this are further features:

In Exod 24:1–18 there is a Solemn Ceremony that includes a list of witnesses and a statement that Moses read the Book of the Covenant to the people. The Stipulations resume in chapter 25, where Moses is commanded to make a sanctuary for the LORD. Next there is a detailed description of the worship tent or tabernacle, its furnishings and the regulations for the priests. However, at Exod 34:8 the stipulations resume through to 35:19. Thereafter there is a statement detailing how the command to make the tabernacle, its furnishings, and the consecration of its priests was fulfilled. The Book of Exodus closes with a description of the glory of the LORD filling the tabernacle.

Interestingly if we continue reading Leviticus, we see the stipulations for the covenant are resumed in chapter 11 with rules for clean and unclean animals. Three more groups of stipulations follow before we reach Leviticus 26, where we have blessings and then curses to conclude the Covenant. Lev 26:46 closes with the main colophon, a notice appended to a text by a scribe, detailing its contents.[3] The colophon reads: "*These are the decrees, the laws and the regulations that the LORD established on Mount Sinai between himself and the Israelites through Moses.*" There is then one additional group of stipulations, probably a supplement (Lev 27:1–33), closed by a final colophon in Lev 27:34 "*These are the commands the LORD gave Moses on Mount Sinai for the Israelites.*"

Summarizing this diagrammatically (figures in brackets refer to then number of verses):

Table 18. Exodus/Leviticus as a covenant document (with extra material)

| |
|---|
| *Title* Exod 20:1 (1) |
| *Historical Prologue* 20:2 (1) |
| *Stipulations* 20:3—23:33 (124) |
| *Solemn Ceremony* 24:1–4a (4) |
| *Witnesses* 24:4b–6 (3) |
| *Reading* 24:7–8 (2) |
| *Solemn Ceremony resumed* 24:9–18 (9) |
| *Stipulations* 25:1–8 |

3. See p. 30 n 3.

| |
|---|
| Extra material 25:9—34:7 |
| Stipulations 34:8–27 |
| Extra material 34:28–35 |
| Stipulations 35:1–19 |
| Extra material 35:20—40:38 |
| Leviticus |
| Extra material Lev 1:1—10:20 |
| Stipulations 11:1—15:33 |
| Extra material 16:1—17:16 |
| Stipulations 18:1—20:27 |
| Extra material 21:1—24:14 |
| Stipulations 24:15—26:2 |
| Blessings 26:3–13 (10) |
| Curses 26:14–45 (31) |
| Main colophon 26:46 (1) |
| Stipulations 27:1–33 (33) |
| Final colophon 27:34 (1) |

It can be concluded that the classic covenantal form can be traced, but there is a lot of extra material often relating to the tabernacle and religious ritual that is inserted. Perhaps, more surprisingly, it is in Leviticus that we find the conclusion of the covenant with the blessings and curses. So what is going on here?

The division between Exodus and Leviticus may not have been original.[4] Exodus 1–19 is really a continuation of the historical narrative begun in Genesis. This material was too long to fit on to one scroll, so it was separated, eventually to be attached to the book later to be known as Exodus. Exodus 20 is the beginning of the covenant. The author recorded the stipulations of the covenant and wove into this the extra material concerning the tabernacle, its furnishings, and the priesthood. This scroll became too long and so was divided at Exodus 40 with the glory of the LORD filling the temple providing a fitting end to the book we now know as Exodus.

So it is only when Exodus and Leviticus are combined that we can clearly discern a covenant document, to which much extra material was added. Taking out this extra material the following framework of a covenant document emerges:

4. *TLC* III, 125.

Table 19. Exodus/Leviticus as a covenant document (without extra material)

| |
|---|
| Title Exod 20:1 (1) |
| Historical Prologue 20:2 (1) |
| Stipulations 20:3—23:33 (124) |
| Solemn Ceremony 24:1–4a (4) |
| Witnesses 24:4b–6 (3) |
| Reading 24:7–8 (2) |
| Solemn Ceremony resumed 24:9–18 (9) |
| Stipulations Exod 25:1-Lev 26:2 (1296) including much extra material now taken out |
| Blessings 26:3–13 (10) |
| Curses 26:14–45 (31) |
| Main colophon 26:46 (1) |
| Additional Stipulations 27:1–33 (33) |
| Final colophon 27:34 (1) |

Exodus/Leviticus can be compared with Deuteronomy thus:

Table 20. Exodus/Leviticus and Deuteronomy as covenant documents

| Exodus/Leviticus | Deuteronomy |
|---|---|
| Title Exod 20:1 | Title 1:1–1:5 |
| Historical Prologue 20:2 | Historical Prologue 1:6—3:29 |
| Stipulations 20:3—23:33 | Stipulations 4:1—26:19 |
| Solemn Ceremony 24:1–4a | Solemn Ceremony 27:1–26 |
| Witnesses 24:6b–6 | |
| Reading 24:7–8 | |
| Solemn Ceremony resumed 24:9–18 | |
| Stipulations 25:1-Lev 26:2 | |
| Blessings 26:3–13 | Blessings 28:1–14 |
| Curses 26:14–45 | Curses 28:15–68 |
| Main colophon 26:46 | Epilogue 29:1—31:8 |
| Additional stipulations 27:1–33 | Deposit and Reading 31:9–13 |
| Final colophon 27:34 | Witnesses 31:14—32:43 |

There is a basic similarity between the covenants of Exodus/Leviticus and Deuteronomy. Both covenants begin with a Title, Historical Prologue, Stipulations, and Solemn Ceremony in that order. Deuteronomy has a simpler structure with only one set of stipulations. The position of the

Witnesses and Reading sections varies between the two texts. Only Exodus/Leviticus has the colophons, but both Exodus/Leviticus and Deuteronomy have blessings followed by curses.

## THE HITTITE TREATIES

The pentateuchal covenants are now viewed in a much wider context, being compared with treaties made by the Hittites of central Anatolia (Turkey) and surrounding states. Among the ruins of the Hittite capital of Hattusas (modern Boğazköy), in the uplands of central Anatolia, no less than thirty-four inter-state treaties have been found.[5] The dates of these treaties cluster around the two centuries ca. 1380–1180 BC. Two treaties from this period were also found at the Syrian sea-port city of Ugarit[6] and one in Thebes in Egypt.[7]

The Hittite treaties with Mesopotamia, Syria, and Egypt were written in Akkadian,[8] the language of the Babylonians and Assyrians from Mesopotamia (modern Iraq), which was used as the language of diplomacy of the time. Hittite was used for treaties with the Anatolian states— Kizzuwatna, Hayasa, Hapalla, Mira, Seha River Land, and Wilusa.[9] It was used for the treaty with the southern Hittite internal satellite kingdom of Tarhuntassa, and also Anatolian people groups like the people of Ismirika and the Kaskeans. Hittite copies of treaties with Amurru (in Syria) and Alasia (Cyprus) are also preserved. Two other languages were also used. The treaty from Thebes between the Hittite king Hattusil III with Ramesses II of Egypt *[71B]* was written in Egyptian, that of the Hittite king Suppiluliuma II with Niqmad III of Ugarit *[77]* was written in Ugaritic. The fact that Akkadian, Ugaritic, and Egyptian were also used suggests that these treaties were not specifically Hittite in origin and that a common treaty format was in use throughout the Near East of the time.[10] For the two centuries in

---

5. The ones quoted in this work are listed in Appendix Two Table 3. See pp. 134–35. This figure excludes several very fragmentary treaties.

6. The Treaty of the Hittite king Suppiluliuma I with Niqmad II of Ugarit *[61]* and the treaty of Suppiluliuma II with Niqmad III of Ugarit *[77]*. Two treaties: the treaty of Idrimi of Alalakh with Pilliya of Kizzuwatna *[41]* and the treaty of Niqmepa of Alalakh with Ir-Adad of Tunip *[42]* from a slightly earlier period were found at Alalakh in Syria.

7. The treaty of Ramesses II of Egypt with the Hittite king Hattusil III *[71B]*.

8. More specifically Middle Babylonian.

9. For locations see *TLC* II, 51; III 99. See Hittite Treaty Partners, map 2, p. 143.

10. Bright, *History of Israel*, 150–51; Kitchen suggests that it was the Kassites in

question, ca. 1380–1180 BC, the conventions for the content and layout of treaties remained remarkably uniform until the whole political framework disappeared, virtually overnight, around 1180 BC when the Hittite Empire fell. As we have seen, this was probably due to a combination of invasions of the Kaskeans from northern Anatolia, and the so-called "Sea Peoples" and by famine and plague in relatively quick succession.[11]

Most of the Hittite treaties were drawn up between the kings of the Hittites and their vassals—subordinate kings who pledged allegiance to the Hittite crown. These are sometimes called "suzerainty" treaties or "vassal" treaties. The notable exception is the treaty of 1259 BC between the Hittite king Hatusil III and his Egyptian counterpart Ramesses II [71]. This is what can be termed a "parity treaty" and exists both in an Akkadian version from the Hittite capital of Hattusas and in two Egyptian copies from Thebes in Egypt.[12]

## THE HITTITE TREATIES AND THE PENTATEUCHAL COVENANTS

These Hittite treaties of the late Second Millennium are sometimes compared with the pentateuchal covenants. This comparison is not new. It can be traced back to V. Korošec some eighty years ago,[13] through G. E. Mendenhall well over fifty years ago[14] and has been taken up by others since.[15] Although some scholars have questioned such a comparison on methodological grounds,[16] it should be noted that the pentateuchal

---

Babylon who applied the old, long-transmitted law-collection format to the Hittite treaties, *TLC* III, 246.

11. See above pp. 26–28.

12. See above p. 20. Although the pair of treaties between the Hittite king Suppiluliuma I and Shattiwaza of Mitanni [55A, 55B] appear to be parity treaties, they are in reality suzerainty treaties disguised as parity treaties *TLC* III, 188.

13. Korošec, *Hethitische Staatsverträge*.

14. Mendenhall, "Covenant Forms," 50–76, who incidentally only compared the so-called "Book of the Covenant" (Exod 20:22—23:33) and Josh 24 with the Hittite treaties. He paid no attention to Exodus/Leviticus as a whole or to Deuteronomy. See Kitchen, *OROT*, 290.

15. E.g., Kline, *Treaty of the Great King*; Kitchen, *Ancient Orient and Old Testament*, 90–102; *Bible in its World*, 79–86; *OROT*, 283–307.

16. E.g., Mayes, *NCB Deuteronomy*, 34, who claims "it is not possible to transfer directly and immediately from the literary context of the extra-biblical treaties to the literary context of Deuteronomy . . . this in turn means that the arguments for the unity

covenants do not slavishly follow a treaty pattern. As P. C. Craigie has observed, "The use of the treaty form in the Hebrew tradition must necessarily have involved adaptation. At the most obvious level, there was the adaptation of a political document for a specifically religious purpose."[17] In fact, the pentateuchal covenants represent a fresh and distinctive formulation, intelligently using the two components of treaty and law, not just a crude pastiche of either or both.[18]

## TREATIES MADE WITH PEOPLES

The Old Testament covenants are in essence treaties made between the LORD and his people, Israel. Treaties made with people groups are also a feature of the late Second Millennium Hittite treaties[19] thus:

1. Three treaties made by the Hittites with the Kaskeans *[46–48]*
2. Treaty of Arnuwandas I with the men of Ismirika[20] *[53]*
3. Treaty of Arnuwandas I with the Kaskeans *[54]*
4. Treaty of Suppiluliuma I with Huqqanas and "the men of Hayasa"[21] *[60]*

Thus treaties made with peoples (The LORD and Israel and the Hittites and their Anatolian vassals) are a feature of both the pentateuchal covenants and the late Second Millennium Hittite treaties.[22] There are no later examples of treaties made with peoples among the First Millennium treaties.[23]

---

of Deuteronomy because of its treaty background; explicit arguments for the unity on this basis—and indeed also for Deuteronomy's origin in Mosaic times are inadmissible."

17. Craigie, *NICOT Deuteronomy*, 27. See further von Rad, *OTL Deuteronomy*, 21.

18. Kitchen, "The Rise and Fall," 128; *TLC* III, 128, 132–36.

19. Since all these are treaties were made with the peoples of Anatolia they were all written in Hittite.

20. An area east of the Euphrates to the Upper Tigris, modern Siverek probably reflects the ancient name. See further *TLC* II, 42.

21. Hayasa is another north Anatolian people. For further discussion of their land see *TLC* II, 48. Some see them as the ancestors of the Armenians. Compare Hayasa with Haik, the Armenians' own name for themselves, and Hayastan, their name for their country.

22. Also compare the treaty made between Joshua and the Gibeonites, Josh 9:1–27.

23. A later Assyrian treaty, the Succession Treaty of Esarhaddon, 672 BC *[94]* enlists the support of Humbaresh, city-ruler of Nahshimarti and all the Nahshimartians (line 4) in recognizing the succession arrangements, but this is not actually a treaty made between the Assyrians and that people group.

## TREATIES MADE WITH SUCCESSIVE GENERATIONS

The covenant made at Mount Sinai was repeated nearly forty years later with the Israelites on the Plains of Moab. This ostensibly forms the book of Deuteronomy. The making of new agreements or treaties with a succeeding generation is something that can be observed within the biblical material as with the two stories of Abraham and Abimelech, and Isaac and Abimelech.[24] It can also be observed within the collection of ancient Near Eastern treaties that has come down to us.[25]
For example:

1. The Hittite king, Suppiluliuma I, made a treaty with Niqmad II of Ugarit [61]; his next-but-one successor, Mursil II, made a treaty with Niqmepa of Ugarit [63].

2. The Hittite king, Tudkhalia IV, made successive treaties with kings of the southern Hittite internal satellite kingdom of Tarhuntassa[26] (a) with Kurunta in ca. 1230 BC [73] and (b) with Ulmi-Tesub [74] in ca. 1210 BC.

From a later period there is:

3. The eighth century BC Syrian ruler, Bar-Gayah, king of KTK[27] who made treaties with two successive kings of Arpad, probably Atar-sumki [86] in ca. 783 BC and Matiel [87] in ca. 775 BC and [88] in ca. 773 BC.

---

24. Gen 21:22–24; 25–33; 26:26–31. See further pp. 40–41.

25. Kitchen argues (*TLC* III, 88) that the Hittite treaty of Tudkhalia II with Sunassura (I) of Kizzuwatna [50] is not from the same generation as an Akkadian version [51], but rather the second is the work of a Tudkhalia II, III or Suppiluliuma I, either at two points in reign of Sunassura I or with two rulers both called Sunassura.

26. See p. 27 n 30.

27. The vocalization and location of KTK is uncertain, hence the use of capitals here. The various suggestions are summarized by Hawkins in *RLA* VI, 254b–256a, who lists three conditions that KTK must satisfy: (1) To dominate previously prominent Arpad it probably was a major power; (2) It must be a neighbor of or be contiguous to Arpad and; (3) It must have the predominantly Assyrian and Babylonian gods listed in Stela I [87] A.7–14. Bar-Gayah may well have been an Assyrian governor (See further *TLC* II, 87; III, 219–20), perhaps even the influential *turtānu* or army commander Shamshi-ilu who is attested from at least 796–752 BC (Lemaire and Durand, *Inscriptions Araméennes*, 1, but the latter is shown beardless on the Antakya (Tavla) and Pazarcık (Kızkapanlı) stelae and may thus have been a eunuch, hardly a suitable candidate for the title "king," unless the title "king" merely means "governor." Bar-Gayah was clearly no eunuch, having sons according to Sefire I [87] B.1.

Furthermore, there are two references within the treaties themselves to treaties made with an earlier generation, thus:

4. The Hittite king Muwatallis II in his treaty with Talmi-sarruma of Aleppo *[67]* refers to an original tablet that was stolen. Muwatallis had a new tablet made, citing his father Mursil (II)'s text (Obv.3–4, 7b–8), "*[A tablet] of the treaty for Talmi-sarruma, king of the land of Aleppo, my father Mursil (II) made for him but the tablet was stolen. I, the Great King, have written another tablet [for him] . . . And the tablet of the treaty which [my] father Mursil (II) made for him is written thus.*"

5. The Hittite king Hattusil III in his treaty with Bentesina of Amurru[28] *[69]* mentions a treaty that his grandfather Suppiluliuma I had made with Aziru of Amurru *[58A]* (lines Obv.5–6), "*My grandfather showed him* [Aziru king of Amurru] (*mercy*), *he wrote a treaty tablet and recorded the boundaries of the land of Amurru of his fathers and gave it* [the tablet] *to him.*"

and Obv.28–30a "*To Bentesina a tablet of the treaty corresponding to the tablet which Suppiluliuma, the Great King [. . .] for Aziru, I, the Great King, have written for Bentesina, king of the land of Amuru, in accordance with the treaty tablet of my grandfather, and I have given it to him.*"

## PATTERNS IN THE HITTITE TREATIES

All the Hittite treaties of the late Second Millennium *[50–80]* start with a title, a historical prologue and the stipulations made between the two parties to the treaty.[29] Thereafter all the sections found in the pentateuchal covenants occur, but with some variation. In the treaties, curses, almost without exception, precede blessings.[30] This is in contrast to Exodus/Leviticus and Deuteronomy. The scheme of a treaty made between king

---

28. An area in Syria between the river Orontes and the Mediterranean.

29. In some texts some or all of these features are lost. See Appendix Two, Table 3 column 5, pp. 135–36. In the treaty of Suppiluliuma I with Shattiwaza of Mitanni *[55A]* the title and historical prologue are combined.

30. The treaties of an unidentified ruler of Hatti with the Kaskeans (no 2) *[47]* and of Suppiluliuma I with Huqqanas of Hayasa *[60]* which may incorporate an earlier treaty made by Tudkhalia III with the Hayasa people *[54bis]*, are exceptions, with blessings preceding curses. Compare too the blessing pregnant in the phrase "*after he has done you good*" in Josh 24:20b that follows the curse.

Shattiwaza of Mitanni and the Hittite king, Suppiluliuma I, *[56A]* can be summarized as follows:

Table 21. Treaty of Shattiwaza of Mitanni and the Hittite king Suppiluliuma I *[56A]*

| |
|---|
| Title/Preamble Obv.1a (1) |
| Historical Prologue 1b–68 (68) |
| Stipulations 69–Rev.6 (?) |
| Deposit 7 (1) |
| Public Reading 8a (1) |
| Witnesses 8b–24 (16) |
| Curses 25–34 (9) |
| Blessings 35–43 (8) |
| Curses 44–53a (9) |
| Blessings 53b–62 (9) |

It can be compared to Deuteronomy 1:1–32:43:

Table 22. Deuteronomy as a covenant document

| |
|---|
| Title/Preamble 1:1–1:5 (5) |
| Historical Prologue 1:6—3:29 (93) |
| Stipulations 4:1–26:19 (581) |
| Solemn Ceremony 27:1–26 (incl. Witnesses 2–8) (26) |
| Blessings 28:1–14 (14) |
| Curses 28:15–68 (53) |
| Epilogue 29:1—31:8 (incl. Oath 29:91–94) (57) |
| Deposit and Public Reading 31:9–13 (4) |
| Witnesses 31:14—32:43 (incl. Deposit 31:26) (59) |

The first three sections (Title/Preamble, Historical Prologue, and Stipulations) are the same; in Deuteronomy blessings precede curses, in the Hittite treaty there is a list of witnesses before a double dose of curses followed by blessings. In Deuteronomy the witnesses conclude the text.

## SYRIAN AND ASSYRIAN TREATIES FROM THE FIRST MILLENNIUM

The Hittite texts are not the only collection of treaties from the ancient Near East. From the First Millennium there are three Aramaic treaties from Sefire[31] in Syria and twelve treaties from the archives of the Neo-Assyrian kings from Nineveh, Nimrud,[32] and Assur in northern Iraq.

There are a number of striking differences between these First Millennium treaties and the late Second Millennium Hittite treaties.[33] Although the beginnings of the First Millennium treaties are often damaged, it is clear, from the surviving examples, that witnesses follow the title.[34] Gone are the historical prologue[35] and blessings. Although a single blessing does occur in the treaty of Bar-Gayah of KTK with Matiel of Arpad, ca. 775 BC, *[87]* (§15) Face C 10–16a "[*Whoever will respect the words . . .*] *may the gods keep* [*all evils*] *away from his day and from his house*," this relates solely to respect for the physical monument, not to detailed obedience to the document proper that characterizes the treaties of the late Second Millennium. In the First Millennium treaties there is no mention of a solemn ceremony, or of the text being read.

The largest of all the Assyrian treaties was a treaty that the Assyrian king Esarhaddon made with seven of his vassals among the Medes in 672 BC[36] *[94]*. It sets out detailed provisions as to who would succeed to his throne.

The scheme of the treaty can be summarized as follows (brackets refer to number of lines):

---

31. Twenty-five km SE of Aleppo. *TLC* II, 87.

32. Calah of Gen 10:11.

33. These differences can be explained at least in part by the historical events relating to the collapse of the Hittite empire and the coming of the Sea Peoples (see pp. 26–28), and the subsequent Assyrian practice of incorporating territories into their empire rather than merely maintaining a clientele of vassals. These differences are minimized in the work of McCarthy, *Treaty and Covenant*, 122.

34. See Appendix Two Table 4 column 5, p. 136. Only the treaty of the Assyrian Queen Zakutu with Shamash-shum-ukin *[96]*, ca. 669 BC, has no demonstrable witness section.

35. It will be argued later p. 92 that the historical prologue claimed in the treaty of the Assyrian king Ashurbanipal with Abiate of Qedar *[97]*, ca. 653/2 BC, is a "historical flashback," not a historical prologue.

36. A colophon (scribal note about the writing of the text) (see p. 30 n 3) consisting of lines 664–69 "*The 18th day of Iyyar* [April–May], *eponymy of Nabu-bel-usur* [672 BC], *governor of Dur-Sharruken* [Khorsabad]. *The treaty of Esarhaddon, king of Assyria, which he concluded on behalf of Ashurbanipal, the great crown prince of the succession of Assyria, and on behalf of Shamash-shum-ukin, the crown prince of the succession of Babylon*" provides the date. It is the only one of the treaties to be so precisely dated.

Table 23. The Succession Treaty of Esarhaddon, 672 BC [94]

| |
|---|
| Title/Preamble 1–12 (12) |
| Witnesses 13–40 (incl. Oath 25–40) (27) |
| Sub-Title 41–45 (4) |
| Stipulations 46–413 (367) |
| Curses 414–493 (79) |
| Stipulations 494–512 (18) |
| Curses 513–663 (150) |

It is when the pattern of this treaty is compared with the pentateuchal covenants that fundamental differences come into focus, showing that the pentateuchal covenants are not First Millennium compositions. The following comparison between Deuteronomy and the Succession Treaty of Esarhaddon will make this clear:

Table 24. Comparison between Deuteronomy and the Succession Treaty of Esarhaddon, 672 BC

| Deuteronomy | Succession Treaty of Esarhaddon, 672 BC |
|---|---|
| Title/Preamble 1:1–1:5 | Title/Preamble 1–12 |
| Historical Prologue 1:6—3:29 | Witnesses 13–40 (incl. Oath 25–40) |
| Stipulations 4:1—26:19 | Sub-Title 41–45 |
| Solemn Ceremony 27:1–26 (incl. Witnesses 2–8) | Stipulations 46–413 |
| Blessings 28:1–14 | |
| Curses 28:15–68 | Curses 414–49 |
| Epilogue 29:1—31:8 (incl. Oath 29:91–94) | Stipulations 494–512 |
| Deposit and Public Reading 31:9–13 | Curses 513–663 |
| Witnesses 31:14—32:43 (incl. Deposit 31:26) | |

## ARE THE BIBLICAL COVENANTS JUST TREATIES?

Although it is clear that the pentateuchal Covenants closely resemble the format of late Second Millennium Hittite treaties, for example in having a witness section, clauses for the deposit and reading of the terms of the covenant, they do not follow the late Second Millennium treaties in having curses before blessings.[37] Rather, in the pentateuchal covenants

37. For two exceptions see p. 56 n 30 .

blessings precede curses. This is a feature found in the Law Collections[38] of Lipit-Ishtar, king of Isin, *[10]* and Hammurabi, king of Babylon, *[14]* as the following schemes make clear:

Table 25. The Laws of Lipit-Ishtar (1934–1924 BC) *[10]*

| Preamble 1:1–55 |
|---|
| Historical Prologue 2:1–40 |
| Stipulations 2:Rev.1—21:4 |
| Epilogue 21:5–38 |
| Blessings 21:39–48 |
| Curses 21:49—22:16 |

Exactly the same scheme is found in the Laws of Hammurabi (1792–1750 BC) *[14]*

Table 26. The Laws of Hammurabi (1792–1750 BC) *[14]*

| Title/Preamble 1:1–1:49 |
|---|
| Historical Prologue 1:50—5:25 |
| Stipulations 5:26–46:102 |
| Epilogue 47:1- 49:1 |
| Blessings 49:2–17 |
| Curses 49:18—51:90 |

## TREATIES AND LAW COLLECTIONS

It is unwise to regard Treaties and Law Collections as unrelated genres. An examination of the non-biblical ancient Near Eastern material shows that this is not the case. Within the treaty of Suppiluliuma I with Huqqanas and the Hayasa people *[60]* there are instructions about sexual morality, such as one would expect to find in a Law Collection. Thus Stipulations §§ 25–29 (3:25–68):

> Now further concerning this my sister whom I have given you to be your wife: She has many full sisters and further relatives, [and you have] gained these as sisters too, because you have their sister

---

38. The term "Law Collection" is deliberate. The concept of a binding written Law Code was completely lacking in Mesopotamia. It seems that the judges of ancient times had neither the custom nor the techniques for arriving at a decision by means or interpreting and applying an authoritative written law code. Landsberger, "Die babylonische Termini," 223 cited in Mendenhall, "Covenant Forms," 32.

in marriage. Now in the land of Hatti, there is an important rule. A full brother does not have sex with his own sister or cousin, for that is improper. But anyone who does such a thing cannot live in Hattusas, but must die! Because your country is barbarous, it is allowed there that a full brother has sex with his own sister or cousin; but in Hattusas it is improper.

Now if it should happen that your wife's sister, further relative or cousin visits you, then give her food and drink; and eat, drink and have a happy time. But do not even desire to take her sexually—it is improper. On account of that deed, people are executed. So don't you try it either! Even if you are tempted to do such a thing by anyone else, then you do not need to heed him, don't do it! For this will be set under oath against you.

Also, you shall keep well clear of any palace-woman. Whatever kind of palace-woman it be, a free person or a serving maid, and do not go near her, do not approach her; do not even utter a word to her. Even your servant or your maidservant must not approach her. Keep a sharp lookout for her. The moment a palace-woman comes along, then jump right out of her way and leave her a clear passage! And to this case about a palace-woman pay the closest attention!

Now who was Maryas and why did he die? Did not a mere serving maid come by and he only looked at her? The father of the Sun-King[39] just glanced out of the window and fastened on him saying: "Why did you look at her?" So he died because of that matter. So, be sharply aware of any such thing by which a man can come to grief.

So, once you return to the land of Hayasa, thus you shall not take your brother's wives sexually or your sisters; in Hattusas, that is improper. Now if you come back up to the palace, then again that kind of behavior is improper. Also you shall not take as a wife a woman from the land of Azzi. But [divorce] that one whom you had taken earlier; she can be your concubine, but you cannot make her to be your wife. Now also take away your daughter from Maryas, and give her to (his) brother. Now give back those deportees belonging to Hatti who had crossed over to Hayasa. And also give back the Hittite borderlands!

Within the Mesopotamian cuneiform tradition there is a further link between a Law Collection and a Treaty. Thus when the Assyrian king Shamshi-Adad V makes a treaty with Marduk-zakir-shumi, king of Babylon, in ca. 824 BC [89] he uses curse formulae from the well-known Law Collection of the Babylonian king Hammurabi [14], which had been written over 900 years earlier, to impress upon his Babylonian treaty part-

---

39. A title of the Hittite king.

ner the importance of adherence to the treaty. Compare Rev.7,10–16 with Hammurabi *[14]* 49:98—50:7; 41–54; 64–68; 81–85.[40]

Table 27. The Laws of Hammurabi *[14]* compared with the Treaty of Shamshi-Adad V *[89]*

| Hammurabi 49:98—50:7 | Shamshi-Adad V Rev.7 |
|---|---|
| *May Ea,*[A] *the great prince, whose decrees go in front, expert of the gods, who knows everything, who lengthens the days of my life, deprive him of understanding and wisdom, and may they lead him into confusion, may he stop up his rivers at their source.* | *May Ea, expert of the gods, who knows everything, stop up his rivers [at their source].* |
| **Hammurabi 50:41–54** | **Shamshi-Adad V Rev.10–12** |
| *May Sin,*[B] *the lord of heaven, the god who created me, whose brilliance is visible among the gods, remove his crown and throne of kingship, may he impose on him a harsh punishment as his great condemnation, which will not disappear from his body, may he bring to an end each day, each month, each year of his reign in sighing and moaning.* | *[May Sin, the lord of heaven whose] brilliance is visible among the gods, [impose on him] a harsh punishment, which is not to be removed from his body, may [he bring to an end the days, months and years] of his reign in sighing and moaning.* |
| **Hammurabi 50:64–68** | **Shamsh-Adad V Rev.13–16a** |
| *May Adad,*[C] *Lord of plenty canal inspector of heaven and earth my helper deprive him of rain from heaven and flood water from the source.* | *[May Adad, canal inspector of heaven and earth deprive him of] rain from heaven and flood water from the source.* |
| **Hammurabi 50:81–85** | **Shamsh-Adad V Rev.16b** |
| *May Zababa,*[D] *great hero, first born in the Ekur, who goes at my right hand.* | *[May Zababa, great hero], who goes [at my right hand].* |
| A. The god of subterranean freshwater ocean. B. The moon god. C. The storm god. D. A warrior god. | |

The pentateuchal covenants, although essentially following the late Second Millennium treaty form, were not its slavish imitators. The stipulations of the covenant were the Laws that the LORD required his people Israel to obey. The pentateuchal covenants were, thus, in K. A. Kitchen's

---

40. This was first pointed out by Borger, "Marduk-zākir-šumi," 168–69.

phrase "a confluence of Treaty and Law."[41] This is further demonstrated by the fact that the pentateuchal covenants follow the tradition of the Law Collections in placing blessings before curses.

## CONCLUSIONS

By way of conclusion, I offer the following:

1. Within Deuteronomy the text of a covenant can clearly be discerned 1:1—32:43. The remaining material 32:44—34:12 was not part of this covenant, but this does not invalidate the demonstration that a covenant document forms the heart of the book.
2. Exodus 20:1 to Leviticus 27:34 constitute another covenant document. Even though much material was added to the stipulations section, the framework of this covenant document is also clearly discernible.
3. The fundamental framework of both the Deuteronomy and Exodus/Leviticus covenants is the same.
4. The fact that the treaties made by the Hittites were written in four languages—Hittite, Akkadian, Egyptian, and Ugaritic—shows that they were not specifically Hittite in their origin or usage and suggests that a common treaty format was in use throughout the Near East of the time.
5. Treaties made by a ruler with people-groups are found both in the pentateuchal covenants and in the late Second Millennium treaties. They are not found later.
6. Deuteronomy is an example of a covenant renewed with a later generation. Several other examples of this can be seen among the Hittite treaties of the late Second Millennium and a single example too from the early First Millennium Sefire treaties from Syria.
7. All the Hittite treaties of the late Second Millennium start with a title, a historical prologue and the stipulations made between the two states making the treaty. This pattern is found too in the pentateuchal covenants. Thereafter, in the pentateuchal covenants, essentially all the sections found in the Hittite treaties occur, but with some minor variation.
8. In the Hittite treaties, with two minor exceptions, curses precede

---

41. Kitchen, *Bible in its World*, 83; "The Rise and Fall," 128; *TLC* III, 128, 132–36.

blessings. By contrast in Exodus/Leviticus and Deuteronomy blessings precede curses—a feature that is found in the Law Collections.

9. With one solitary exception blessings are absent from the First Millennium treaties. The fact that, along with the late Second Millennium Hittite treaties, the pentateuchal covenants have blessings, is an indication that the pentateuchal covenants are also late Second Millennium compositions in origin.

10. That the covenants in Exodus/Leviticus and Deuteronomy fit closely with the treaty form current towards the end of the Second Millennium is a further indication that Exodus/Leviticus and Deuteronomy are also late Second Millennium compositions.

11. That there is no real similarity in form between the covenants in Exodus/Leviticus and Deuteronomy and treaties of the First Millennium is strong evidence that Exodus/Leviticus and Deuteronomy are not First Millennium compositions.

12. The pentateuchal covenants were not slavish imitators of the treaty form. They were rather "a confluence of Treaty and Law."

So by way of a summary: It can be concluded that the form of the pentateuchal covenants has much more in common with the Second Millennium BC treaties than their counterparts from the First Millennium BC. This suggests that the pentateuchal covenants are Second Millennium BC in their origin.

# Chapter 5

## Detail, Detail: The Heart of the Matter

IN THE PREVIOUS CHAPTER we saw how the form of the large biblical covenants in the Pentateuch, namely Exodus/Leviticus and Deuteronomy, mirrors the form of the Hittite treaties of the late Second Millennium BC. Significant though this observation may be, it does not, in itself, prove that Exodus/Leviticus and Deuteronomy are authentic late Second Millennium compositions, since the "author," while keeping this format, could have added later material. We therefore need to look more closely at specific features of the covenants to see if these too are corroborated by features found in late Second Millennium treaties. This chapter contains much detail—titles, historical prologues, stipulations, deposit of the treaty, and the reading of the treaty terms, blessings and curses, not to mention epilogues and historical flashbacks—some of which readers may wish to skip, but it is this detail that provides arguably the most compelling evidence for the Pentateuch being an authentic composition of the late Second Millennium BC.

### TITLES

Both the pentateuchal covenants are introduced by a title containing the verb "spoke," thus:

Exod 20:1 "God *spoke* all these words saying"

Deut 1:1 "These are the words that Moses *spoke* . . . and so it was . . . Moses *spoke* . . . to Israel . . . saying":

This pattern is also clearly seen in Josh 24:2 "Thus *says* YHWH, God of Israel." These titles can thus be termed "verbal."

66  THE BOOKS OF MOSES REVISITED

The title in the late Second Millennium Hittite treaties, (in both languages Akkadian and Hittite), does not actually contain a verb, they all have the same basic format:

"Thus KING'S NAME + titles"

Both languages use the Akkadian word *umma* "thus," which implies a verb of speech.[1]

Linguistically it can be said that the title in the Hittite treaties, if not in its purist sense verbal, has an implied verb "in ellipsis." So, in detail [All kings whose origin is left unspecified are Hittites]:

1. Treaty of Tudkhalia II or Suppiluliuma I with Sunassura (II ?) of Kizzuwatna[2] *[51]* Obv.1

"Thus (says) the Tabarna[3] [Tudkhalia II or Suppiluliuma I]"

2. Treaty of Arnuwandas I with the people of Ismirika *[53]* Obv.1a

"Thus (says) Arnuwandas, [Great King, king of the land of Hatti]"

3. Treaty of Shattiwaza of Mitanni with Suppiluliuma I *[56A]* Obv.1

"[Thus] (says) Shattiwaza, son of Tushratta, king of the land of Mitanni"

4. Treaty of Suppiluliuma I with Tette of Nuhasse[4] *[57]* 1–2a

"Thus (says) the Sun-King, Great King, king of the land of Hatti, hero"

5. Treaty of Suppiluliuma I with Huqqanas of Hayasa *[60]* 1:1

"Thus (says) the Sun-King, Suppiluliuma I, king of the land of Hatti"

6. Treaty of Suppiluliuma I with Niqmad II of Ugarit *[61]* Obv.1

"Thus (says) the Sun-King Suppiluliuma, Great King, king of the land of Hatti, hero"

7. Treaties of Mursil II with Duppi-Tesub of Amurru *[62A and 62B]* 1a

"Thus (says) the Sun-King, Mursil (II), Great King, king of the land of Hatti"

8. Treaty of Mursil II with Niqmepa of Ugarit *[63]* 1

"Thus (says) the Sun-King, Mursil (II), [Great King], king of the land of Hatti"

9. Treaty of Mursil II with Kupanta-Kurunta of Mira[5] *[65]* 1

"Thus (says) the Sun-King, Mursil (II), Great King, king of the land of Hatti, hero"

---

1. See further Deutscher, *Syntactic Change*, 67, 79–82.
2. A kingdom in S Anatolia, classical Cilicia.
3. A title of the Hittite king.
4. An area south of the Euphrates in Syria.
5. A kingdom in W Anatolia.

10. Treaty of Mursil II with Manapa-Tarhunta of Seha River Land[6] *[66]* 1

"Thus (says) the Sun-King, Mursil (II), Great King, king [of the land of Hatti]"

11. Treaty of Muwatallis II with Talmi-sarruma of Aleppo *[67]* Obv.1a

"[Thus] (says) the Tabarna, Muwatallis, Great King, king of the land of Hatti, hero"

12. Treaty of Muwatallis II with Alaksandus[7] of Wilusa[8] *[68]* 1a

"Thus says the Sun-King, Muwatallis (II), Great King, king of the land of Hatti"

13. Treaty of Hattusil III with Bentesina of Amurru *[69]* 1a

"[Thus (says) the Tabarna, Hattusil (III)], the Great [King], king [of the land of Hatti, hero]"

14. Treaty of Tudkhalia IV with Sausga-muwa of Amurru *[72]* 1–2a

"[Thus (says) the Tabarna, Tudkhalia] (IV), the Great King, [king of the] land [of Hatti], hero"

15. Treaty of Tudkhalia IV with Kurunta of Tarhuntassa *[73]* 1

"Thus (says) the Tabarna, Tudkhalia (IV), the Great King, king of the land of Hatti, hero"

The title in Deut 1:1 has the same fundamental structure as the title in the Akkadian version of the treaty of Egyptian king Ramesses II with the Hittite king Hattusil III, 1259 BC *[71A]*, where there is a repeated personal name with two verbs so compare:

> Deut 1:1. "These are the words that Moses spoke . . . and so it was . . . Moses spoke . . . to Israel . . . saying"

with Treaty of Ramesses II with Hattusil III *[71A]* Obv.1–7:

---

6. Another kingdom in W Anatolia. The river in question may be *either* the Kaikos of antiquity, the modern Bakır Çayı that flows near Pergamum, Lloyd, *Ancient Turkey*, 45 *or* further south the Hermos of antiquity, the modern Gediz, *TLC* III, 99.

7. Many equate Alaksandus with Alexandros, another name for Priam's son Paris, in Homer's *Iliad*, who is first mentioned in 3.16. Even if this Alexandros is too early to be the Alexandros of the Trojan War the name could have been passed down the family line to be used again at a slightly later date. Muwatallis may find an echo in the Greek name Motylos, preserved in the *Ethnika* (554.5) of Stephanus Byzantius, (ca. AD 530).

8. Probably a state in NW Anatolia. Wilusa may reflect the Greek Ilion, another name for Troy.

> *The treaty which Ramesses (II) [beloved] of Amun, Great King, king [of Egypt made on a tablet of silver] with Hattusil (III), [Great King], king of Hatti, his brother, for [Egypt with the land of Hatti], in order to establish [great] peace and great [brotherhood] between them forever. Thus says Ramesses (II), beloved of Amun, Great King, king of Egypt, hero of all lands; son of Minmuarea [Sethos I], Great King, king of Egypt, hero; grandson of Minpahtarea [Ramesses I], Great King, king of Egypt, hero to Hattusil (III), Great King, king of the land of Hatti, hero; grandson of Suppiluliuma (I), Great King, king of the land of Hatti, hero.*[9]

This use contrasts with the titles used for the treaties from the First Millennium. These only have "descriptive" title lines, no verbs are used. Thus the general form is:

> *Treaty of PN1, king of x with PN2, king of y*

So, in detail [All the rulers left unspecified are Assyrian]:

1. Treaty of Bar-Gayah, king of KTK with Matiel of Arpad. Sefire I, ca. 775 BC, *[87]* 1:

    > *The treaty of Bar-Gayah, king of KTK with Matiel, son of Atar-sumki, king of [Arpad].*

2. Treaty of Esarhaddon with Baal of Tyre, ca. 676 BC, *[93]* 1:1–2a:

    > *The treaty of Esarhaddon, king of Assyria, son of [Sennacherib, king of Assyria] with Baal, king of Tyre.*

3. Treaty with the rulers of the Medes concerning Esarhaddon's succession, 672 BC, *[94]* 1–3:

    > *The treaty of Esarhaddon, king of the world, king of Assyria, son of Sennacherib, king of the world, king of Assyria, with Humbaresh, city-ruler of Nahshimarti.*

4. Treaty of Queen Zakutu with Shamash-shum-ukin of Babylon, ca. 669 BC, *[96]* Obv.1–3:

---

9. The parallel Egyptian version *[71B]* from Thebes 5b–7a just has one verb thus: "*The treaty, which the Great Ruler of Hatti, Hattusil III, the hero, the son of Mursil II, the Great Ruler of Hatti, the hero, the grandson of Suppiluliuma I, [the Great Ruler of Hatti] the hero, made upon a silver tablet for Usimare Setepenre [Ramesses II], the Great Ruler of Egypt, the hero, the son of Menmare [Sethos I], the Great Ruler of Egypt, the hero, the grandson of Menpehtyre [Ramesses I], the Great Ruler of Egypt, the hero, the good treaty of peace and brotherhood, to bring in [good] peace [and good brotherhood between us], forever.*"

*The treaty of Zakutu, the Queen of Sennacherib, king of Assyria, mother of Esarhaddon, king of Assyria, with Shamash-shum-ukin, his equal brother.*

5. Treaty of Sin-shar-ishkun (died 612 BC) with Babylonian allies, *[99]* 1–3:

    *The treaty of Sin-shar-ishkun, [king of Assyria], son of Ashurbanipal, [king of the world, king of Assyria] with Nabu-apla-iddina (and two other personal names).*

In summary, the verbal titles in the pentateuchal covenants are closer to the implied verbal (in ellipsis) titles of the Second Millennium Hittite treaties than to non-verbal descriptive title lines of the First Millennium Assyrian treaties.

## HISTORICAL PROLOGUES

Exod 20:2 has a very brief historical prologue— "*I am the LORD your God, who brought you out of Egypt, out of the land of slavery,*"—whereas Deuteronomy has a much more extensive prologue 1:6—3:9.[10]

Historical Prologues are found in the earliest of all our texts, Eannatum's Stele of the Vultures *[1]* ca. 2500 BC and in each of the monumental Law Collections, Ur-Nammu, ca. 2100 BC; *[9]* Lipit-Ishtar, ca. 1930 BC; *[10]* and Hammurabi (1792–1750 BC) *[14]*. Then there was a veritable explosion of this feature in the fourteenth and thirteenth centuries BC. The vast majority of the late Second Millennium Hittite treaties, twenty-four in all, have historical prologues.[11] This burgeoning use of Historical Prologues may stem from the Hittites' deliberate use of past history to highlight their neighbors' indebtedness to the Hittites' supposedly gracious dealings with them. It is striking that Historical Prologues do not occur in the Aramaic and Neo-Assyrian treaties of the First Millennium.[12]

---

10. Interestingly in Josh 24:2c–13 the historical prologue is the largest section.

11. See Appendix Two Table 3 column 6, pp. 134–35.

12. Despite numerous claims made about the Ashurbanipal's treaty with Abiate of Qedar, 653/2 BC, *[97]* it will be pointed out below p. 92 that its so-called "Historical Prologue" is really a "historical flashback"—what Kitchen terms a HRAF "Historical reminiscence, archaeological flashback." See p. 89.

## STIPULATIONS

### *A Basic Ruling Followed by the Fine Print*

The stipulations form the heart of any treaty, law-collection or covenant. One hundred and thirty-five stipulations can be identified in Exodus/Leviticus and 101 in Deuteronomy.[13] This total, though large, is not as large as those of the Hammurabi or Hittite Law Collections as the following table illustrates:[14]

Table 28. The number of stipulations in ancient Near Eastern law collections

| Law Collection | Date BC | No. of paragraphs |
|---|---|---|
| Ur-Nammu [9] | ca. 2100 | 52 |
| Lipit-Ishtar [10] | ca. 1930 | 38 |
| Old Assyrian Laws [12] | ca. 1900 | 11 |
| Sumerian Laws on exercise tablets [11] | ca. 1800 | 42 |
| Eshnunna [13] | ca. 1800 | 55 |
| Hammurabi [14] | ca. 1750 | 275[A] |
| Laws from Hazor[B] | 18th–17th C | |
| Hittite Laws Old Series [36] | 16th–14th C | 202 |
| Hittite Laws New Series [36] | 13th C | 36 |
| Middle Assyrian Laws [81] | 12th–11th C | 128 |
| Exodus/Leviticus | | 135[C] |
| Deuteronomy | | 101 |
| Neo-Babylonian Laws [102] | ca. 600 | 15 |
| Demotic Laws from Hermopolis, Egypt [103] | 8th – late 4th C | 117 |
| Laws from Gortyn, Crete [104] | 5th C | 18 |

A. Traditionally 282 paragraphs, but this figure is obtained by starting with a notional paragraph 100 after a break.

B. A tiny fragment, roughly one inch (2.5 cm) square, part of a Law Collection has recently been found at Hazor. It is reported to have close similarities to the Law Collection of Hammurabi [14]. See further Shanks, "On the Trail," 16; *TLC* III, 287.

C. Three extra stipulations in Num 5:11–31; 27:6–11 and 36:5–9 could also be added here. See p. 96.

13. *TLC* I, 767; 865.

14. It should be noted that all the non-biblical texts, apart from the Laws from Gortyn, are in some way incomplete.

## Detail, Detail: The Heart of the Matter

A striking feature of these two biblical covenants is that they begin with the basic topic (the Ten Commandments), which is followed by the detail, the "fine print" so to speak. Thus Exodus starts with 20:2–17 "The Ten Commandments." After recording the effect of the revelation on the Israelites (20:18–21) the detailed stipulations begin with 20:22.

In Deuteronomy the stipulations are prefaced by a lengthy introduction 4:1—5:6. "The Ten Commandments" follow in 5:7–21. In keeping with Deuteronomy's style of "preached law,"[15] a lengthy call to loyalty follows, 5:22—11:32. The main stipulations do not begin until 12:1.

The "Ten Commandments" are a classic case of what is called apodictic law or outright commands of the form "*You shall . . . / You shall not.*" Another type of law is the casuistic that deals with contingencies and is often introduced by "*if.*" See how Exodus moves from the apodictic to the casuistic:[16]

> *Exod 20:17. You shall not covet your neighbor's house. You shall not covet your neighbor's wife, or his manservant or maidservant, his ox or donkey, or anything that belongs to your neighbor.* (NIV)

> *Exod 21:2–6. If you buy a Hebrew servant, he is to serve you for six years. But in the seventh year, he shall go free, without paying anything. If he comes alone, he is to go free alone; but if he has a wife when he comes, she is to go with him. If his master gives him a wife and she bears him sons or daughters, the woman and her children shall belong to her master, and only the man shall go free. But if the servant declares, 'I love my master and my wife and children and do not want to go free,' then his master must take him before the judges. He shall take him to the door or the doorpost and pierce his ear with an awl. Then he will be his servant for life.* (NIV)

The Treaty of Suppiluliuma I with Shattiwaza of Mitanni *[55A]* exhibits this same shift from apodictic to casuistic thus:[17]

---

15. A phrase that is sometimes used to describe the style of Deuteronomy. E.g., Norrback, *Fatherless and the Widow*, 82.

16. Kitchen observes the writers "desired to get to most essential issues first and then could fill in other messy details . . . inherently rebellious folk needed to hear the basics of what they were in for, before they got too bored to listen to more," *TLC* III, 253.

17. Both the apodictic and the casuistic can be traced back to the earliest known treaty, Eannatum's Stele of the Vultures *[1]* ca. 2500 BC.

> You Shattiwaza, the king's son *shall not* [. . .] the great king, the king of the land of Hatti. (Obv.74)

> *If* a fugitive flees from the land of Hatti [and goes to the land of Mitanni, the people of Mitanni shall arrest him] and hand him over. (Rev.9–10a)

A further example is provided by the treaty of the Hittite king Suppiluliuma I with Tette of Nuhasse *[57]*:

> And Tette *shall come* to the Sun-King, his master, in the land of Hatti annually. (2:4–5)

> *If*, I, the king of the land of Hatti, am in the Hurrian land or in the land of Egypt or in the land of Karduniash.[18] (2:7–8)

The same pattern can also be observed in treaties of the First Millennium, e.g., the treaty of Bar-Gayah, king of KTK, ca. 783 BC *[86]*:

> *You shall not accept* such utterances from any man who fulminates and utters wicked words against me. *You shall surely deliver* them up to me. (1b–2)

> Now *if* a fugitive or any of my officials, brothers, courtiers or any of the people under my authority flees from me, and they go off to Aleppo. (4b–5a)

However, as K. A. Kitchen notes, the "basic ruling followed by the fine print principle" is particularly evident in the epoch ca. 1400–1180 BC, where it relates to matters of vassal-loyalty.[19]

### Splitting up the Stipulations

One of the most obvious differences between Exodus/Leviticus and Deuteronomy is that whereas the Stipulations in Deuteronomy are in a single block 4:1—26:19, in Exodus/Leviticus several features interleave them such as the Solemn Ceremony, Exod 24:1–4a, 9–14; Witnesses 24:4b–6; Reading 24:7–8; Deposit of the text 25:10, 16, 17, 21, and much additional material.[20]

The Hittite treaties also provide similar examples thus:

---

18. I.e., Babylonia.

19. *TLC* III, 276.

20. I.e., Exod 25:9—34:7; 34:28–35; 35:20—40:28; Lev 1:1—10:20; 16:1—17:16; 21:1—24:14 for consideration of this material see pp. 48–52.

1. The treaty of an unnamed Hittite king with the Kaskeans *[47]* Stipulations I (Obv.1:1'–Obv.2:7') + Witnesses + Oaths, Stipulations II (Rev.3:9—4:3)

2. Treaty of Suppiluliuma I with Huqqanas and "the men of Hayasa" *[60]*
Stipulations I (1:8–40) + Witnesses + Curses + Blessings, Stipulations II (2:14—4:40)

3. Treaty of Tudkhalia IV with Ulmi-Tesub of Tarhuntassa *[74]*. Here the stipulations are briefly interrupted (38'–39') with a short section dealing with the deposit of the treaty in a sanctuary. Thereafter the stipulations continue with a supplementary paragraph on military matters.

K. A. Kitchen sees this splitting up of otherwise extensive rulings with intervening rites as a device to hold people's attention.[21]

## Additional Stipulations after Curses

Exodus/Leviticus has additional stipulations after the curses that close the covenant (Lev 27:1–33). This is also a feature of the treaty of the Hittite king, Arnuwandas I, with the Kaskeans *[54]* Rev.2.18'–20'; 3:1–2 where specific stipulations are added for specific sub-groups. It is also a feature of the Egyptian version of the treaty of Ramesses II with the Hittite king, Hattusil III, from Thebes *[71B]* 32a–36b. Here the reason may have been much more banal, the Egyptian scribe, copying from a master-copy, seems to have omitted some of his material and was obliged to add it to the end of his text.[22]

## Where Does the Balance Lie?

K. A. Kitchen has analyzed the topics covered by the stipulations of Exodus/Leviticus and Deuteronomy. He notes that eighty-two of the topics covered by Exodus/Leviticus occur in the material from the Third and Second Millennia.[23] Only two occur exclusively in the First Millennium material. Similarly, forty-three of the topics covered by Deuteronomy

---

21. *TLC* III, 253.
22. *TLC* III, 100, 127.
23. This excludes any comparison between Exodus/Leviticus and Deuteronomy themselves.

occur in the material from the third and second millennia.[24] Likewise only two topics exclusively occur in the First Millennium material.

### DEPOSIT OF THE TREATY DOCUMENT

In Deuteronomy 27 Moses commands the people, after they have crossed the river Jordan, to set up stones, coat them with plaster and write on them the text of the covenant. Thus: 27:4–8:

> And when you have crossed the Jordan, set up these stones on Mount Ebal,[25] as I command you today, and coat them with plaster. Build there an altar to the LORD your God, an altar of stones. Do not use any iron tool upon them. Build the altar of the LORD your God with stones from the field and offer burnt offerings on it to the LORD your God. Sacrifice fellowship offerings there, eating them and rejoicing in the presence of the LORD your God. And you shall write very clearly all the words of this law on these stones you have set up. (NIV)

This can be paralleled in the treaties of the Second Millennium: [all the unspecified kings are Hittite]

1. Treaty of Suppiluliuma I with Shattiwaza of Mitanni *[55A]* Rev.35–36a:

   > A duplicate of this tablet is deposited before the Sun-goddess of Arinna,[26] since the Sun-goddess of Arinna directs kingship and queenship. Also in the land of Mitanni, a copy is deposited before the Storm-god, Lord of the kurinnu of Kahat.

2. Treaty of Shattiwaza of Mitanni with Suppiluliuma I *[56A]* Rev.7:

   > In the land of [Mitanni, before the Storm-god, Lord of the kurinnu of Kahat a duplicate of this tablet is deposited].

3. Treaty of Tudkhalia IV with Kurunta of Tarhuntassa *[73]* 4:44–46:

   > Now this tablet has been prepared as the seventh copy; and with the seal of the Sun-goddess of Arinna, and with the seal of the Storm-god of Hatti has it been sealed. Thus one tablet is deposited before the Sun-goddess of Arinna [then details of deposit of the other six tablets are given].

24. This also excludes any comparison between Deuteronomy and Exodus/Leviticus.
25. A mountain near Shechem.
26. The Hittite cultic center in the vicinity of Hattusas. Its location is unknown, though some identify it with Büyük Nefesköy, south of Hattusas. Cornelius, "Geographie," 244.

4. Treaty of Tudkhalia IV with Ulmi-Tesub of Tarhuntassa *[74]* Obv. 38'-39':

> This tablet of the treaty has already been produced, and in the city of Arinna, before the Sun-goddess of Arinna, shall it be deposited. Since a military agreement for that tablet had not been produced, so then I, the Sun-King, have now made for him hereafter a military agreement per the following.

5. Treaty of Suppiluliuma II with the rulers of Alasia (Cyprus) *[80]* 12'-15':

> [...] the treaty tablets, I, the Sun-King, [have prepared...] all lands with weapons [have I smitten ... in lands] from the sunrise to [the sunset I have had tribute. The temple] of the Sun-goddess of Arinna, with silver [and gold I endowed].

Significantly this feature is not present in treaties from the First Millennium.

## READING THE TERMS OF THE TREATY

In Deut 31:10-11 Moses commands that the law be read aloud at the end of every seven years:

> Then Moses commanded them: "At the end of every seven years, in the year for cancelling debts, during the Feast of Tabernacles, when all Israel comes to appear before the LORD your God at the place he will choose, you shall read this law before them in their hearing. (NIV)

Provision for reading the treaty is mentioned in several of the Second Millennium treaties: [all the unspecified kings are Hittite]

1. Treaty of Suppiluliuma I with Shattiwaza of Mitanni *[55A]* Rev.36b-37a:

> Regularly, before the king of the land of Mitanni, and before the people of the land of Hurri, let it be read out.[27]

2. Treaty of Mursil II with Kupanta-Kurunta of Mira *[65]* J1-3:

> [Furthermore, this tablet which I have] drawn up [for you, Kapunta-Kurunta, this shall be read out for you year by year, three times, and you Kapunta-Kurunta], keep [these] words.

---

27. The same sentence can also be restored in the treaty of Shattiwaza of Mitanni with Suppiluliuma I *[56A]* Rev.7b-8a.

3. Similarly the Treaty of Muwatallis II of Hatti with Alaksandus of Wilusa *[68]* 3:73–77 specifies reading the treaty three times a year:

> *Now, Alaksandus, this tablet which I have [prepared] for you shall be [read] out to you year by year, three times a year, and so, Alaksandus, you shall know it well. These provisions are not upon equals, but issue from Hatti.*

A clause providing for the reading of the treaty is absent from treaties of the First Millennium.

## BLESSINGS

Blessing formulae are normally used less than curses.[28] For example, the Law Collection of Hammurabi (1792–1750 BC) *[14]* only has two blessings,[29] but has fifty curses. In the biblical material Exodus/Leviticus has 10 curses to 5 blessings, Deuteronomy has forty curses to eight blessings.

Most of the late Second Millennium treaties have blessings.[30] There was much standardization of the blessing-formulae in the treaties of the Hittite kings.[31] There are no blessings in the First Millennium Assyrian treaties, for which several explanations have been advanced. According to M. Weinfeld, "The Assyrians did not feel that someone who maintains loyalty deserves special blessings; therefore, blessings were altogether eliminated from the treaty formulation."[32] Alternatively, R. Frankena, somewhat more positively and arguably much less plausibly, suggests "The omission

---

28. The only two texts where this is marginally not the case are the treaties of Suppuliuma I with Tette of Nuhasse *[57]* and Muwatallis with Alaksandus of Wilusa *[68]*.

29. Thus 49:2–17: *"If that man has heeded my words which I have inscribed on my stela and has not cast aside my rules, if he has not altered my words, if he has not changed my plan, (1) may Shamash [the sun god] extend the sceptre of that man, a king of justice like me. (2) May he pasture his people in justice."*

30. See Appendix Two Table 3 Column 7, pp. 134–35.

31. Compare the blessing formulae in the treaties of Suppuliuma I with Tette of Nuhasse *[57]*, 53–57 and with Aziru of Amurru *[58A]*, 3:17–20; the treaties of Mursil II with Duppi-Tesub of Amurru *[62B]*, 4:27–32; and with Niqmepa of Ugarit *[63]*, 116–18. Apart from changes to the names of the parties these blessings are virtually identical. Only Mursil II's treaty with Duppi-Tesub is in Hittite, the rest are in Akkadian.

32. Weinfeld, "Covenant Making," 136.

of blessings in the Assyrian treaties might be due to the fact that the treaty would bestow automatically blessings on the faithful vassal."[33]

### Matching Blessings and Curses

In all the Second Millennium treaties, blessings are accompanied by curses. Sometimes blessings are paralleled by an accompanying curse section in which the wording is similar, even at times virtually identical. Compare Deut 28:3–6:

As a blessing:

> You will be blessed in the city and blessed in the country.
>
> The fruit of your womb will be blessed, and the crops of your land and the young of your livestock–the calves of your herds and the lambs of your flocks.
>
> Your basket and your kneading trough will be blessed.
>
> You will be blessed when you come in and blessed when you go out. (NIV)

with Deut 28:16–19:

As a curse:

> You will be cursed in the city and cursed in the country.
>
> Your basket and your kneading trough will be cursed.
>
> The fruit of your womb will be cursed, and the crops of your land, and the calves of your herds and the lambs of your flocks.
>
> You will be cursed when you come in and cursed when you go out. (NIV)

A similar parallelism can be traced back in time to the Law Collection of Hammurabi *[14]*.

As a blessing:

> If a man has heeded my word which I have inscribed upon my stela ... if he has not changed my plans. (49:2–5, 9–10)

As a curse:

> If that man has heeded my words which I have inscribed upon my stela ... if he has changed my plans." (49:18–22, 31–32)

---

33. Frankena, "The Vassal Treaties," 136.

Extensive parallels between blessings and curses are also found in the Hittite treaties thus:

1. The treaty of an unnamed Hittite king with the Kaskeans *[47]*

As a blessing:

> *If you observe this oath, then shall the gods protect you.* (Obv.2:14')

As a curse:

> *But if you break this oath, then shall all the gods of the oath destroy you.* (Obv.2:16')

2. Treaty of Arnuwandas I with the Kaskeans *[54]*:

As a curse:

> *May they* [=the gods] *destroy their wives, their sons, their cattle, their flocks and their vineyards.* (Obv.II.14'-15')

As a blessing:

> [*May the gods bless his wives*], *children, flocks, fields* [*and vineyards*]. (Obv.II.17')

3. Treaty of Shattiwaza of Mitanni with Suppiluliuma I *[56A]*:

As a curse:

> *If you, Shattiwaza and the people of the land of* [*Hurri, do not observe*] *these words of this treaty . . . with your land, with your wives, with* [*your sons*], *and with your property, may these gods of the oath* [*destroy you*]. (Rev.26–27a)

As a blessing:

> *If you Shattiwaza, and the Hurrian people, observe this treaty and oath . . . with your wives, your sons, and with your land, may these gods protect you.* (Rev.35–36)

The next four examples have a virtually identical form:

4a. Treaty of Suppiluliuma I with Tette of Nuhasse *[57]*:

As a curse:

> *If Tette does not hold to these words of the treaty and oath and transgresses the oath by these gods, may they* [=the gods] *destroy Tette*

[his head], his wives, his sons, his grandsons, his house, his city, his land along with all his property. (4:48–52)

As a blessing:

> If Tette holds to [these] words [of the treaty] and the oath which are [written] on [this tablet], may they [=the gods] protect Tette, his head, his wives, [his sons, his grandsons], his cattle, [his house], his city, his land along with all his property. (4:53–57)

### 4b. Treaty of Suppiluliuma I with Aziru of Amurru [58A]:

As a curse:

> [If Aziru does not observe these words of] the treaty and the oath, [but breaks the oath] may these gods destroy Aziru [his head, his wives, his sons, his grandsons, his house], his city, his land, and also [his property]. (3:13b–16)

As a blessing:

> [But if Aziru observes these words of the treaty] and the oath which are [written on this tablet] may these gods protect [Aziru] his head, his wives, his sons, his grandsons, his cattle, his house, his city, his land [and also his property]. (3:17–20)

### 4c. Treaty of Mursil II with Duppi-Tesub of Amurru [62B]:

As a curse:

> If Duppi-Tesub [does not observe these words] of the treaty and oath, so may these oath-gods destroy Duppi-Tesub, [his head], his wife, his sons, his grandsons, his house, [his city, his land, and] all his possessions. (4:22b–26)

As a blessing:

> [If Duppi-Tesub observes] these [words of the treaty and oath . . .] then may [these oath-gods] protect Duppi-Tesub, his head, his wife, [his sons, his grandsons, his city, his land] even your house [your servants and all your possessions]. (4:27–32)

### 4d. Treaty of Mursil II with Niqmepa of Ugarit [63]:

As a curse:

> If Niqmepa does not observe these [words of the] treaty and of the oath, may these [gods] destroy Niqmepa, [his head], his wives, his

sons, his grandsons, his [house], his city, his land, and also his property. (113b–15)

As a blessing:

If Niqmepa observes [these] words [of the treaty] and the oath ... may these [gods] protect Niqmepa, his head, his wives, his sons, [his grandsons, his cattle, his house, his city, his land], and also his property. (116–19)

5. Treaty of Muwatallis II with Alaksandus of Wilusa *[68]*:

As a curse:

If you, Alaksandus, breach the terms of this record, which are found on this tablet, then these Thousand gods shall sweep you away along with your head, your wife, your sons, your lands, your towns, your vineyards, your threshing-floors, your fields, your cattle, and your flocks, along with your other property. (4:31–37)

As a blessing:

If you keep to these terms, then these Thousand gods ... shall guard you well, along with your wife, your sons, your [lands], your towns, your threshing-floors, your vineyards, [your fields], your cattle, and your flocks, along with your other property. (4:37b–45)

6. Treaty of Hattusil III with Ramesses II *[71B]* Egyptian version:[34]

As a curse:

As for these terms that are written upon this silver tablet for the land of Hatti and for the land of Egypt—the Thousand gods of the land of Hatti along with the Thousand gods of the land of Egypt shall destroy whoever shall not keep them, his household, his territory, and his servants. (30b–31a)

As a blessing:

As for whosoever shall keep to these terms that are written upon this silver tablet, be they in Hatti or be they Egyptians, and they do not at all neglect them, the Thousand gods of the land of Hatti along with the Thousand gods of the land of Egypt shall act to keep them

---

34. The Akkadian version here is too fragmentary here to quote, but it can be reconstructed from the Egyptian version.

alive and healthy, with his household, his territory, and his servants. (31b–32a)

7. Treaty of Tudkhalia IV with Kurunta of Tarhuntassa *[73]*:

As a curse:

> If you, Kurunta, do not observe the word of this tablet and do not support me, the Sun-King, and thereafter the Sun-King's descendants, in kingly rule ... if anyone makes difficulties for me, the Sun-King, and his descendants regarding the kingship of the land of Hatti, but you favor him, and do not oppose him, then shall these gods of the oath destroy you along with your descendants. (4:5–11)

As a blessing:

> But if you, Kurunta, take the words of this tablet to heart, and strive for the Sun-King and also for the Sun-King's descendants and support them, so shall these gods support you with health. (4:12–14)

8. Treaty of Tudkhalia IV with Ulmi-Tesub of Tarhuntassa *[74]*:

As a curse:

> Now if you, Ulmi-Tesub, do not observe the words of this tablet, and do not support me, the Sun-King, the Queen, and thereafter my, the Sun-King's, son in kingly rule ... then the Thousand gods shall blot you out, along with your head, your wife, your offspring, your land, your house, your threshing-floor, your orchard, your fields, your cattle, your flocks, and all your property. (Rev 5–7)

As a blessing:

> But if you observe the words of this tablet, and support me, the Sun-King, the Queen, and thereafter support my, the Sun-King's, son in kingly rule ... then these gods of the oath shall support you, along with your head, your wife, your offspring, your land, your house, your threshing-floor, your orchard, your fields, your cattle, your flocks, and all your property. (Rev 8–11)

Since, with one solitary exception noted above,[35] blessings are absent from the First Millennium treaties, the feature of matching blessings and curses also disappears.

---

35. See p. 58.

## CURSES

### The Biblical Curses and Supposed Parallels Elsewhere

One particular curse is often compared, both between the biblical covenants and wider afield with a particular Assyrian example.

1. Heavens as bronze, earth as iron:

> Lev 26:19. *And I will break the pride of your power, and I will make your heavens like iron and your earth like bronze.* (ESV)[36]

> Deut 28:23. *And the heavens over your head shall be bronze, and the earth under you shall be iron.* (ESV)

We should note that the points of comparison differ. In the Leviticus example the heavens are compared to iron and the ground to bronze. In the Deuteronomy example the heavens are compared to bronze and the earth to iron. This comparison is also shared by a curse found in Esarhaddon's Succession Treaty, dating from 672 BC, *[94]*:

> *May they [=the gods] make your earth like iron, so that nothing can sprout from it. Just as rain does not fall from a heaven of bronze.* (528–530)

It is true that in both Deuteronomy and Esarhaddon's Succession Treaty *[94]*, (in contrast to Leviticus), the earth is compared to iron and the heavens to bronze. Even so, the order of elements in both texts is reversed. Thus in Deuteronomy first the pairing of "heavens" with "bronze," then the pairing of "earth" with "iron" contrasts with the pairings in Esarhaddon of, first, "earth" with "iron," then of "heaven(s)" with bronze.[37] Furthermore, the Assyrian scribes drew a line before line 530 suggesting that they considered this a new idea with no special connection with what went before.[38] The lines can therefore be seen in a wider context thus:

---

36. Kitchen, *TLC* III, 195 argues that this usage in Leviticus, not surprisingly for a group that had just left Egypt, reflects the Egyptian belief in the heavenly origin of iron.

37. This reversal invalidates or certainly weakens the claim of Weinfeld, "Traces of Assyrian treaty Formulae," 417 n 4, that because the Deuteronomic order is identical with that in the Esarhaddon treaty, the Deuteronomic formulation (unlike that of Lev 26:19) is the direct result of Assyrian influence.

38. *TLC* II, 227.

> *May the gods, as many as are [mentioned by name] in this treaty tablet make the ground as narrow for you as a brick. May they make your earth like iron, so that nothing can sprout from it.*

---

> *Just as rain does not fall from a heaven of bronze, so may rain and dew not come upon your fields and your meadows.* (526–532a)

It is clear that whatever relationship exists between the three texts, it is far from straightforward and should certainly caution us against assuming that the writer of Deuteronomy borrowed his material from Assyria.[39]

A number of other curses in Deuteronomy 28 are sometimes compared with those in the Succession Treaty of Esarhaddon *[94]*. Thus:

2. A dead body devoured by birds:[40]

> 28:26. *And your dead body shall be food for all the birds of the air and for all the beasts of the earth, and there shall be no one to frighten them away.* (ESV)

> §41 425–427. *May Ninurta*[41] *... fell you with his fierce arrow; may he fill the plain with your blood and feed your flesh to the eagle and vulture.*

3. Infliction of skin complaints:[42]

> 28:27. *The LORD will strike you with the boils of Egypt, and with tumors and scabs and itch, of which you cannot be healed.* (ESV)

> §39 419–420. *May Sin*[43] *... clothe you with "leprosy".*[44]

4. Infliction of blindness:

> 28:28–29. *The LORD will strike you with madness and blindness and confusion of mind and you shall grope at noonday, as the blind grope in darkness, and you shall not prosper in your ways. And you shall be only oppressed and robbed continually, and there shall be no one to help you.* (ESV)

---

39. E.g., Borger, "Asarhaddon," 191–92 who proposed that the writer of Deuteronomy borrowed his material from a treaty between Assyria and Judah.
40. Deuteronomy has a broader remit with its addition of "beasts of the earth."
41. The warrior god.
42. This category is made as broad as possible to facilitate some kind of comparison.
43. The moon god.
44. The Akkadian *saḫaršupu* traditionally translated "leprosy" *CAD* 15/S, 36b, but see p. 91 n 60.

84   THE BOOKS OF MOSES REVISITED

§40 422–424. *May Shamash*[45] *. . . not judge you justly, may he remove your eyesight. Walk about in darkness.*

5. The rape of a wife:

28:30a. *You shall betroth a wife, but another man shall ravish her.* (ESV)

§42 428–429a. *May (the planet) Venus . . . before your eyes make your wives lie in the lap of your enemy.*

6. An enemy takes property:

28:33. *A nation that you have not known shall eat up the fruit of your ground and of all your labors, and you shall be only oppressed and crushed continually.* (ESV)

§42 430b. *May a strange enemy divide your goods.*

7. Locusts:

28:38. *You shall carry much seed into the field and gather in little for the locust*[46] *shall consume it.* (ESV)

§47 442b–443. *May the locust that diminishes the land devour your harvest.*

8. Cannibalism:

28:53–57. *And you shall eat the fruit of your womb, the flesh of your sons and daughters, whom the LORD your God has given you, in the siege and in the distress with which your enemies shall distress you. The man who is the most tender and refined among you will begrudge food to his brother, to the wife he embraces, and to the last of the children whom he has left, so that he will not give to any of them any of the flesh of his children whom he is eating, because he has nothing else left, in the siege and in the distress with which your enemy shall distress you in all your towns. The most tender and refined woman among you, who would not venture to set the sole of her foot upon the ground because she is so delicate and tender, will begrudge to the husband she embraces, to her son and to her daughter, her afterbirth that comes out from between her feet and her children whom she bears, because lacking everything she will eat*

---

45. The sun god.

46. The destructive power of locusts can be measured in the modern world, where locusts have been known to cover 370 km$^2$ at a density of over 600,000 per hectare.

*them secretly, in the siege and in the distress with which your enemy shall distress you in your towns.* (ESV)

§47 449–450. *In your hunger eat the flesh of your sons! In want and famine may one man eat the flesh of another.*

Although some claim a correlation between the two texts, and thus a seventh century BC composition date for Deuteronomy,[47] a careful examination shows that such a correlation is riddled with several gaps and inversions that make it unworkable. Thus:

Table 29. A comparison between the curses in Deut 28 and the Succession Treaty of Esarhaddon *[94]*, 672 BC

| Deuteronomy 28 | Succession Treaty of Esarhaddon |
|---|---|
| 23 (1) heavens = bronze, earth = iron | 528–531 (1) heavens = bronze, earth = iron |
| *Gap 24–25* | |
| 26 (2) A body devoured by birds | 425–427 (2) A body devoured by birds |
| 27 (3) Infliction of skin complaints | 419–420 (3) Infliction of skin complaints |
| 28–29a (4) Infliction of blindness | 422–424 (4) Infliction of blindness |
| *Gap 29b* | |
| 30a (5) Rape of a wife | 428–429 (5) Rape of a wife |
| *Gap 30b–32* | |
| 33 (6) An enemy takes property | 430b (6) An enemy takes property |
| *Gap 34–37* | |
| 38 (7) Locusts | 442b–443 (7) Locusts |
| *Large Gap 39–53* | |
| 53–57 (8) Cannibalism | 449–450 (8) Cannibalism |

The topics of Deuteronomy appear in the order 3,4,2,5,6,7, 8,1 in the Succession Treaty of Esarhaddon, which has many other curses not paralleled by Deuteronomy.

The curse of "blindness" was known as early ca. 2100 BC in the Sumerian Laws of Ur-Nammu of Ur, End-part *[9B]* Rev.3:17' "*May the young men of his city lose their sight.*" Other practices mentioned in curses do not occur in the collection of ancient Near Eastern Treaties and Laws that has come down to us, but they can be illustrated graphically from other texts. This shows that they were part of the ancient Near Eastern

---

47. So Frankena, "The Vassal Treaties," 122–54.

worldview long before they were used as curses in our texts. Thus the curse of "a body devoured by birds (and beasts)" can be illustrated by several Egyptian slate palettes, dated to ca. 3000 BC and showing slain foes left to be mauled by lions and birds of prey. Similarly, Eannatum of Lagash in his celebrated "Stele of the Vultures" [1] from Tello (ancient Girsu) in Mesopotamia, ca. 2500 BC, shows his enemies being attacked by vultures.

As for "cannibalism," this too can be illustrated by early evidence. In the late third millennium BC Ankhtifi, a local Egyptian governor, boasts on his tomb-chapel at Mo'alla in Upper Egypt "*While all of Upper Egypt was dying of hunger, and everybody else reduced to eating their children, I never allowed that death by famine should happen in this province!*" In the Assyrian version of the Atrahasis Epic,[48] cannibalism was considered a punishment from the gods "[*When the sixth year arrived] they served up a daughter for dinner and [a son for food]*" (Rev.5.22-23). Those who seek to draw parallels between the curses in Deuteronomy and the Succession Treaty of Esarhaddon should not ignore the fact that a number of parallels also exist between the curses in Deuteronomy and the curses in the eighteenth century Laws of Hammurabi of Babylon [14], thus:

Table 30. A comparison between the curses in Deut 28 and the Laws of Hammurabi [14]

| Deuteronomy 28 | Laws of Hammurabi |
|---|---|
| 24 *the rain of your land be powder and dust* | 50:68 *deprive him of rain from heaven* |
| 25 *defeated before your enemies* | 50:90 *let his enemy stand victor over him* |
| 27 *boils of Egypt, tumors, scabs, and itch* | 50:47 *a harsh punishment that will not disappear from his body* |
| 28a *blindness* | 49:68 *darkness, without any light* |
| 29b *confusion* | 50:5 *may they lead him into confusion* |
| 37 *among all the peoples where the LORD will lead you away* <br> 41 *they shall go into captivity* | 49:74 *the exile*[D] *of his people* <br><br> 51:22 *lead him as captive to the land of his enemy* |

---

48. The extant version is from the Assyrian Ashurbanipal's (668-627 BC) library at Nineveh, but may represent a much earlier work. Text: Lambert and Millard, *Atrahasis*, 112-13.

| | |
|---|---|
| 38–40 *description of a failed harvest* | 49:65 *days of need, years of famine*<br>50:10 *may there be no grain in his land* |
| D. The use of exile as a punishment at the time of Hammurabi over a thousand years before the exile of the Israelites from Samaria in 721 BC is worthy of note. There were many other examples of exile in the intervening millennium, for which see *TLC II*, 225–26. Exile certainly cannot be used as evidence of a seventh century date for Deuteronomy. | |

Thus it is clearly at best simplistic to claim a special relationship between the curses of Deuteronomy with those of the Succession Treaty of Esarhaddon[49] and to use this as evidence of Deuteronomy's composition in the seventh century BC.

### Sevenfold Curses

Within the curses in Leviticus 26, the LORD says four times that he will discipline or strike his people "sevenfold for your sins":

> Lev 26:18b. *I will discipline you again sevenfold for your sins.* (ESV)
> Lev 26:21b. *I will continue striking you, sevenfold for your sins.* (ESV)
> Lev 26:24b. *And I myself will strike you sevenfold for your sins.* (ESV)
> Lev 26:28b. *And I myself will discipline you sevenfold for your sins.* (ESV)

In the curses in Deuteronomy the LORD states that Israel will flee seven ways before their enemies:

> Deut 28:25b. *You shall go out one way against them* [=your enemies] *and flee seven ways before them.* (ESV)

The Aramaic treaty from Sefire (Sefire I), ca. 775 BC, *[87]* has some complex curse formulae involving the number seven. It is partly paralleled by Sefire II, ca. 773 BC, *[88]*:

> *And if seven lambs cover a ewe, may she not conceive!*
> *And if seven nurses anoint their breasts and suckle a boy-child, may he not be sated!*
> *And if seven mares suckle a colt, may it not be sated!*

---

49. As Frankena, "The Vassal Treaties," 122–54.

> *And if seven cows suckle a calf, may it not be sated!*
>
> *And if seven ewes suckle a lamb, may it not be sated!*
>
> *And if seven hens go seeking food, may they kill nothing!* (21–24a)[50]
>
> *So for seven years, may the locust devour,*
>
> *and for seven years, may the worm devour,*
>
> *and for seven years may a pest arise over the face of the land* (27b–28a)[51]

Significantly there is no trace of sevenfold curses continuing into the First Millennium. The sevenfold curse could well have been a "Western" (i.e., Syrian) idiom not taken up further east in Assyria proper.[52]

## EPILOGUES

After all the main elements, except for witnesses and reading/deposit, Deuteronomy has a full-scale epilogue (Deut 29:1—31:8) that exalts the LORD as the caring ruler of his people.[53]

There is only one clear example of an epilogue among the collection of Hittite treaties.

In the treaty of Tudkhalia IV with Ulmi-Tesub of Tarhuntassa *[74]* he affirms the rules on boundaries with his subordinate:

> Now whatever I, the Sun-King, have given to Ulmi-Tesub, king of the land of Tarhuntassa, whatever boundaries I have set for him and whatever else I have later given him—that have I inscribed upon an iron tablet. In the future nobody shall take it from Ulmi-Tesub's offspring, and nobody shall legally challenge it. The Hittite King shall not take it over himself, nor shall he give it to his son; nor to any other of his offspring shall it be given. In the future, the kingship of Tarhuntassa shall be held only by the offspring of Ulmi-Tesub. Whoever makes trouble for him, or whoever takes land from him, or alters even one word of this tablet—him and his descendants shall the storm-god, king of heaven, the sun-goddess of Arinna,

---

50. Sefire II *[88]* places some of these curses in a different order and adds: "And if seven goats suckle a kid, may it not be sated!"

51. Sefire II *[88]* is less well preserved here, but there is a reference to "thorns."

52. *TLC* III, 221. See further Younger, *CoS* 3, xxxix, who cites additional examples from Tell Fekheriyeh in Syria (ca. 850–825 BC) and Bukān (ca. 725–700 BC) in what is now NW Iran.

53. *TLC* III, 258.

the Mistress of the Hatti-lands, Sarruma, the son of the storm-god, Ishtar, and the Thousand gods of this tablet blot out from the land of Hatti. (Rev.21–27)

A solitary epilogue has survived from the First Millennium. In Sefire I, ca. 775 BC, *[87]* Matiel of Arpad, passes on an epilogue of counsel to his son:

> Thus we have spoken [and thus] we have written. What I, Matiel, have written is here as a reminder for my son [and for] my grandson who shall rule in my [place]. For good relations shall they strive [under] the sun, [for the house] of my kingship, so that no evil [should be wrought against] the house of Matiel and his son, and his grandson, forever. (C:1–9)

It then goes on to include a blessing (10–15a) and a curse (16b–24).

The feature "epilogue" is too infrequently used for a firm conclusion to be drawn.

## HISTORICAL FLASHBACKS

A final feature is what K. A. Kitchen[54] terms a "HRAF"—"Historical reminiscence and archaeological flashback," simplified here to "historical flashback."

Within the curses section of Lev 26:14–45 the LORD goes back to his foundational covenants with the Hebrews, first with Abraham, Isaac and Jacob and then in relation to rescuing his people from Egypt (Lev 26:40–45).

Up to twenty "historical flashbacks" can be identified in Deuteronomy. They can be grouped into three types:

a. Information about travel in the title:
1. 1:2. *(It takes eleven days to go from Horeb[55] to Kadesh Barnea[56] by the Mount Seir road.)* (NIV)

b. Historical background notes in the Historical Prologue:
1. 2:10–12. *(The Emites used to live there–a people strong and numerous, and as tall as the Anakites. Like the Anakites, they too were considered Rephaites, but the Moabites called them Emites. Horites used to live in Seir, but the descendants of Esau drove them out. They destroyed the Horites from before*

---

54. *TLC* III, 211–13.
55. I.e., Mount Sinai.
56. Modern Ain el-Qudeirat in the Sinai peninsula.

them and settled in their place, just as Israel did in the land the LORD gave them as their possession.) (NIV)

2. 2:20–23. (*That too was considered a land of the Rephaites, who used to live there; but the Ammonites called them Zamzummites. They were a people strong and numerous, and as tall as the Anakites. The LORD destroyed them from before the Ammonites, who drove them out and settled in their place. The LORD had done the same for the descendants of Esau, who lived in Seir, when he destroyed the Horites from before them. They drove them out and have lived in their place to this day. And as for the Avvites who lived in villages as far as Gaza, the Caphtorites coming out from Caphtor*[57] *destroyed them and settled in their place.*) (NIV)

3. 3:9. (*Hermon is called Sirion by the Sidonians; the Amorites call it Senir.*) (NIV)

4. 3:11. (*Only Og king of Bashan was left of the remnant of the Rephaites. His bed was made of iron and was nine cubits long and four cubits wide.*[58] *It is still in Rabbah of the Ammonites.*[59]) (NIV)

5. 3:13b–14. (*The whole region of Argob in Bashan used to be known as a land of the Rephaites. Jair, a descendant of Manasseh, took the whole region of Argob as far as the border of the Geshurites and the Maacathites; it was named after him, so that to this day Bashan is called Havvoth Jair.*) (NIV)

The two references to "*to this day*" (b2 [2:22] and b5 [3:14a]) and the reference to "*still*" (b4 [3:11]) would seem to describe the situation of the writer's own time.

   c. References (in the Stipulations) to events in Israel's previous history:

   4:45a–49. Recent Israelite successes east of the river Jordan.

   5:2–5. The LORD's covenant with his people at Horeb.

   5:22–31. The LORD's covenant with his people at Horeb.

We should note that these two frame the Ten Commandments 5:6–21:

---

57. I.e., Crete. See p. 24.
58. About 4 meters long and 1.8 meters wide.
59. Modern Amman.

6:10–12. The promise to the Patriarchs and deliverance from Egypt.

6:21–23 and 7:18–19. Deliverance from Egypt.

8:2–4. The LORD's discipline through forty years of desert wanderings.

8:14–16. The LORD's preservation of his people in the desert.

9:7–10:11. The rebellion with the Golden Calf.

11:2–7. Deliverance from Egypt, the rebellion of Dathan and Abiram.

23:3–6. Recent Ammonite and Moabite hostility towards the Israelites.

24:9. Miriam's "leprosy".[60]

25:17–18. The Amalekites' attack on the Israel.

26:5b–9. The LORD's faithfulness to his people from the time of the Patriarchs to the present.

Among the Hittite treaties the following most notable "historical flashbacks" are to be found:

1. Treaty of Suppiluliuma I with Huqqanas and "the men of Hayasa" 3:53–58 *[60]*:

> Now who was Maryas and why did he die? Did not a mere serving maid come by and he only looked at her? The father of the Sun-King just glanced out of the window and fastened on him saying: "Why did you look at her?" So he died because of that matter. So, be sharply aware of any such thing by which a man can come to grief.

2. The Hittite king Muwatallis II, in his treaty with Talmi-sarruma of Aleppo *[67]*, refers to an original tablet that was stolen. Muwatallis had a new tablet made, citing his father Mursil (II)'s text (Obv.3–4, 7b–8):

> [A tablet] of the treaty for Talmi-sarruma, king of the land of Aleppo, my father Mursil (II) made for him but the tablet was stolen. I, the

---

60. The Hebrew term *ṣāraʿat* has traditionally been translated "leprosy." The term is now used for a specific medical condition known as Hansen's disease (identified by Hansen in 1874). However, since "leprosy" (as now understood) only entered the Near East when the soldiers of Alexander the Great brought it back from India in the late fourth century BC, Old Testament references to leprosy are, in its strictest sense, anachronistic. See further: Hulse, "Biblical Leprosy," 88; Roberts and Manchester, *Archaeology of Disease*, 201; Lawrence, "Avoiding Anachronism," 14–17; and "Anachronism."

> Great King, have written another tablet [for him] ... And the tablet of the treaty which [my] father Mursil (II) made for him is written thus.

3. Treaty of Tudkhalia IV with Sausga-muwa of Amurru *[72]* (2:15–19, 24–27):

> You must not act as Masturi did. Muwattalis (II) appointed Masturi who was king of the Seha River Land and took him on as a brother-in-law; so he had given him Massanuzzi his sister in marriage and made him king of Seha River Land. (2:15–19) ... But Masturi whom Muwatallis had installed, whom he had taken as brother-in-law, failed to protect his son Urhi-Tesub[61] and opted for treason. (2:24–27)

4. In a treaty between Tudkhalia IV and his cousin Kurunta of Tarhuntassa *[73]* Tudkhalia remembers their adolescence when (2:31–34):

> The god had already brought me and Kurunta together in friendship and we were already dear and good friends and we shared a common oath "Each shall protect the other!"

There are only two examples of "historical flashbacks" in the First Millennium treaties.

1. In Sefire III, ca. 783 BC, *[86]* Bar-Gayah, king of KTK insists on his country's ownership of the town of Talayim:

> [Now] Talayim and its villages and its masters, and its territory belonged to my father and to [my father's house from] of old. Now when the gods smote [my father's] house it [=Talayim] belonged to another. (§9 23a–24)

2. The treaty of Ashurbanipal with Abiate of Qedar, ca. 653–652 BC, *[97]* also contains a "historical flashback":[62]

> [Considering] that Yauta, the malefactor, [through a] sword, handed all [Arabs] over to destruction and put you to the sword, [and that Ashurbanipal], king of Assyria, your lord, has put oil on you, and

---

61. The Hittite king also known as Mursil III. *TLC* III, 211.

62. This is commonly claimed to be the single Neo-Assyrian example of a Historical Prologue. E.g., Campbell, "A Historical Prologue," 534; Weinfeld, *Deuteronomy*, 131; Riemann, "Covenant, Mosaic," 193b; McCarthy, *Treaty and Covenant*, 119, 141; Parpola and Watanabe, *Neo Assyrian Treaties*, XXXVIII; Mendenhall and Herion, "Covenant," 1182; Norrback, *Fatherless and the Widow*, 95. However, after the Witness section we cannot be in a Historical Prologue, we are already a third of the way down the obverse of the reconstructed tablet as reference to plate 9 in Parpola and Watanabe makes clear.

> he has turned his friendly face towards you, you shall not strive for peace with Yauta, you shall not [ . . . with] your brothers, [your] uncles [. . .]. You shall [. . .] his feet [. . .] after him you shall not send [. . .] by the hand of anyone, but considering the terrible things which he did, you shall make every effort to kill him. (Obv.4'–14'; Rev 1–7)

So, to conclude, the feature "historical flashback" frequent in Deuteronomy, is also found in the late Second Millennium treaties and to a much more limited extent in the First Millennium treaties.

## CONCLUSIONS

By way of conclusion, I offer the following:

1. The pentateuchal covenants (and also Josh 24) have verbal titles, the late Second Millennium Hittite treaties have implied verbal (in ellipsis) titles. By contrast the First Millennium Assyrian treaties have descriptive, non-verbal titles.
2. The pentateuchal covenants agree with the late Second Millennium treaties in having Historical Prologues. By contrast Historical Prologues are not found in the First Millennium treaties.
3. Additional stipulations that follow the curses is a feature that Exodus/Leviticus shares with two treaties of the late Second Millennium. By contrast this does not occur in the First Millennium treaties.
4. Of the topics covered by the stipulations in the pentateuchal covenants the large majority have already occurred in the Law Collections of the Second Millennium. By contrast the number of stipulations shared by the pentateuchal covenants and the material from the First Millennium is minuscule. This supports the view that the stipulations in the pentateuchal covenants are (substantially at the very least) of second millennium origin.
5. Deuteronomy shares the feature of the deposit of the covenant document with a number of late Second Millennium treaties. By contrast this feature is not present in the First Millennium treaties.
6. Deuteronomy shares the feature of reading the covenant document with several late Second Millennium treaties. By contrast this feature is not present in the First Millennium treaties.
7. The pentateuchal covenants agree with the late Second Millennium treaties in having blessings and, on occasions, sets of match-

ing blessings and curses. By contrast, with one solitary exception (itself of a different type), blessings are absent from the First Millennium treaties.

8. Although some claim a correlation between the curses in Deuteronomy and the Succession Treaty of Esarhaddon, and thus a seventh-century BC composition date for Deuteronomy, careful examination shows that such a correlation is riddled with gaps and inversions that make it unworkable. Parallels between the curses in Deuteronomy and the curses in the earlier Laws of Hammurabi can be demonstrated. The precise significance of this latter observation is uncertain, but it does show a common and ancient tradition of curses, invalidating any claim to a unique relationship between Deuteronomy and the Succession Treaty of Esarhaddon.

9. The feature "historical flashback" frequent in Deuteronomy, is also found in the late Second Millennium treaties and, to a much more limited extent, in the First Millennium treaties also.

In summary, in five out of the nine conclusions (1,2,3,5,6) cited above the Pentateuch agrees exclusively with the Second Millennium treaties as opposed to the First Millennium treaties. In three other examples (4,7,9) there is a general, though not exclusive, concurrence. A further conclusion (8) demonstrates that a suggested parallel between Deuteronomy and a First Millennium treaty is invalid.

In conclusion, the study of the specific features of the pentateuchal covenants shows that they have five cases of exclusive agreement with the late Second Millennium Hittite treaties, three other examples show general, though not exclusive, concurrence. The clear conclusion is that the pentateuchal covenants, like the Hittite treaties, have authentic late Second Millennium origins.

# Chapter 6

## The Rest of the Pentateuch

HAVING CONSIDERED GENESIS, AND the covenants contained in Exodus/Leviticus and Deuteronomy it is now time to look at the rest of the Pentateuch.

### THE FIRST HALF OF EXODUS AND THE BOOK OF NUMBERS AS BRIDGES

It should not be forgotten that Genesis and the covenants preserved in Exodus/Leviticus and Deuteronomy are not the whole Pentateuch. The first half of Exodus and the whole of the book of Numbers have not been considered up until now.

The first half of Exodus, being the record of the Israelites' oppression in Egypt and their escape under Moses' leadership, forms a bridge between the Joseph story, which closes Genesis, and the giving of the Law on Mount Sinai, which leads into the covenant of Exodus/Leviticus.

The book of Numbers also forms a bridge between the Exodus/Leviticus covenant given at Mount Sinai and the covenant made between the LORD and his people on the Plains of Moab, a generation later, which forms the basis of the book of Deuteronomy. The name Numbers[1] is loosely derived from the two censuses, recorded in the book (1:1–46 and 26:1–65), between which a period of thirty-eight years elapses. The book of Numbers details the rebellion of the Israelites that led to their prolonged wandering in the desert (13:1—14:45; 16:1—17:12; 20:1–13). It is

---

1. See p. 3 n B.

also possible that some parts of Numbers such as 5:11–31; 27:6–11 and 36:5–9 may be additional stipulations to the first covenant.[2]

## EVIDENCE FOR A SECOND MILLENNIUM DATE

In the first half of Exodus and in the book of Numbers there are several pieces of evidence that point to a Second Millennium date:

1. In Exod 2:3 there is a description of the basket into which the baby Moses was placed. In this description there is a cluster of Egyptian loan-words. Thus:

Table 31. Egyptian loan-words in Exod 2:3

| Hebrew word | Egyptian word | Meaning |
|---|---|---|
| tēḇā (basket) | dbʿt/tbt | "sarcophagus"/"chest" |
| gōmeʾ | qmʾ | "papyrus" |
| ḥēmār[A] | mrḥ | "bitumen" |
| zāp̱eṯ | sft | "pitch" |
| yeʾōr | yrw | "Nile" |
| A. Here the Hebrew form transposes the consonants. | | |

As we saw earlier[3] the presence of an odd loan-word may just be accidental, but when there is a cluster of loan-words from the same language, all in the same verse, it surely carries greater weight. It is an indication that the writer knew the cultural setting that he was writing about, not making it up in another land centuries after the event.

2. In Exod 16 the Israelites first encounter the miraculous food "manna"—Hebrew mān (16:31). The popular etymology of this word is explained earlier in 16:15 "what is it?" Here the Hebrew for "what" is again mān, though the normal form is māh, used later in the same verse *they did not know what it was*. It is perhaps significant that the form manna, meaning "what," is found in a letter from Abdi-Heba of Jerusalem (one of the Amarna Letters from Egypt), dated to the fourteenth century BC.[4] This is evidence that the form mān "what" may have been current in the fourteenth century BC.

2. So *TLC* I, 770–73; *TLC* III, 142. See p. 70 n C.
3. See pp. 38–39.
4. See pp. 22–23 Amarna Letter 286.5. *CAD* 10/M1, 212b a; Rainey, *Canaanite in the Amarna Letters*, 111.

3. In Exod 19:5 Israel is described as a "treasured possession." The Hebrew word here is *sᵉgullā*. It is a word with a venerable history. Its Akkadian counterpart *sikiltu* is used in the Laws of Hammurabi (1792–1750 BC) *[14]* Law 141 (30:39).[5] It is also used on the fifteenth-century BC treaty seal of king Niqmepa of Alalakh in Syria in his treaty with Ir-Adad of Tunip *[42]*. The presence of one ancient word, also used in Deut 7:6; 14:2 and 26:18, in a text does not prove its antiquity, but it certainly points earlier rather than later for the date of its composition.

4. In Exod 28:17–20 the twelve precious stones mounted on the high priest's breastpiece are listed.[6] Among the stones three are loan-words from Egyptian thus:

Table 32. Egyptian loan-words in the high priest's breastpiece (Exod 28:17–20)

| Hebrew word | Egyptian word | Meaning |
|---|---|---|
| 18a *nōp̄ek̠* | *mfk't* | "green/blue turquoise" |
| 19a *lešem* | *nšm.t* | "whitish blue feldspar" |
| 19c *aḥlāmā* | *ḥnm.t* | "a red precious stone" |

The last word is particularly interesting. In Egyptian it is the name of a red precious stone brought to Egypt from the Eighteenth Dynasty (1540–1295 BC) and onwards from Nubia (modern Sudan). It is likely that this word is derived from some African language.[7]

Once again, a cluster of loan-words, all from the same language, requires serious consideration.[8]

It should also be noted that the names of two of the other precious stones would appear to be loan-words from Akkadian thus:

---

5. The meaning there is disputed, several options are possible: Meek, "Code of Hammurabi," 172, "engage in business"; Roth, "Laws of Hammurabi," 344b, "appropriates goods"; Richardson, *Hammurabi's Laws*, 85, "has dealt deviously"; *TLC* I, 145, "acquires (goods) fraudulently."

6. This is in the material added into the covenant stipulations, but for convenience is considered here.

7. Ellenbogen, *Foreign Words*, 22.

8. See pp. 38–39.

Table 33. Akkadian loan-words in the high priest's breastpiece (Exod 28:17–20)

| Hebrew word | Akkadian word | Meaning |
|---|---|---|
| 19b šᵉḇô | šubû | "agate" |
| 20c yāšp̄ē | (y)ašpu | "jasper" |

The first is itself a loan-word into Akkadian from Sumerian; the second could well have been borrowed from Hurrian, a language spoken in Upper Mesopotamia and Syria.[9] It is attested in a letter from the Hurrian ruler Tushratta to the Egyptian king Amenophis III (1391–1353 BC).[10] Both words have clearly demonstrable antiquity. Finally Exod 28:18b *sappîr* "lapis lazuli" (TNIV) should be noted. Although the Hebrew term *sappîr* is the origin of the term "sapphire," modern sapphire (blue corundum) was scarcely known to the ancients.[11] The rendering "lapis-lazuli" is to be preferred. This was used widely in the ancient world, and was obtained from Badakshan in NE Afghanistan, being attested as early as 2500 BC on the celebrated "Standard of Ur."[12]

Thus etymology and archaeology show that the names of six out of the twelve precious stones in the High Priest's breastpiece can be clearly demonstrated to have forms current in the Second Millennium or earlier.

5. In Num 13:22 there is a curious parenthetical comment about the Canaanite town Hebron:

*(Hebron had been built seven years before Zoan in Egypt.)* (NIV)

Zoan, known as Tanis to the Greeks, is the modern San-el-Hagar near the south shore of Lake Menzaleh in the northeast Delta.[13] It was close to Goshen where the Israelites settled in Egypt. Comparison of Hebron with a named town in Egypt would only be relevant to someone who had personal experience of Egypt.[14]

6. In Num 22:5 the false prophet Balaam is summoned from near the

---

9. For further see p. 22 n 10.
10. Ellenbogen, *Foreign Words*, 81.
11. Marshall, "Jewels," 785c.
12. Picture: Lawrence, *Atlas of Bible History*, 24. Although Sanskrit (an ancient Indian language) etymologies are sometimes also claimed for 17b *piṭdā* (topaz) and 17c *bāreqet* (emerald) these words may have been borrowed into Sanskrit from the Near East, Ellenbogen, *Foreign Words*, 133.
13. Kitchen, *IllBD*, 1684c; for map see 1686, see p. 18 n 2 on Qantir.
14. The precise significance of this comment remains obscure.

river Euphrates in the land of Amaw.[15] The place-name Amaw is known from an inscription (lines 23,37) on a statue of king Idrimi of Alalakh in Syria (ca. 1480–1450 BC) and is known to be in Syria between Aleppo and Carchemish. In Egypt it is also used to mean "Asiatic" or "Syrian" in the tomb of Qen-Amun, an officer of Amenophis II (1427–1401 BC).[16] It is not used in later periods.[17]

7. In Num 34:1–29 there is a description of the boundaries of the Land of Canaan. It corresponds to the geographical entity of Canaan as known from Egyptian texts of the fourteenth and thirteenth centuries BC.[18]

## LATER ADDITIONS

1. In Num 12:3 there is a somewhat curious parenthetical statement:

*(Now Moses was a very humble man, more humble than anyone else on the face of the earth.)* (NIV)

The question is, if Moses were so humble, as is claimed, would he have written it about himself? This could be a later addition to the text, alerting the reader to the great unfairness of the charge of arrogance against Moses,[19] or alternatively the translation "humble" needs to be revised. "Miserable" has been suggested as an alternative.[20]

2. Num 32:39–42 records the exploits of descendants of Makir, son of Manasseh, capturing land in Transjordan and giving it to their descendants. This could well be after the initial conquest of Transjordan under Moses and thus be an addition to the text.

## FIERY LAW?

In the Hebrew text of Deut 33:2 (the beginning of Moses' blessing on the tribes of Israel) the last but one word is *ēšdāt*. Traditionally this has been

---

15. The Hebrew *ereṣ bᵉnê 'ammô* "land of the sons of his people" is now commonly emended to *ereṣ bᵉnê 'Amaw* "land of the sons of Amaw" so RSV, NRSV, ESV, NEB, REB, GNT. NIV and TNIV, however, retain "in his native land."
16. Grohman, "Amaw," 104a; Thompson, "Amaw," 183b.
17. See Marín, *Répertoire Géographique*, 18.
18. Wenham, *TC Numbers*, 232.
19. *NIV Study Bible*, 206a.
20. Rogers, "Moses," 257–63.

understood as two words *ēš dāt*,²¹ meaning "fiery law."²² The word *dāt* is derived from the Persian *dāta* "law," which occurs in inscriptions of the second, fifteenth, and thirty-fifth years of Darius I (522–486 BC). Such an attempt to bring meaning to an obscure word that occurs only once in the Old Testament cannot be advanced as evidence of a date as late as the Persian period (Late sixth century and onwards). Other options are possible.²³ Actually, the total absence of Persian words in the Pentateuch must be compelling evidence of its composition before that period.²⁴

## CONCLUSIONS

By way of conclusion, I offer the following:

1. The cluster of Egyptian loan-words in Exod 2:3 and the statement about Zoan in Num 13:22 would seem derive from someone with a first-hand knowledge of Egypt.

2. The names of six out of the twelve stones in the high priest's breast-piece (Exod 28:17–20) can be clearly shown to have etymologies or archaeological evidence in the Second Millennium BC or earlier.

3. The following evidence points to a Second Millennium date:

    A. The etymology of *mān* "what" (Exod 16:31), the explanation for the Hebrew word "manna," can be explained by reference to the fourteenth-century BC Amarna Letters.

    B. The place name Amaw (Num 22:5) is known from fifteenth-century BC material, not later.

    C. The description of the land of Canaan in (Num 34:1–29) corresponds to the Egyptian view of Canaan in the fourteenth and thirteenth centuries.

    D. The antiquity of the word *sᵉgullā* "treasured possession" (Exod 19:5) may also be relevant here.

4. In contrast to the above the statement that Moses was more hum-

---

21. So the Bomberg edition of the Hebrew text (Jacob ben Hayim, Venice 1524–25).

22. Thus the Latin Vulgate version *"ignea lex"* of Jerome (Sophronius Eusebius Hieronymus) and the English Authorized Version.

23. NIV, TNIV "mountain slopes" so Christensen, *WBC Deuteronomy*, 833; RSV, ESV "flaming fire"; NASB "flashing lightning" Cf. NJPS "lightning flashing."

24. Eskhult, "Importance of Loanwords," 369, 23.

ble than anyone else (Num 12:3) and the list of exploits of the descendants of Makir (Num 32:39–43) may be evidence of later additions being made to the text.
5. There is no compelling case to translate *ēšdāt* in Deut 33:2 as "fiery law" and thus rely on the Persian loan-word *dāta*. The total absence of Persian words in the Pentateuch must be compelling evidence of its composition before that period.

# Chapter 7

# On Kidnapping, Oxen, and Fruit Trees

## *A Few Specific Laws*

SEVERAL OF THE LAWS in the Pentateuch have parallels in the Old Babylonian Law Collections of the early Second Millennium. The study offered below is selective (based on straightforward examples), rather than novel or exhaustive. The two collections cited here are the laws from the small central Mesopotamian kingdom of Eshnunna[1] *[13]*, dated to ca. 1800 BC[2] and the Laws of the celebrated Old Babylonian king Hammurabi (1792–1750 BC) *[14]*.

There are several cases where the offence and the penalty are identical in the pentateuchal and Old Babylonian material.[3]

### KIDNAPPING

Exod 21:16:

> Anyone who kidnaps another and either sells him or still has him when he is caught must be put to death.

---

1. Eshnunna is to be identified with Tell Asmar in central Mesopotamia (Iraq). Most of the texts of the Laws of Eshnunna were found at Tell Harmal (ancient Shaduppum) on the outskirts of Baghdad.

2. The laws are generally dated to the reign of Dadusha, which ended a year or two before Hammurabi ascended the throne. Westbrook, *Old Babylonian Marriage Law*, 4.

3. A principle elucidated by Greengus, "Law," 533.

And Deut 24:7:

> If a man is caught kidnapping one of his brother Israelites and treats him as a slave or sells him, the kidnapper must die. You must purge the evil from among you.

These can be compared with Hammurabi 8:25–29 (§14):

> If a man has kidnapped the young son of another man, he shall be put to death.

In all three texts the object of kidnap is male, in all three texts the kidnapper is put to death.

An identical offence and penalty can be seen in our next example.

## LAWS ABOUT A GORING OX

### A Goring Ox Kills another Ox

> Exod 21:35. *If a man's ox injures the ox of another and it dies, they are to sell the live one and divide both the money and the dead animal equally.* (NIV slightly modified)[4]

This can be compared with a law from Eshnunna Aiv13b–15 (§53):

> *If an ox gores and kills another ox, both owners shall divide the value of the live ox and the carcass of the dead ox.*

In both Exodus and Eshnunna the offence and the penalty are identical. Both texts ordain that the surviving ox be sold and the proceeds divided equally between the two parties; the carcass of the dead ox is to be divided as well.

### A Goring Ox Kills a Bystander

> Exod 21:28. *If an ox gores a man or a woman to death, the ox must be stoned to death, and its meat must not be eaten. But the owner of the ox will not be held responsible.* (NIV slightly modified)

and Exod 21:31–32:

---

4. Here and in subsequent examples "ox" is substituted for NIV's "bull."

> This law also applies if the ox gores a son or daughter. If the ox gores a male or female slave, the owner must pay thirty shekels[5] of silver to the master of the slave, and the ox must be stoned. (NIV slightly modified)

These can be compared with the Laws of Hammurabi 44:44-49 (§250):

> If an ox while it is going along a road has gored a man, and caused him to die, that case has no claim.

Both Exodus and Hammurabi have an ox that gores. In both collections it is an action that results in death, though Exod 21:31-32 does not state this explicitly. Hammurabi only has a "man" as the object of the goring. Both Exodus passages have both man and woman as the object, thus both sexes are treated equally. In Hammurabi no statement is made of the fate of the ox, whereas both Exodus laws require the stoning of the ox.

### Willful Negligence of an Ox

> Exod 21:29. If, however, the ox has had the habit of goring and the owner has been warned but has not kept it penned up and it kills a man or woman, the ox must be stoned and the owner also must be put to death. (NIV slightly modified)

This can be compared with Eshnunna Aiv15b-18 (§ 54):

> If the ox has the habit of goring and the community authorities notify its owner, but he does not keep his ox under control and it gores and kills a man, the owner of the ox shall weigh out two thirds of a mina of silver.

and with Hammurabi 44:52-64 (§251):

> If the ox of a man has the habit of goring and his city quarter know that it has the habit of goring, and the owner has not trimmed his horns, and has not kept his ox under control, and if that ox has gored the son of a man and caused him to die, he shall pay half a mina of silver.

All three laws concern an ox that "*has the habit of goring.*" In Exodus and Hammurabi the ox had a previous "conviction" of goring, but its owner did not take sensible precautions, in the case of Exodus "*has not penned*

---

5. About 300 grams.

it up" and in the case of Hammurabi "*has not trimmed his horns, and has not kept his ox under control.*"

In all three cases the ox takes human life, but the response is contrasting. In Exodus the ox is stoned and the owner put to death, in Eshnunna and Hammurabi the owner escapes with a fine. The differing value placed on human life in Exodus and the Old Babylonian law collections should be noted.[6]

## RAISING FRUIT TREES

Lev 19:23–25:

> *When you enter the land and plant any kind of fruit tree, regard its fruit as forbidden. For three years you are to consider it forbidden; it must not be eaten. In the fourth year all its fruit will be holy, an offering of praise to the LORD. But in the fifth year you may eat its fruit. In this way your harvest will be increased. I am the LORD your God.*

This can be compared with Hammurabi 16:10–26 (§60):

> *If a man has given to a gardener a field to plant as an orchard, when the gardener has planted the orchard, he shall let the orchard grow for four years. In the fifth year the owner of the orchard and the gardener shall divide it equally. But the owner of the orchard shall choose his share and take it first.*

Interestingly both texts share a common time scale regarding not eating fruit from a developing fruit tree or orchard. They were to be left for four years and eaten only in the fifth year.

It should be noted that there are no equally clear parallels between the pentateuchal laws and Law Collections of the First Millennium—the New Babylonian Laws, the Demotic Laws from Hermopolis in Egypt and the Laws from Gortyn in Crete.

## CONCLUSIONS

By way of conclusion, I offer the following:
1. That there are some parallels between the pentateuchal and Old Babylonian Law collections cannot be denied. Particularly interesting are the cases where the offence and the penalty are identical.

---

6. For further discussion of these examples see Finkelstein, *Ox that gored*.

2. However, there are significant differences even in the small number of examples selected.
3. As both similarity and difference between the pentateuchal and the Old Babylonian laws can be seen, the proper inference is not that the Hebrew law is derived from the Babylonian, but that both represent the formulation of old and widespread Semitic customs, pre-Mosaic in their origin, which may well have already been in force in the patriarchal period (i.e., contemporary with the Old Babylonian laws).[7] There was thus a legal tradition common to both the Old Testament and the ancient Near East.[8]
4. The fact that there is some kind of relationship between the pentateuchal and Old Babylonian Laws suggests that the time gap between the two is smaller (as demanded by a late Second Millennium date for the pentateuchal Laws) rather than greater (as required by a date for the Pentateuch in the First Millennium).
5. The fact that there are no clear parallels between the pentateuchal laws and those of the First Millennium BC is evidence that the pentateuchal laws are not First Millennium in origin.

---

7. Manley, *Book of the Law*, 80.
8. Greengus, "Law," 247.

# Chapter 8

## Wider Horizons

*A Comparison with Epic Poems of the Ancient World*

Having considered the Pentateuch in the light of ancient Near Eastern treaties and Law Collections, we shall briefly consider the Pentateuch from an even wider perspective.

Three famous works from the ancient world are selected thus:[1]

1. The Story of Sinuhe
2. The *Epic of Gilgamesh*
3. The *Iliad* and *Odyssey*

These works provide *independent* confirmation or otherwise of the principles observable in the Pentateuch (or allegedly observable in the Pentateuch) of its composition and transmission. It is only in the celebrated Flood Story (11.9–196), which forms a small part of the *Epic of Gilgamesh*, that a direct relationship to the Pentateuch can be traced or even postulated.[2]

---

1. These works were selected primarily because the transmission of their texts can be observed over many centuries.

2. There is not the space to consider this question in detail. Many have rightly noted several striking similarities to the Flood Story in Gen 6:1—9:19, but there are also significant differences between the two stories, such as the shape of the boat, the length of the flood, and the order in which the birds are sent out. See further Heidel, *Gilgamesh Epic*, 224–69; Lawrence, *Atlas of Bible History*, 17.

## THE STORY OF SINUHE

The Story of Sinuhe is a well-known Egyptian autobiographical text. The story begins with a brief announcement of the death of the Twelfth-Dynasty Egyptian pharaoh Amenemhat I in 1944 BC. Sinuhe was in the service of princess Nefru, wife of the Sesostris I (1953–1908 BC), but he went into voluntary exile in Syria-Palestine for about twenty years. Later he was to receive a royal invitation to return and join the court some time before the death of Sesostris I in 1908 BC.[3]

Maybe the original was written on Sinuhe's tomb, but this has not been found. However, the Story of Sinuhe is preserved on five papyri and some twenty-eight later copies.[4] Two late Twelfth Dynasty papyri contain substantial parts of the story, written about a century after Sinuhe's death, i.e., ca. 1800 BC,[5] but the most widely known version is of 130 lines of the story written in the Nineteenth Dynasty (1295–1186 BC).[6] Interestingly this version shows clear signs of being updated.[7] Some later copies are as late as the Twenty-First Dynasty (1070–945 BC),[8] so it is possible to trace the development of the text for a minimum of 730 years.

So in summary:

Table 34. Textual transmission of the Story of Sinuhe

| Historical placement of hero | before 1908 BC |
|---|---|
| Date of author | before 1908 BC |
| Total number of manuscripts | 5 papyri + ca. 28 later copies = ca. 33 |
| Earliest manuscript | ca. 1800 BC |
| Latest manuscript | after ca. 1070 BC |
| Textual transmission | minimum 730 years |

---

3. Kitchen, *Sinuhe: Scholarly method*, 61.

4. Wilson, "Story of Sinuhe," 18b; Parkinson, *Tale of Sinuhe*, 26.

5. Papyrus Berlin 3022 and Papyrus Berlin 10499 contain 311 and 203 lines of text respectively.

6. Lichtheim, "Story of Sinuhe," 222–23.

7. The ostracon replaces the Middle-Egyptian negative -*n* by its Late-Egyptian counterpart *bw*. It also substitutes the Semitic *yam* for the older *nwy* "sea." Kitchen, *Ancient Orient and Old Testament*, 143.

8. Wilson, "Story of Sinuhe," 18b.

## THE EPIC OF GILGAMESH, ATTRIBUTED TO SIN-LEQI-UNNINNI

The *Epic of Gilgamesh* is one of the best known examples of Mesopotamian literature. It consists of twelve tablets describing the adventures of Gilgamesh, the celebrated king of Uruk[9] in what is now southern Iraq. No single complete version of the epic survives, but to date seventy-three tablets or fragments of tablets have been discovered. These are mainly from Mesopotamia, but also from as far afield as Hattusas, the Hittite capital in central Anatolia (Turkey), Ugarit, and Emar (Tell Meskene) in Syria and Megiddo in ancient Canaan.[10] Parts of the Gilgamesh story are preserved in Sumerian, Hittite, and very fragmentarily in Hurrian,[11] but the large majority of texts were written in Akkadian (the language of Mesopotamia). The earliest attested tablet dates from ca. 2000 BC, the latest from ca. 130 BC.[12] In Babylonian tradition the *Epic of Gilgamesh* is attributed to a certain incantation priest from Uruk named Sin-leqi-unninni. Current opinion supposes he lived some time in the thirteenth to eleventh centuries BC.[13] He is thus to be seen not as the epic's original composer, but the editor who gave it its standardized (or canonical) form.

Gilgamesh, whose name appears in the Sumerian King List (3.17), is to be dated to ca. 2700 BC.[14] He thus lived some 700 years before the earliest surviving tablet of the Epic.

So in summary:

Table 35. Textual transmission of the Epic of Gilgamesh

| Historical placement of hero | c 2700 BC |
| --- | --- |
| Date of "compiler" | 13–11th centuries BC |
| Total number of manuscripts | 73 |

---

9. I.e., Erech of Gen 10:10, modern Warka.

10. George, *Epic of Gilgamesh*, xxvii. For a map showing the find spots of the Gilgamesh Epic tablets see West, *East Face of Helicon*, 591. The Megiddo example is to be dated to fourteenth century BC.

11. See p. 22 n 10.

12. George, *Epic of Gilgamesh*, xxvii.

13. Ibid., xxiv–xxv.

14. He was contemporary with Mes-anne-padda, ruler of Ur, who is mentioned as a son of A-anne-padda in an inscription from Ur, and a contemporary of Agga, king of Kish, whose father En-me-baragesi is mentioned on two fragments of vases contemporary with him of unknown origin.

| Earliest manuscript | ca. 2000 BC |
| --- | --- |
| Latest manuscript | ca. 130 BC |
| Textual transmission | ca. 1,870 years |

Tablets 1–11 would seem to constitute the original work. Tablet 1 starts with Gilgamesh *building the wall of Uruk, the sheepfold, of Holy Enanna,*[15] *the sacred storehouse* (1.10–11). Tablet 11 closes with a reference to the wall of Uruk: *O Ur-shanabi,*[16] *climb Uruk's wall and walk back and forth. Survey its foundations, examine its brickwork* (11.325–326). In Tablet 12, Gilgamesh's friend Enkidu appears, despite his death in Tablet 7. It would thus seem that Tablet 12 was a parallel version of an earlier story, which was eventually appended to the series, even being considered an integral part of the Epic in the First Millennium.[17] The Flood Story (11.9–196) would also seem to be an addition within Tablet 11.[18] This can be schematized thus (the figures in brackets are the number of lines, or estimated number of lines):[19]

Table 36. The Epic of Gilgamesh

| Tablet 1 (300) |
| --- |
| Tablet 2 (est.320) |
| Tablet 3 (est.245) |
| Tablet 4 (250) |
| Tablet 5 (est.302) |
| Tablet 6 (183) |
| Tablet 7 (est.275) |
| Tablet 8 (est.250) |
| Tablet 9 (est.261) |
| Tablet 10 (322) |
| Tablet 11 (328) Flood Story 11.9–196 (187) |
| Later addition: Tablet 12 (est.153) |

15. The Sumerian goddess of sex and war.

16. Ur-shanabi is the ferryman of Utnapishtim, (the hero of the Flood Story).

17. Tigay, *Evolution of the Gilgamesh Epic*, 27, 105, 232–40.

18. This can be traced back to the third tablet of the Akkadian Epic of Atrahasis, which is dated to the reign of the Old Babylonian king Ammisaduqa (1648–1626 BC) and a seventeenth century BC Old Babylonian Sumerian version. For texts see Lambert and Millard, *Atrahasis*, 88–105, 138–45. Both these additions may have been incorporated into the text by Sin-leqi-unninni— George, *Babylonian Gilgamesh Epic*, 32.

19. Figures are those of George, *Babylonian Gilgamesh Epic*, 418.

The book of Genesis can also be divided into eleven documents.[20] Although this similarity is probably just accidental, it certainly shows that the Genesis scheme is not without parallel in the ancient world.[21]

It is clear that the *Epic of Gilgamesh* provides us with a manuscript tradition that spans nearly two millennia. This is unparalleled in the ancient Near East and provides a real model to trace the development of an ancient text. The work of editors in updating vocabulary, reworking the text and sometimes adding new lines and deleting others can be traced.[22] Further careful study may unlock further clues as to how other ancient works of literature (including the Pentateuch) were put together.

## THE ILIAD AND THE ODYSSEY, ATTRIBUTED TO HOMER

The Greek poet Homer is credited with the authorship of the two great Greek epics the *Iliad* and the *Odyssey*. Each work has been divided into twenty-four books. The *Iliad* is the longer work consisting of 15,693 lines and the *Odyssey* of 12,109 lines. The *Odyssey* is normally considered the later composition. The *Iliad* is the account of a critical phase of the Greek action against Troy,[23] lasting 54 days. The *Odyssey* concentrates on Odysseus' forty-day struggle to regain his home from a band of suitors encamped in his palace on the island of Ithaca. The ten-year story of Odysseus' wanderings on his return from Troy is described through a flashback technique as Odysseus relates his previous adventures to the Phaeacians in books 9–12.

According to the Greek historian Herodotus ca. 490–425 BC (*Histories* 2.53) Homer lived no more than four hundred years before his

---

20. See pp. 30–32.

21. If the analogy is extended, Tablet 12 may be compared to the first part of Exodus, i.e., chapters 1–19.

22. Tigay, *Evolution of the Gilgamesh Epic*, 72. For specific examples see George, *Babylonian Gilgamesh Epic*, 39–47. I do not, however, endorse Tigay's claim (*Empirical Models*, 27) that what is known of the evolution of the Gilgamesh Epic shows that some of the results of biblical criticism are at least realistic. George, (*Babylonian Gilgamesh Epic*, 17–33) has argued that the Gilgamesh Epic has a more continuous transmissional tradition than Tigay claims. There is no evidence to be found in the Gilgamesh Epic of weaving rival manuscripts into a conflated text as envisaged by the JEDP hypothesis. See further *TLC* III, 261.

23. Troy can be identified with the mound of Hısarlık near the southern end of the Dardanelles, first excavated by Heinrich Schliemann 1870–1873 and 1878–1879. Troy, also called Ilion, may be the same as the Hittite Wilusa, for which see p. 67 n 8.

own time. This would place him at ca. 850 BC or thereabouts. Later accounts state that Homer was born in Smyrna (modern Izmir in Turkey), traveled to mainland Greece and returned to Colophon in western Anatolia (Turkey) where he lost his sight.[24] He died on the insignificant Cycladic island of Ios. The Homeric dialect was chiefly a mixture of two Greek dialects, Ionic and Aeolic, spoken along the western coast of Anatolia. The name Homer may mean "hostage" or "pledge,"[25] so it is possible that Homer's origins lay further afield.

Nowadays Homer's work is generally dated to ca. 750 BC, perhaps as early as ca. 800 BC when the Greeks adopted the Phoenician writing system. Some argue that an inscription on a jug from the Greek colony of Pithekoussai on the island of Ischia in the Bay of Naples, dated to 735–720 BC, provides the latest date for the *Iliad* at least, since the jug, perhaps in jest, mentions "Nestor's cup" described in detail in *Il.*11.632–637.[26] At least twelve late eighth-century bronze tripods have been found in a cave at Polis in Odysseus' homeland, the island of Ithaca. The cave appears to have housed a cult of Odysseus that must have been inspired by the story of the hero bringing home thirteen tripods from the Phaeacians.[27] Scenes derived from Homer's poems begin to appear on Greek vases from 675 BC onwards.[28]

Many of the customs and objects that Homer describes in his poems appear to stem from the earlier Mycenaean world of 1450–1200 BC, some 400 years before his own time. Following the research of Milman Parry on the oral tradition surviving in Croatia[29] it is generally agreed that the *Iliad* and *Odyssey* are the result of a long process of oral composition. Homer may have been the exceptionally good bard at the end of the tradition who knitted together all the episodes so well that the works were

---

24. The matter of Homer's blindness can be traced to *Hymn to Apollo* 169–73, a work once wrongly attributed to Homer. Some see the blind bard Demodocus (*Od.*8.62–82) as a self-description.

25. Curiously the Roman writer Lucian of Samosata (AD 115/125–190) *True Histories* 2.20 mocks those who claim Homer was a Babylonian with the name of Tigranes. Others derive his name from the Semitic *ōmer* "speaker" or "seer." West, *East Face of Helicon*, 622.

26. Picture in Powell, *Homer*, 16.

27. Taplin, *Oxford History of the Classical World*, 62.

28. Kirk in *Cambridge History of Classical Literature*, 48.

29. Parry, *Making of Homeric Verse*.

considered complete. It is also possible that he was the one who committed this long oral tradition to writing.

In Homer's works the absence of references to scribes and writing and the almost total prevalence of illiteracy is striking.[30] In the *Iliad* there is a cryptic reference in the Bellerophon story to a folding writing tablet: "*He gave him a writing tablet (pinax) on which he had traced a number of baneful signs*" (*Il*.6.168b–169).[31] The Greek hero Aias (Ajax) is able to recognize the mark he had scratched on a lot (*Il*.7.175–176).

The view is sometimes advanced, following a remark of the Roman orator Cicero,[32] that the Homeric poems were collected and given their final form in Athens during the reign of the tyrant Peisistratus 546–528 BC.[33] It is clear that the poems were recited in the four-yearly Panathenaic festival. This in turn affected the text, although only minimally. The poems are characterized by several "Atticisms" (Attica = the region around Athens).[34]

The standard edition of Homer's *Iliad* is the Aristarchean Vulgate, compiled by Aristarchus of Samothrace (220–143 BC), head of the library at Alexandria in Egypt. This became the Byzantine and modern text. The *Iliad* has a manuscript tradition starting from tenth century AD in Constantinople. The two best and earliest manuscripts are from that time. There are some 200 extant manuscripts of the *Iliad* and 70 of

---

30. The Pentateuch presents a graphic contrast with no less than twenty-five references to writing thus: Exod 17:14; 24:12; 32:16,32; 34:1,27; Num 5:23; 17:2,3; Deut 6:9; 10:2, 4; 11:20; 17:18; 24:1, 3; 27:3, 8; 28:58; 29:20, 21, 27; 30:10; 31:19, 24.

31. It is possible that the "baneful (or mournful) signs" (*sēmata lygra*) were pictograms, such as Mycenaean Linear B, cuneiform (Mesopotamian or Hittite) or hieroglyphs (Egyptian or Hittite), rather than an alphabetic script. The folding tablet was probably oriental, so was not Mycenaean. Compare the boxwood writing tablet found in a shipwreck off Uluburun on the south coast of Turkey and dated to ca. 1300 BC. Payton, "The Uluburun Writing-Board Set," 41, 99–106.

32. Cicero (106–43 BC), *De Oratore*, 3.137 may be giving credence to a story propagated by the librarian of Pergamum and Homeric scholar, Crates of Mallos, that Pergamum possessed the true text of Homer established by Peisistratus. Not surprisingly this view was bitterly contested by the rival library at Alexandria that boasted Homeric texts from the private library of Aristotle. See further Whitman, *Homer*, 4; Davison, "Homeric Question," 234–65; Wyrick, *Ascension of Authorship*, 143, 144, 150, 214.

33. This is further endorsed by Pausanias (ca. AD 130–180), *Guide to Greece*, 7.26.

34. E.g., *Il*.7.334–43 apparently depicts an Attic custom of building a mound over the remains of a funeral pyre and looks like a later Athenian addition. Smaller so-called Atticisms may be the corruptions of Attic scribes— Stanford, *Odyssey of Homer* 1, liii and 2, lxi.

the *Odyssey*.³⁵ The most authoritative edition of the *Iliad* is the Venetus Marcianus 822 dating from before 947 AD, a superb, annotated text, packed with marginal notes, now in St. Mark's, Venice.

The fact that the *Iliad* was frequently used in Egypt as a "schoolboy exercise text" explains why there are more copies of the *Iliad* from Egypt than any other ancient text. There are some 1,500 papyrus fragments of Homer's *Iliad* and some 500 of the *Odyssey* from Egypt, the earliest dating to the third century BC.³⁶ They are essentially the same text. The papyri contain few omissions but comparatively frequent additional lines or groups of lines, some of them displaced or repeated from other Homeric contexts. These would seem to have been subsequently excluded from the tradition by Aristarchus and his circle.

So in summary:

Table 37. Textual transmission of the Iliad

| Historical placement of heroes | latest ca. 1200 BC |
| --- | --- |
| Date of author | ca. 800–750 BC |
| Total number of manuscripts | 1,500 papyri + 200 MSS = 1,700 |
| Earliest manuscript | 3rd C BC |
| Latest manuscript | before AD 947[A] |
| Textual transmission | minimum 1,147 years |

A. There are of course many later copies, but these are excluded as being of little textual value.

Even in antiquity the so-called *chōrizontes* (separators) did not accept that Homer wrote the *Odyssey*. In the late eighteenth century, F. A. Wolf attempted to isolate sources from which Homer's poems were reputably constructed.³⁷ K. Lachmann³⁸ claimed to have identified eighteen separate and distinct "lays" (short lyric or narrative poems) out of which the *Iliad* had been composed. More recently, R. Merkelbach, adopting an approach resembling that of the Documentary Hypothesis, posited four main sources for the *Odyssey*³⁹ thus:

---

35. Latacz, "Homerus," 462; Landfester and Egger in *Dictionary of Ancient Greek and Latin Authors and Texts*, 325.

36. Ibid. The papyri cover about 10,400 lines of the Iliad and 4,200 of the Odyssey. Bolling, *External Evidence*, 7.

37. So Wolf, *Prologomena ad Homerum*.

38. Lachmann, *Betrachtungen über Homers Ilias*.

39. Merkelbach, *Untersuchungen zur Odysee*.

R Vengeance (German Rache) poem
A The Older (German älter) *Odyssey*
T The Telemachy (The story of Odysseus' son Telemachus)
B The work of the Reviser and compiler (German Bearbeiter)

However, scholars now generally accept Milman Parry's[40] view that the poems were developed orally before they were committed to writing (possibly by Homer himself),[41] consequently written source documents such as those Merkelbach suggested are regarded as irrelevant.[42]

The unity of the *Iliad* is generally accepted, but three substantial sections are often regarded as additions. Two sections are commonly regarded as being written before the main text of the poem, but incorporated later, thus:

1. The so-called "Catalogue of Ships" (2.484–762) lists the contingents of the various Achaean (Greek) states arrayed against Troy. In its details it contradicts a number of statements made elsewhere in the *Iliad*. Outside the "Catalogue of Ships" Agamemnon, the Greek commander-in-chief, is referred to as *"ruler of many islands and of all Argos,"* e.g., 2.108, whereas the Catalogue (2.569–580) limits his personal kingdom to Mycenae, the northern part of Argolis, Corinth, and the country between Arcadia and the Gulf of Corinth. Many see the Catalogue as being earlier than Homer's work.[43]

2. A shorter Catalogue 2.816–877 that lists the Trojan Allies, is thought to represent western Anatolia (Turkey) at the time of the Trojan War.[44]

---

40. See p. 112.

41. Thus it is argued that Homer's works are products of the transition from orality to literacy. Latacz, "The Homeric Question," 976.

42. The Pentateuch does not have the type of poetry that is clearly seen in Homer, so Parry's oral composition model cannot be applied there. The abandonment of a "Documentary Hypothesis" approach to Homeric studies, however, should be noted, see further Lewis, *Fern-seed and Elephants*, 119.

43. Stubbings, "Recession of Mycenaean Civilization," 343. Further passages within the "Catalogue of Ships" such as the references to the Athenian contingent 2.546–56 and perhaps more credibly a single line reference (following Aristarchus and Diogenes Laertius 1.57) to the Athenians' control of the island of Salamis in 2.558, thereby justifying their seizure of Salamis from the Megarians, are considered later additions to the Catalogue.

44. Stubbings, "Recession of Mycenaean Civilization," 349; Hope Simpson and Lazenby, *Catalogue of Ships in Homer's Iliad*, 177, considers that the Trojan Catalogue is

Another addition is the whole of Book 10 (1–579), the story of a "Night Expedition" in which the Greek warriors Odysseus and Diomedes seize a Trojan spy named Dolon, slaughter the Thracian king, Rhesus, and capture his horses. This is often regarded as a later, perhaps seventh century BC, addition.[45]

Thus the following scheme for the *Iliad* can be proposed (figures in brackets give number of lines):

Table 38. Additions to the Iliad

| 1.1—2.483 (1094) |
| --- |
| *The Catalogue of Greek (Achaean) ships* <br> 2.484–762 (278) |
| 2.763–815 (52) |
| *Catalogue of Trojan Allies* <br> 2.816–877 (61) (Total 339) |
| 3.1—9.713 (4200) |
| *A Night Expedition* <br> 10.1–579 (579) |
| 11.1—24.804 (9419) |

Curiously, a similar scheme is also observable in the book of Genesis, where two sections the "The Table of the Nations" and "The List of the Kings of Edom" contain some later material. It is curious too that the first of these sections in both the *Iliad* and Genesis is a geographical list (in the case of the *Iliad* written before the main text, in the case of Genesis apparently after). Although these similarities may just be accidental, it certainly shows that the Genesis scheme was not without parallel in the ancient world.

More significantly it is surprising just how many similarities there are in the transmission of the Homeric poems and the Pentateuch as this table shows:

---

even more independent of the *Iliad* as a whole than the Achaean Catalogue. See further Bryce, *Trojans and their Neighbours*, 135–50.

45 According to Whitman's *Homer and the Heroic Tradition*, 257, Book 10 is chronologically right in the middle of the action described in the *Iliad*, twenty-seven days of action precede it, twenty-seven follow. Latacz, *Troy and Homer*, 193, has a slightly different scheme totaling fifty-one days.

Table 39. The similarity of the transmission of Homer's Iliad and the Pentateuch

| Point of comparison | Homer's Iliad | Pentateuch |
|---|---|---|
| Date of author | 800–750 BC | 13th C BC |
| Earlier oral tradition/ sources | Describes many customs and objects of the Mycenaean age 1400–1250 BC—perhaps 400 years before | Genesis 12–50 describes events earlier in Second Millennium 700–450 years before |
| Process of Composition | Use of oral material handed down 1250–800/750 BC | Use of pre-13th C sources in Genesis |
| Earliest citation of a portion of text in the archaeological record | Ischian jug 735–720 BC —perhaps 15–80 years after Homer | Ketef Hinnom amulets late 7th BC—6 centuries after |
| Possible editing | Under Peisistratus 546–528 BC—over 200 years later | Some geographical and linguistic updating perhaps under David and Solomon 1010–930 BC—250–300 years later |
| Earliest papyrus/leather scroll | 3rd C BC—350 years minimum | 3rd C BC—1,000 years minimum |
| Place of preservation of Papyri/Scrolls | Egypt | Near Dead Sea shore, Nash papyrus from Egypt |
| Largest number of papyri/leather scroll copies | ca. 1,500 Iliad | 33 Deuteronomy |
| Creation of standard edition | Aristarchean Vulgate 2nd C BC | Masoretic Text 5th–6th C AD, but it can be traced back to Dead Sea Scrolls 250 BC–mid 1st C BC |
| Earliest extant standard text | 10th C AD | Late 9th C AD |

It is clear that the textual processes affecting the development of the *Iliad* and the Pentateuch are surprisingly similar, even down to the first citation of a portion of text coming on a tiny archaeological artifact, and subsequent possible editing. Furthermore, both works are known at least in part from papyri or leather scroll copies that were made before the production of the standard text. The dates for the production of the earliest extant standard text are also surprisingly similar. It can thus be concluded that the Homeric poems show that the process by which the Pentateuch was composed and transmitted was not unique in the ancient world.

## POLYBIUS' HISTORIES

We should also briefly consider the work of the Greek Historian Polybius ca. 204–122 BC. In his *Histories* 7.9.1–17 Polybius quotes the text of a treaty between Hannibal of Carthage with Philip V of Macedonia *[105]*. This treaty is to be dated to 215 BC,[46] yet the earliest extant manuscript of Polybius' *Histories*, Vaticanus Urbinas Graecus 102, dates from the late tenth century or very early eleventh century AD.[47] Thus there is a case of the text of a treaty being transmitted for ca. 1,200 years between its first writing and its first appearance in a manuscript. This treaty recorded in Polybius' *Histories* thus outstrips the biblical covenants by perhaps two centuries in the duration between its composition and its earliest surviving manuscript.[48]

## CONCLUSIONS

By way of conclusion, I offer the following:

1. Both the Egyptian Story of Sinuhe and the *Epic of Gilgamesh* show examples of editing and updating of texts. The transmission of both texts can be traced over long periods, in the case of the Story of Sinuhe some eight hundred years, and in the case of the *Epic of Gilgamesh* nearly two millennia.

2. With the very small exception of the Ketef Hinnom amulets, the fact that the textual transmission of the Pentateuch text cannot be traced before the earliest Dead Sea Scrolls of the third century BC has to be accepted. However, the evidence from the Story of Sinuhe and the *Epic of Gilgamesh* show that a thousand year transmission of the Pentateuch text prior to the third century BC (as yet unattested in the archaeological record) is not impossible.

3. The principles visible in the Story of Sinuhe and the *Epic of Gilgamesh* provide a real and contemporary model for any proposed editing or updating of the Pentateuch.

4. Curiously, the division of the main text of the *Epic of Gilgamesh*

---

46. Interestingly this treaty has clear parallels with the treaty of the Assyrian King Esarhaddon with Baal of Tyre ca. 676 BC *[93]*. This illustrates the close links between Tyre and its colony of Carthage.

47. Moore, *Manuscript Tradition of Polybius*, 19, or alternatively eleventh/twelfth century AD so Landfester and Egger in *Dictionary of Ancient Greek and Latin Authors*, 519.

48. *TLC* II, 109.

into eleven tablets is parallel to the eleven tablets (strictly speaking 11+1 tablets)[49] postulated for Genesis. At least it shows that the Genesis scheme is not without parallel in the ancient Near East.

5. There are a number of aspects of the composition and transmission of the *Iliad* and *Odyssey* of Homer and the Pentateuch that are surprisingly similar. It certainly cannot be claimed that the Pentateuch was unique in its composition and transmission, neither is there any need to resort to "special pleading" for the Pentateuch.

6. The additions to the *Iliad*, "the Catalogue of (Achaean) Ships and the Catalogue of Trojan Allies" and "The Night Expedition" provide a curious parallel to the sections in Genesis "The Table of the Nations" and the "List of the Rulers of Edom" that may contain later material. Again it shows that the Genesis pattern is not without parallel within the ancient world.

7. A Documentary-Hypothesis approach to the *Iliad* and *Odyssey* has not won lasting scholarly acceptance.

8. Polybius' *Histories* gives us a case of a treaty/covenant being preserved from composition to earliest extant manuscript that is even longer than is observable in the case of the Pentateuch.

---

49. For which see pp. 30–31.

# Chapter 9

# Conclusion

### LOOKING BACK

IN THE FIRST CHAPTER we looked at the claims of the New Testament, the Apocrypha and Jewish tradition for Moses being the "author"[1] of at least parts of the so-called "Pentateuch" Genesis, Exodus, Leviticus, Numbers, and Deuteronomy. We also outlined the history of the so-called Documentary (or JEDP Hypothesis) and saw how it has been applied to the books of the Pentateuch.

In chapters 3 to 7 we looked at the pentateuchal material primarily in the light of ancient Near Eastern Treaties and Law Collections. Our study aimed at being as objective and impartial as possible, but the clear conclusion is that the covenants contained in the Pentateuch have far more similarities with material of the Second Millennium than with material of the First Millennium. In case we fail to grasp the importance of this statement, the Second Millennium is when, by virtue of their attribution and association with Moses, the books of the Pentateuch claim to have been written and the First Millennium, when the books of the Pentateuch were supposedly compiled according to the JEDP Hypothesis. The Second Millennium origin of the following pentateuchal material is set forth in summary below:

---

1. See the remarks about the term "author" p. 3 n 14.

Table 40. Evidence for a Second Millennium date for the Pentateuch

| Conclusion no. | Feature | Date BC | Reference[A] |
|---|---|---|---|
| 3.8 | ḥānîk "trained man" | 19th–15th | Gen 14:14 |
| 3.10 | Genesis covenants | Early 2M | Gen 21:23–24 |
| 3.11 | price of slave "20 shekels of silver" | 18th C | Gen 37:28 |
| 4.5 | People group treaties | Late 2M | Exod/Lev, Deut |
| 4.6 | Covenant with later generation | Late 2M[B] | Deut |
| 4.7 | Order: Title, Historical Prologue, Stipulations | Late 2M | Deut 1:1—26:19 |
| 4.9; 5.7 | Blessings in the covenant/treaty | Late 2M[C] | Lev 26:3–13 |
| 4.10 | Covenant = Treaty Form | Late 2M | Exod/Lev; Deut |
| 5.1 | Verbal Title Lines | Late 2M | Exod 20:1; Deut 1:1 |
| 5.2 | Historical Prologues | Late 2M | Exod 20:2; Deut 1:6—3:9 |
| 5.3 | Additional stipulations after curses | Late 2M | Lev 27:1–33 |
| 5.4 | Greater similarity of stipulations with 2M material | 2M | Exod 20:3—23:33 |
| 5.5 | Deposit of the covenant/treaty | Late 2M | Deut 27:4–8 |
| 5.6 | Reading of the covenant/treaty | Late 2M | Deut 31:10–11 |
| 5.9 | Historical flashback | Late 2M[D] | Deut 1:2; 2:10–11 |
| 6.2 | Six stones on high priest's breastpiece | 2M or earlier | Exod 28:17–20 |
| 6.3a | mān "what" | 14th C | Exod 16:31 |
| 6.3b | Amaw | 15th C | Num 22:5 |
| 6.3c | Description of Canaan | 14th–13th C | Num 34:1–29 |
| 6.3d | sᵉgullā "treasured possession" | 18th, 15th C | Exod 19.5 |
| 7.4 | Similarity between pentateuchal Laws and Old Babylonian Laws | Suggests 2M | Exod 20:3—23:33 |

A. The references in this and the following table are in places representative, not exhaustive.

B. There is also a single First Millennium example in the eighth century BC Sefire treaties see p. 55.

C. There is one solitary First Millennium example of a blessing, but see p. 58.

D. Also in First Millennium to a lesser extent. See pp. 92–93.

## THE BASIC CONCLUSION

The basic conclusion of this work, therefore, is that the pentateuchal covenants, like the late Second Millennium Hittite treaties, are authentic late Second Millennium compositions. They thus come from the times in which they are purportedly set.

## THE AUTHOR'S ACQUAINTANCE WITH EGYPT

We noted that the clustering of Egyptian loan-words in Gen 41:1–42 (The Joseph Story) and Exod 2:3 (The Description of Moses' basket), suggests that the writer knew the cultural setting that he was writing about, and that he was not making it up in another land centuries after the event (as the JEDP Hypothesis clearly implies) [Conclusions 3.9 and 6.1]. The author's comment about Egypt in Gen 13:10, and his statement about Zoan in Num 13:22 also suggest a first-hand knowledge of Egypt [Conclusions 3.2 and 6.1]. Moses fits such a writer well.

## THE LACK OF SIMILARITY WITH FIRST MILLENNIUM TREATIES

In addition, the lack of similarity between the pentateuchal covenants and the First Millennium treaties and the problems in establishing valid parallels between the curses of Deuteronomy and those of the seventh century BC Succession Treaty of Esarhaddon *[94]* is evidence against a First Millennium composition of the Pentateuch [Conclusions 4.11 and 5.8].

## EVIDENCE FOR SUBSEQUENT EDITING OF THE PENTATEUCH

There are, however, examples where the text of the Pentateuch seems to have been subsequently edited. Thus:

Table 41. Evidence for subsequent updating of Pentateuch

| Conclusion no. | Feature | Date BC | Reference |
| --- | --- | --- | --- |
| 3.4 | Dan | Judges period | Gen 14:14 |
| 3.4 | Ur of the Chaldeans | 9th C | Gen 11:28,31; 15:7 |
| 3.4 | "to this day" |  | Gen 24:14; 26:33; 32:32; 35:20 |
| 3.4 | perhaps Philistines | 1177+?? | Gen 21:32,34; 26:1,8,14,15,18 |

| 3.5 | Table of Nations | Final form 9th C? | Gen 10:1–32 |
| 3.5 | List of Rulers of Edom | Final form 11th C? | Gen 36:31–43 |
| 6.4 | Moses more humble | After Moses? | Num 12:3 |
| 6.4 | List of exploits of descendants of Makir | After conquest | Num 32:39–42 |

## THE JEDP HYPOTHESIS REVISITED

So the main contention of this book is that there is much evidence[2] to suggest that the form of the Pentateuch is essentially of Second Millennium origin. The similarity of the biblical covenants—Exodus/Leviticus and Deuteronomy—to contemporary treaties suggests that they were compiled by someone with a diplomatic background. With his education in the Egyptian court Moses would seem to fit the bill well.

So it can be concluded that the Pentateuch is not a work crafted from disparate sources (First Millennium in date), written centuries after the date that the Pentateuch suggests for its own composition. This evidence, at the very least, begs the question whether we should re-examine the JEDP Hypothesis. All "Documentary Hypothesis" approaches to the *Iliad* and *Odyssey* of the Greek poet Homer have long since been abandoned [Conclusion 8.7]. So why not re-examine the Documentary Hypothesis approach to the Pentateuch too? It is hoped that this book shows that there is no compelling reason to reject the traditional view, that Moses was the "author" of the Pentateuch or at least a very substantial part of it, with Deuteronomy 34, the account of Moses' own death, being a clear exception.

We saw how divine names were used in the Pentateuch for clear theological reasons, not just to mark different source documents, as the JEDP Hypothesis claims [Conclusion 1.1].

Actually we can go further than this. Assigning different sources on the basis of divine names and duplicate incidents naively assumes that the redactor (or editor) did not alter his material. However, surely any redactor would have been as aware, as any modern reader, of changes of divine names or of supposed duplicate incidents. The JEDP Hypothesis assumes that the redactor chose to leave these "inconsistencies" as they were, and, moreover, does not offer any reason as to why any redactor should have done so.

2. See Table 40, p. 121.

Subsidiary to this main conclusion I offer three others:

## NOTHING IN ANCIENT LITERATURE RESEMBLES THE DOCUMENTARY HYPOTHESIS

1. There is nothing in the whole of ancient literature that even remotely resembles the stages of composition that the Documentary Hypothesis assumes. In fact the patterns observable in the composition and transmission of the Pentateuch are paralleled in other works of ancient literature, most notably (but surely not uniquely) the Story of Sinuhe, the *Epic of Gilgamesh*, the *Iliad* and *Odyssey* of Homer and Polybius' *Histories*. [Conclusions 8.1, 8.3 and 8.6]

## "SIMPLICITY IS A SIGN OF TRUTH"

2. If the contention that has just been made is correct then it would be good to re-examine how the books of the Pentateuch look according to the JEDP hypothesis. Let us again compare Genesis according to JEP with the eleven document hypothesis that we advanced in chapter three.[3]

---

3. See pp. 30–32.

Conclusion 125

Table 42. Genesis according to the JEDP Hypothesis and the
Eleven Document Hypothesis

**Genesis according to the JEDP Hypothesis**

This diagram shows the text of Genesis as divided by the JEDP Hypothesis. J is shown in dark gray, E in medium gray and P in off-white. Chapter 14 is not commonly assigned to any of these sources, and it is shown in black.

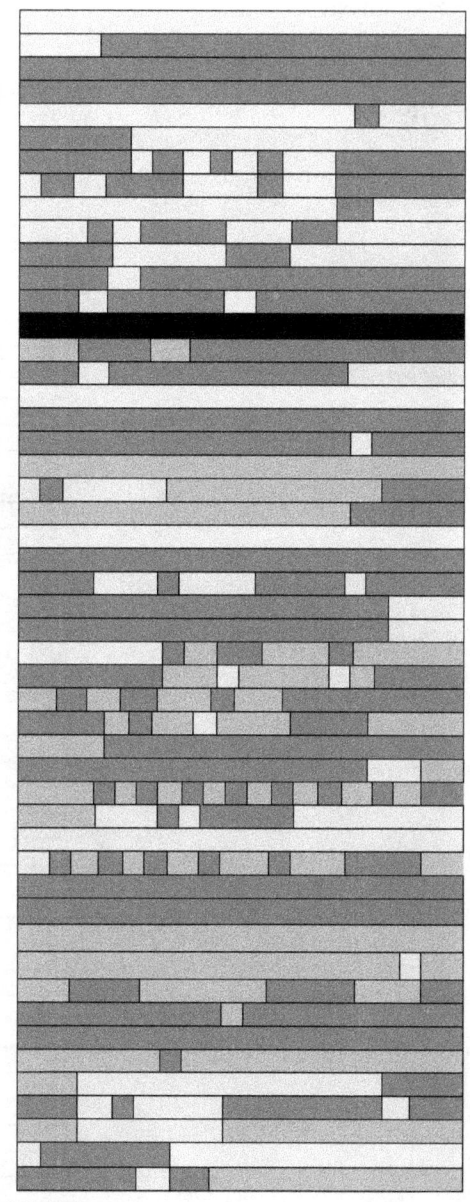

126  THE BOOKS OF MOSES REVISITED

**Genesis according to the Eleven Document Hypothesis**

This diagram shows the text of Genesis as divided into the eleven proposed documents. Each line represents one chapter of text.

The diagram makes it very clear just how fundamentally different the two different hypotheses are. The motto above the Physics Auditorium at the University of Göttingen "*Simplex sigillum veri*," (Simplicity is a sign of truth) is apposite here.[4] In essence it invokes the philosophical principle of parsimony, famously expressed in the so-called "Ockham's razor" "*Entia non sunt multiplicanda praeter necessitate*": "*Entities should not be multiplied beyond necessity.*"[5] In short, the simpler model is more likely to be the right one.

The JEDP Hypothesis envisages a complex pastiche of documents forming what is now known as the Pentateuch. With our modern "cut and paste" word-processor technology we can create a complex pastiche of documents (such as the JEDP Hypothesis envisages). The question, however, remains: "Did ancient writers have the wherewithal, let alone the desire to produce one?"

And finally:

## THE PENTATEUCH IS A CRAFTED COMPOSITION

3. As we saw with the example of Flood Story in Genesis[6] the Documentary Hypothesis obscures complex literary structures present in the text. The Pentateuch certainly does not read as a collection of interwoven sources, but as a carefully crafted, unified composition.

---

4. Two ironical remarks may be appropriate here. (1) Such a statement may not be wholly appropriate to the complexities of physics, indeed of much modern science. (2) Göttingen was the university where Wellhausen finished his career.

5. Actually the saying in its classic form does not occur in the works of the medieval English philosopher and Franciscan monk William of Ockham (ca. 1288–1347), but similar expressions do occur in his works. E.g., "*Frustra fit per plura quod potest fieri per pauciora*," "It is pointless to do with more [principles] what can be done with fewer" Sent.I.17.3; 16:1,2; II.12–13. It was hardly a brand new principle, having antecedents in the works of the Greek philosopher Aristotle (384–322 BC), e.g., *Posterior Analytics* 1.25.86a.33–35 "[All] other things being equal, let that demonstration be better which depends on fewer assumptions, suppositions or propositions" and *Physics* 1.4.188a.17–18 "It is better to assume a smaller and finite number of principles."

6. See p. 13.

## LOOKING FORWARD

If our conclusions are true it is time to leave behind the constraints that the JEDP Hypothesis places on our understanding of the pentateuchal text. The evidence that we have considered clearly points to the Late Second Millennium BC as the period when the first five books of the Bible were written. So I contend that it is also time to reinstate Moses as the "author," or, in case of Genesis, as the "compiler."[7] It is good to be aware that assigning the authorship of a text to some anonymous and later redactor is hardly the norm in world literature. So why resort to it in the case of the Pentateuch? Diligent study of any author's life and times is to be seen as a prerequisite to effective understanding of their work.[8] I hope that this book will further that understanding.

---

7. See the remarks about the term "author" p. 3 n 14.
8. See further: Lawrence, "Authorship, Date and Bible Translation."

# Appendix 1

# Chronology

Any serious historical study is not possible without the framework provided by chronology. The chronology adopted here is conventional [all dates here are BC]. It accepts the commonly accepted Egyptian chronology of K. A. Kitchen.[1] This segment is relevant to our wider discussions:

### 1. EGYPTIAN KINGS 1479–1153

*EIGHTEENTH DYNASTY*
    Tuthmosis III 1479–1425 (including Hatshepsut 1479–1457)
    Amenophis II 1427–1401
    Tuthmosis IV 1401–1391
    Amenophis III 1391–1353
    Amenophis IV 1353–1337
    Smenkhkare 1338–1336
    Tutankhamun 1336–1327
    Ay 1327–1323
    Haremhab 1323–1295
*NINETEENTH DYNASTY*
    Ramesses I 1295–1294
    Sethos I 1294–1279
    Ramesses II 1279–1213
    Merenptah 1213–1203

---

1. Kitchen, *Synchronisation of Civilisations*, 39–51.

Amenmesses 1203–1200[2]
Sethos II 1200–1194
Siptah 1194–1188
Tewosret 1188–1186

*Twentieth Dynasty*
Setnakht 1186–1184
Ramesses III 1184–1153

NB. In year 5 of his reign (1275) Ramesses II fights the Hittite king Muwatallis II at Qadesh and in year 21 (1259) Ramesses II concludes a peace treaty with the Hittite king Hattusil III.

## 2. HITTITE KINGS

The following is the sequence of Hittite kings relevant to our discussions, but there is not enough data to offer a precise sequence of regnal years. It is tied in two fixed points to the chronology of Egypt, marked below with *. The relationship of each king to his immediate predecessor is specified thus:

Suppiluliuma I, son of Tudkhalia III
Arnuwandas II, son of Suppiluliuma I
Mursil II, brother of Arnuwandas Alalakh with
Suppiluliuma I, son of Tudkhalia III
Arnuwandas II, son of Suppiluliuma I
Mursil II, brother of Arnuwandas

> Muwatallis II, son of Mursil II * battle of Qadesh 1275
> Mursil III (Urhi-Tesub), son of Muwatallis
> Hattusil III, uncle of Mursil III * treaty with Egypt 1259
> Tudkhalia IV, son of Hattusil III

Arnuwandas III, son of Tudkhalia IV
Suppiluliuma II, brother of Arnuwandas III
Hittite Empire falls 1177

Note that the Hittite kings within the box were contemporary with Ramesses II of Egypt. Note also that Hattusil III was contemporary with

---

2. It is possible that Amenmesses was a rival to Sethos II and so ruled concurrently with him. Consequently the date before this point could be reduced by three years. See ibid., 42.

the Assyrian king Adad-nirari I (1305–1274) and Tudkhalia IV was contemporary with the Assyrian king Tukulti-Ninurta I (1243–1207).[3]

## 3. ASSYRIAN KINGS

The convention implied in the chronology of J. A. Brinkman in A. L. Oppenheim, *Ancient Mesopotamia*, 346, is followed here. It adopts Mesopotamian usage, starting a new king's reign with a new year. This of course was not the reality! This segment is relevant to our wider discussions:

Sennacherib 704–681
Esarhaddon 680–669
Ashurbanipal 668–627[4]
Sin-shar-ishkun died 612

---

3. Assyrian chronology is based on the Assyrian King List, one king Ninurta-epil-ekur, however, is credited with either a thirteen- or a three-year reign in different versions of the list. A thirteen-year reign is assumed here.

4. It is now known from a reference by Adad-guppi, mother of the Neo-Babylonian king Nabonidus (556–539 BC) to a forty-two-year reign for Ashurbanipal that his reign lasted until 627 BC, not 631 BC, as was earlier claimed. Gadd, *Harran Inscriptions*, 70.

# Appendix 2

## List of Ancient Law Collections and Treaties

Here is a list of the ancient Treaties and Law Collections cited in this work. The italic numbers in brackets, e.g., *[14]* refer to the number given to the text in K. A. Kitchen and P. J. N. Lawrence, *Treaty Law and Covenant in the Ancient Near East*. For find-spots of the documents, see maps 3 and 4.

### 1. Law Collections

| Law collection | Date BC | Found at |
|---|---|---|
| Ur-Nammu *[9]* | ca. 2100 | Nippur, Sippar, Ur, Iraq |
| Lipit-Ishtar *[10]* | ca. 1930 | Nippur, Iraq |
| Old Assyrian Laws *[12]* | ca. 1900 | Kanesh (Kültepe), Turkey |
| Sumerian Laws on exercise tablets *[11]* | ca. 1800 | Nippur, Iraq |
| Eshnunna *[13]* | ca. 1800 | Tell Harmal, Iraq[A] |
| Hammurabi *[14]* | ca. 1750 | Susa, Iran[B] |
| Laws from Hazor | 18th–17th C | Hazor, Israel |
| Hittite Laws Old Series *[36]* | 16th–14th C | Hattusas (Boğazköy), Turkey |
| Hittite Laws New Series *[36]* | 13th C | Hattusas (Boğazköy), Turkey |
| Middle Assyrian Laws *[81]* | 12th–11th C | Assur, Iraq |
| Neo-Babylonian Laws *[102]* | ca. 600 | Sippar ?, Iraq |
| Demotic Laws *[103]* | 8th –late 4th C | Hermopolis, Egypt |
| Laws from Gortyn, Crete *[104]* | 5th C | Gortyn, Crete |

## 2. Early Treaties

| Maker of treaty | With | Date BC | Found at |
|---|---|---|---|
| Eannatum of Lagash [1] | Ruler of Umma | ca. 2500 | Tello, Iraq |
| Ruler of Kanesh [16] | Old Assyrian merchants | ca. 1900 | Kanesh (Kültepe), Turkey |
| Ruler of Assur [17] | Ruler of Hahhum | ca. 1900 | Kanesh (Kültepe), Turkey |
| Zimri-Lim of Mari [20] | Ibal-pi-el of Eshnunna | early 18th C | Mari, Syria |
| Zimri-Lim of Mari [21] | Hammurabi of Babylon | early 18th C | Mari, Syria |
| Zimri-Lim of Mari [22] | Atamrum of Andarig | early 18th C | Mari, Syria |
| Zimri-Lim of Mari [23] | Ruler of Kurda | early 18th C | Mari, Syria |
| Till-Abnu of Apum [24] | City of Assur | 18th C | Tell Leilan, Syria |
| Till-Abnu of Apum [25] | Yamsi-Hadnu of Kahat | 18th C | Tell Leilan, Syria |
| Abba-An of Aleppo [29] | Yarim-Lim of Alalakh | 18th–17th C | Alalakh, Syria |
| Idrimi of Alalakh [41] | Pilliya of Kizzuwatna | 15th C | Alalakh, Syria |
| Niqmepa of Alalakh [42] | Ir-Adad of Tunip | 15th C | Alalakh, Syria |

A. An additional tablet was discovered in the early 1980s at Tell Haddad near the river Diyala, in central Iraq.

B. The celebrated monumental stela was taken from either Sippar or Babylon in modern Iraq to Susa in SW Iran as part of the spoils of war by the Elamite king Shutruk-nahhunte in ca. 1158 BC. The text of the Law Collection also partially exists in many copies from various Mesopotamian sites.

## 134 APPENDIX 2

3. The Hittite Treaties of the Late Second Millennium BC [all unspecified rulers are Hittite]

| Maker of treaty | With | Date C BC | Found at | Title and/or H Prologue and/or Stipulations lost | With Historical Prologue | With Blessings |
|---|---|---|---|---|---|---|
| Ruler [39] | Paddatissu of Kizzuwatna | 15th | Hattusas | | | |
| Zidantas II [40] | Pilliya of Kizzuwatna | 15th | Hattusas | | | |
| Ruler [46] | Kaskeans | 15th | Hattusas | | | |
| Ruler [47] | Kaskeans | 15th | Hattusas | | | |
| Ruler [48] | Kaskeans | 15th | Hattusas | | | |
| Tudkhalia II [50] | Sunassura of Kizzuwatna | 14th | Hattusas | Yes | | |
| Tudkhalia II or Suppiluliuma I [51] | Sunassura II (?) of Kizzuwatna | 14th | Hattusas | | | |
| Tudkhalia II or Suppiluliuma I [52] | Lab'u and the Elders of Tunip | 14th | Hattusas | | | |
| Arnuwandas I [53] | People of Ismirika | 14th | Hattusas | | | |
| Arnuwandas I [54] | Kaskeans | 14th | Hattusas | Yes | Yes | Yes |
| Suppiluliuma I [55A] | Shattiwaza of Mitanni | 14th | Hattusas | | Yes | Yes |
| Suppiluliuma I [55B] | Shattiwaza of Mitanni | 14th | Hattusas | Yes | Yes | |
| Shattiwaza of Mitanni [56A] | Suppiluliuma I | 14th | Hattusas | | Yes | Yes |
| Shattiwaza of Mitanni [56B] | Suppiluliuma I | 14th | Hattusas | Yes | Yes | |
| Suppiluliuma I [57] | Tette of Nuhasse | 14th | Hattusas | | Yes | Yes |
| Suppiluliuma I [58A] | Aziru of Amurru | 14th | Hattusas | Yes | Yes | Yes |
| Suppiluliuma I [58B] | Aziru of Amurru | 14th | Hattusas | | Yes | |
| Suppiluliuma I [60] | Huqqanas of Hayasa | 14th | Hattusas | | Yes | Yes |
| Suppiluliuma I [61] | Niqmad II of Ugarit | 14th | Ugarit, Syria | | Yes | |
| Mursil II [62A] | Duppi-Tesub of Amurru | 14th | Hattusas | Yes | Yes | |

List of Ancient Law Collections and Treaties  135

| Maker of treaty | With | Date C BC | Found at | Title and/or H Prologue and/or Stipulations lost | With Historical Prologue | With Blessings |
|---|---|---|---|---|---|---|
| Mursil II [62B] | Duppi-Tesub of Amurru | 14th | Hattusas | | Yes | Yes |
| Mursil II [63] | Niqmepa of Ugarit | 14th | Hattusas | | Yes | Yes |
| Mursil II [64] | Targasnallis of Hapalla | 14th | Hattusas | Yes | | Yes |
| Mursil II [65] | Kupanta-Kurunta of Mira | 14th | Hattusas | | Yes | |
| Mursil II [66] | Manapa-Tarhunta of Seha River Land | 14th | Hattusas | | Yes | Yes |
| Muwatallis II [67] | Talmi-sarruma of Aleppo | 13th | Hattusas | | Yes | |
| Muwatallis II [68] | Alaksandus of Wilusa | 13th | Hattusas | | Yes | Yes |
| Hattusil III [69] | Bentesina of Amurru | 13th | Hattusas | | Yes | |
| Harrusil III [70] | Town of Tiliura | 13th | Hattusas | | Yes | |
| Hattusil III [71A] | Ramesses II of Egypt | 1259 | Hattusas | | Yes | Yes |
| Ramesses II of Egypt [71B] | Hattusil III | 1259 | Thebes, Egypt | | Yes | Yes |
| Tudkhalia IV [72] | Sausga-muwa of Amurru | 13th | Hattusas | | Yes | Yes |
| Tudkhalia IV [73] | Kurunta of Tarhuntassa | 13th | Hattusas | | Yes | Yes |
| Tudkhalia IV [74] | Ulmi-Tesub of Tarhuntassa | 13th | Hattusas | Yes | | |
| Suppiluliuma II [77] | Niqmad III of Ugarit | early 12th | Ugarit, Syria | Yes | Yes | |
| Tudkhalia IV/Suppiluliuma II [80] | Rulers of Alasia | early 12th | Hattusas | Yes | | Yes |

The following is also added here for the sake of convenience:

| Tukulti-Ninurta of Assyria [75] | Kashtiliash of Babylonia | late 13th | Nineveh, Iraq | | | Yes |

## 4. Syrian and Assyrian Treaties of the First Millennium BC

| Maker of treaty | With | Date BC | Found at | Witnesses following title |
|---|---|---|---|---|
| Shamshi-Adad V [89] | Marduk-zakir-shumi of Babylon | ca. 824 | Nineveh, Iraq | |
| Bar-Gayah of KTK [86] | Attar-sumki of Arpad | ca. 783 | Sefire, Syria (III) | |
| Bar-Gayah of KTK [87] | Matiel of Arpad | ca. 775 | Sefire, Syria (I) | Yes |
| Bar-Gayah of KTK [88] | Matiel of Arpad | ca. 773 | Sefire, Syria (II) | |
| Sennacherib [91] | Unknown ruler | 683/2 | Assur, Iraq | Yes |
| Esarhaddon [93] | Baal of Tyre | ca. 676 | Nineveh, Iraq | |
| Esarhaddon [94] | Rulers of Medes | 672 | Nimrud, Iraq | Yes |
| Queen Zakutu [96] | Shamash-shum-ukin of Babylon | ca. 669 | Nineveh, Iraq | |
| Ashurbanipal [97] | Abiate of Qedar | ca. 653/2 | Nineveh, Iraq | Yes |
| Ashurbanipal [98] | Elders of Babylonia | ca. 653/2 | Nineveh, Iraq | |
| Sin-shar-ishkun [99] | Babylonian allies | died 612 | Nineveh, Iraq | Yes |
| Hannibal of Carthage [105] | Philip V of Macedon | 215 | In medieval manuscript | Yes |

# Appendix 3

## A Possible Outline of the Pentateuch

### 1. THE BOOK OF BEGINNINGS: GEN 1:1—EXOD 19:25

#### (A) *The Primeval World*

1:1 Title: In the beginning God created the heavens and the earth

1:2—2:3 Document 1: Creation

2:4a Title or perhaps colophon (looking back): These are the generations of the heavens and the earth when they were created

2:4b–4:26 Document 2: Adam and Eve, Cain and Abel

5:1 Title: This is the book of the generations of Adam

5:1—6:8 Document 3: From Adam to Noah

6:9a Title: These are the generations of Noah

6:9b–9:29 Document 4: Noah

10:1 Title: These are the generations of the sons of Noah, Shem, Ham, and Japheth

10:2–32: The Table of the Nations

### (B) The Patriarchs in Palestine (Canaan)

11:1-9 Rest of Document 5: The Tower of Babel

11:10a Title: These are the generations of Shem

11:10b-11:26 Document 6: From Shem to Abram

11:27a Title: These are the generations of Terah

11:27—25:11 Document 7: Abraham

25:12 Title: These are the generations of Ishmael, Abraham's son, whom Hagar the Egyptian, Sarah's servant bore to Abraham

25:13-18 Document 8: Ishmael

25:19a Title: These are the generations of Isaac, Abraham's son

25:19b-35:29 Document 9: Isaac and Jacob

36:1 Title: These are the generations of Esau (that is Edom).

36:2-8 Document 10a: Esau part 1

36:9 These are the generations of Esau the father of the Edomites in the hill country of Seir

36:10—36:30 Document 10b: Esau part 2

36:31-43 The List of the Rulers of Edom

### (C) Israel in Egypt—Joseph and Moses

37:1 Introduction to Document 11

37:2a Title: These are the generations of Jacob

37:2b-50:26 Document 11: Joseph, including Poetic Section 49:2-27

Exod 1:1—19:25 Document 12: Moses, including Poetic Section 15:1-18

## A Possible Outline of the Pentateuch 139

### 2. THE BOOK OF THE COVENANT: EXOD 20:1—LEV 27:37

Exod 20:1 Title

20:2 Historical Prologue

20:3—23:33 Stipulations

24:1-4a Solemn Ceremony

24:4b-6 Witnesses

24:7-8 Reading

24:9-18 Solemn Ceremony resumed

25:1—40:28 Stipulations (into which may be added later material 25:9—34:7; 34:28-35; 35:20—40:28 (also written by Moses) regarding the tabernacle, its furnishings, and the priesthood)

Lev 1:1—26:2 Stipulations (into which may be added later material 1:1—10:20; 16:1—17:16; 21:1—24:14 (also written by Moses) regarding the sacrifices, offerings, and the priesthood)

26:3-13 Blessings

26:14-45 Curses

26:46 Main Colophon

27:1-33 Additional Stipulations

27:34 Final Colophon

### 3. THE BOOK OF THE TWO CENSUSES: NUM 1:1—36:13

1:1—5:10 Narrative

5:11-31 Additional Stipulations from the Book of the Covenant

6:1—27:5 Narrative resumed, including Poetic Sections with several prose connectives 23:1-24:25

27:6-11 Additional Stipulations from the Book of the Covenant

27:12—36:4 Narrative resumed

36:5-9 Additional Stipulations from the Book of the Covenant

36:10-12 Narrative resumed

36:13 Final Colophon

## 4. THE BOOK OF THE COVENANT REITERATED: DEUT 1:1—34:12

### (A) The Book of the Covenant reiterated

1:1–1:5 Title/Preamble
1:6—3:29 Historical Prologue
4:1—26:19 Stipulations
27:1-26 Solemn Ceremony (incl. Witnesses 2–8)
28:1-14 Blessings
28:15-68 Curses
29:1—31:8 Epilogue (incl. Oath 29:9–14)
31:9-13 Deposit and Public Reading
31:14—32:43 Witnesses (incl. Deposit 31:26), including Poetic Section 32:1-32:43

### (B) Postscript to the Book of the Covenant

32:44-47 Exhortation
32:48-52 Prediction of Moses' death
33:1—33:29 Moses blesses the tribes of Israel (Poetic Section)

### (C) Final postscript

34:1-12 The Death of Moses

Another way of looking at the Outline of the Pentateuch is to note where poetic sections are placed in the largely prose narratives thus[5]:

1. **Genesis**
   Prose Narrative 1:1-49:1
   Poetic Section 49:2-27
   Prose Narrative 49:28-50:26

2. **Exodus**
   Prose Narrative 1:1-14:31
   Poetic Section 15:1-18
   Prose Narrative 15:19-40:38

3. **Leviticus**
   Prose Narrative throughout 1:1-27:34

4. **Numbers**
   Prose Narrative 1:22:41
   Poetic Sections with several prose connectives 23:1-24:25
   Prose Narrative 25:1-36-13

5. **Deuteronomy**
   Prose Narrative 1:1-31:30
   Poetic Sections with a prose connective 32:1-33:29
   Prose Narrative 34:1-34:12

---

5. I am grateful to Lunn for pointing this out to me.

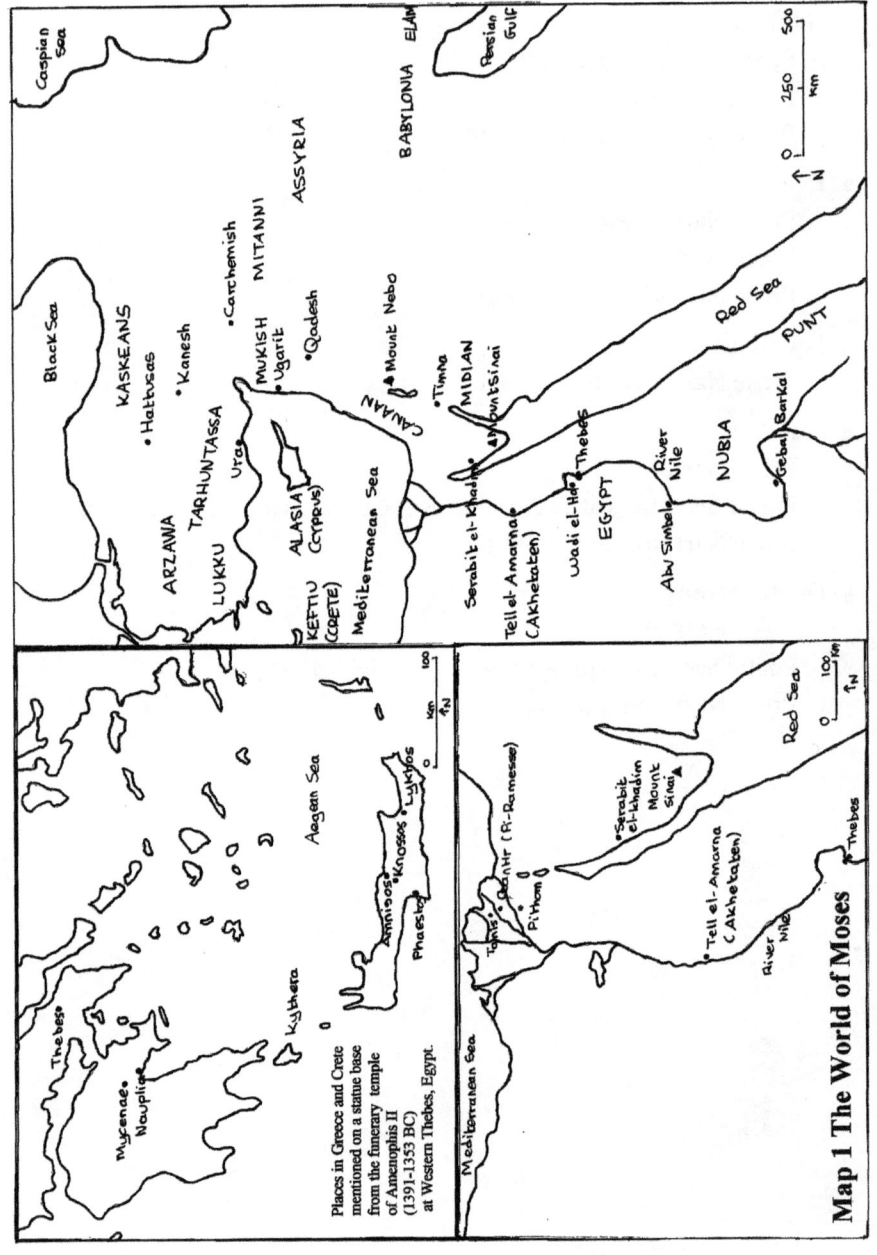

Map 1 The World of Moses

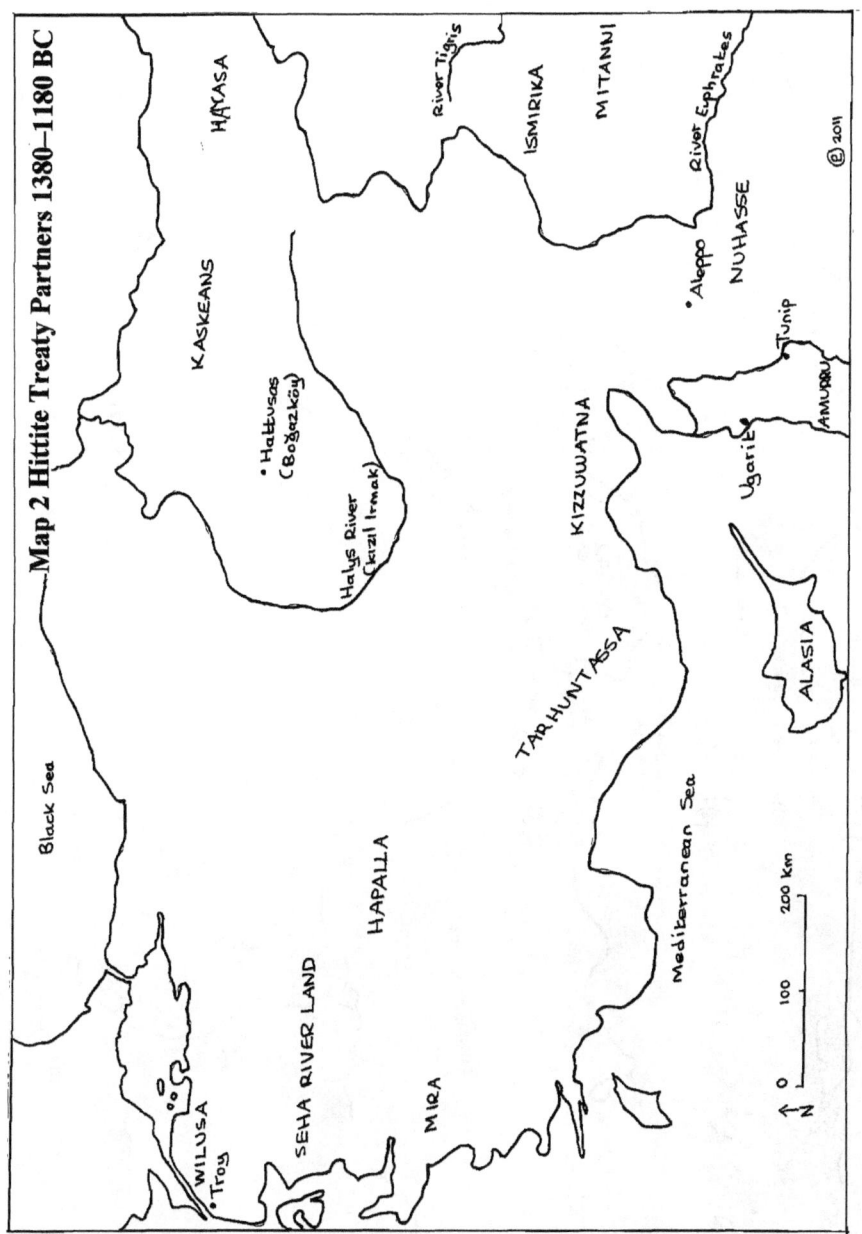

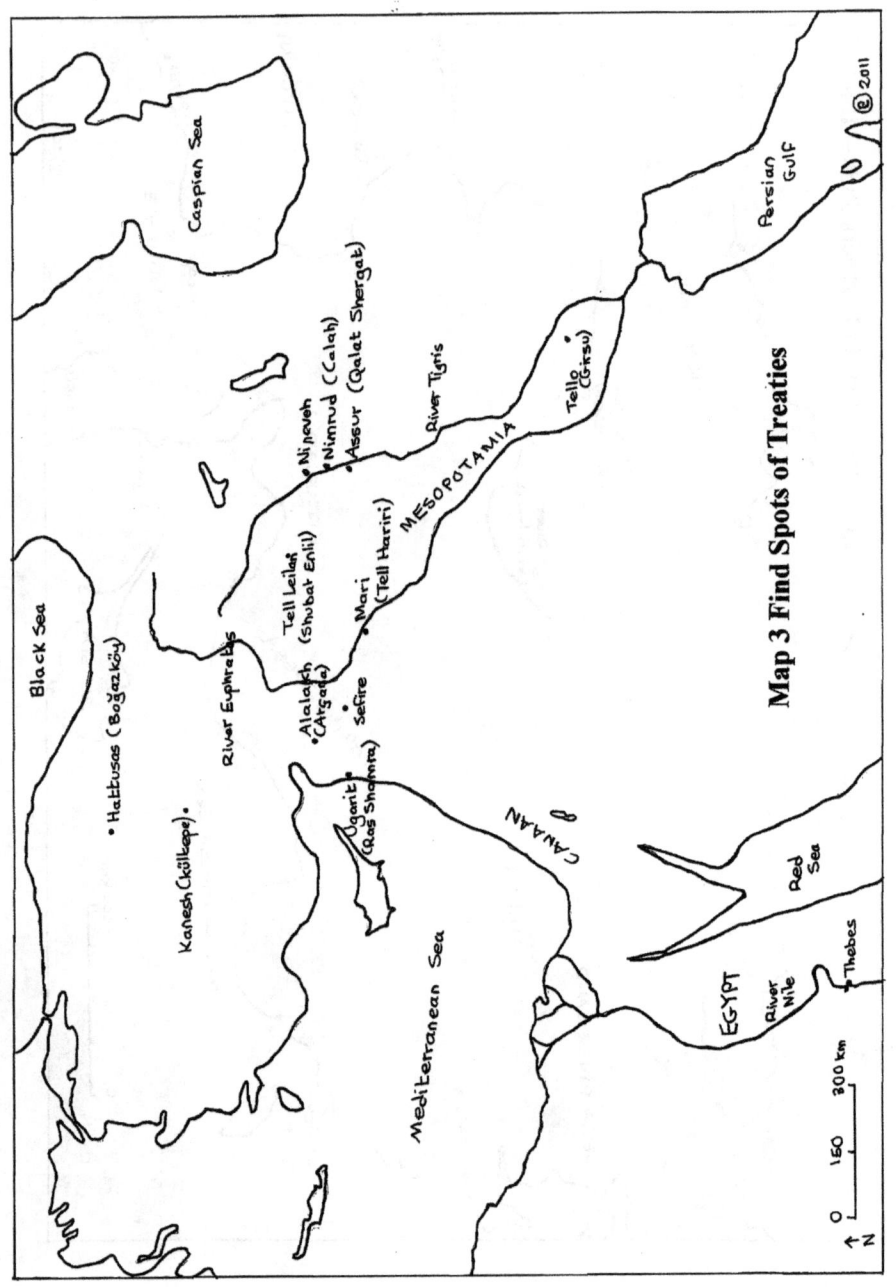

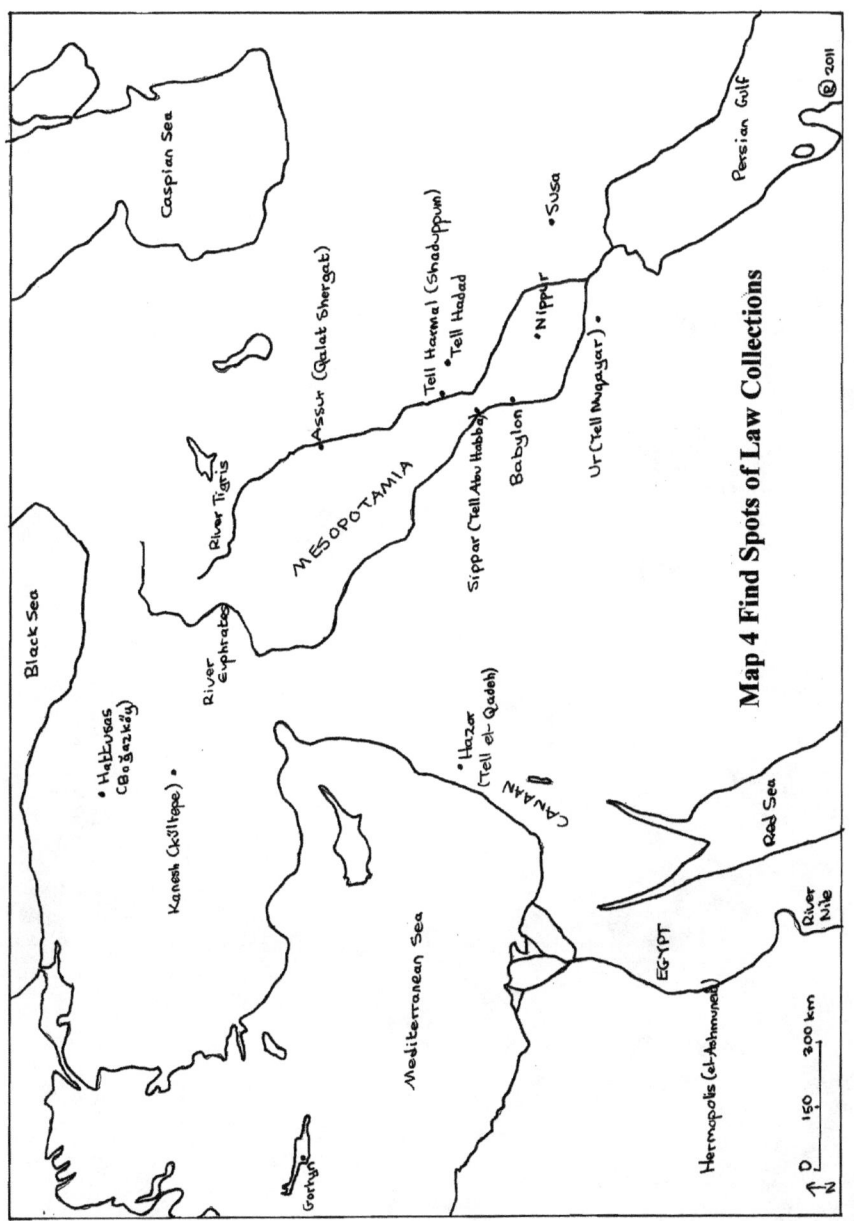

Map 4 Find Spots of Law Collections

# Bibliography

Abegg, Jr., M., P. Flint, and E. Ulrich. *The Dead Sea Scrolls Bible*. New York: Harper Collins, 1999.
Albright, W. F. "The Amarna Letters from Palestine." In *CAH II/2*: 98–116.
———. *From Stone Age to Christianity*. New York: Doubleday / Anchor, 1957.
Aldred, C. *The Egyptians*. London: Thames & Hudson, 1962.
Anderson, B. W. "From Analysis to Synthesis: The Interpretation of Genesis 1–11." *JBL* 97 (1978) 23–39.
Astruc, J. (published anonymously). *Conjectures sur les Mémoires originaux dont il paroit que Moyse s'est servi pour composer le Livre de la Genèse*. 1753.
Baker, D. W. "Source Criticism." In *DOTP*: 798a–805b.
Bolling, G. M. *The External Evidence for Interpolation in Homer*. Oxford: Clarendon, 1925.
Borger, R. "Zu den Asarhaddon-Verträgen aus Nimrud." *ZA* 54 (1961) 173–96.
———. "Marduk-zākir-šumi I und der Kodex Ḫammurapi." *Orientalia* 34 (1965) 168–69.
Breasted, J. H. *Ancient Records of Egypt* IV. Chicago UP, 1906.
Bright, J. *History of Israel* (with appendix by W. P. Brown). 4th ed. Louisville: John Knox, Louisville, 2000.
Bryce, T. *The Trojans and their Neighbours*. London: Routledge, 2006.
Burney, C. F. *The Book of Judges*. London: Rivingtons, 1918.
Campbell, A. F. "A Historical Prologue in a seventh-century Treaty." *Biblica* 50 (1969) 534–35.
Cassuto, U. *The Documentary Hypothesis*. Jerusalem: Magnes, 1961.
Christensen, D. L. *WBC Deuteronomy*. Nashville: Nelson, 2001.
Cornelius, F. "Geographie des Hethitreiches." *Orientalia* 27 (1955) 225–51.
Craigie, P. C. *NICOT Deuteronomy*. London: Hodder and Stoughton, 1976.
Cross, F. M. "Palaeography." In *The Encylopaedia of the Dead Sea Scrolls*, 629a–34b. Oxford UP, 2000.
Davison, J. A. "The Homeric Question." In *Companion to Homer*, edited by A. J. B. Wayce and F. H. Stubbings. London: Macmillan, 1962.
Deutscher, G. *Syntactic Change in Akkadian*. Oxford UP, 2000.
Dobel, A., F. Asaro, and H.V. Michael. "Neutron Activation Analysis and the Location of Waššukanni." *Orientalia* 46 (1977) 375–82.
Eskhult, M. "The Importance of Loanwords for dating Biblical Hebrew Texts." In *Biblical Hebrew Studies in Chronology and Typology JSOT Supplement Series* 369, 8–23. London/New York: T&T Clark International, 2003.
Field, F. *Origenis Hexaplorum*. Hildesheim: Olms, 1964.

Finkelstein, J. J.. *The Ox that gored*. Transactions of the American Philosophical Society 71 (1981).

Frankena, R. "The Vassal Treaties of Esarhaddon and the Dating of Deuteronomy." *OTS* 14 (1965) 122–54.

Gadd, C. J. "The Harran Inscriptions of Nabonidus." *AnSt* 8 (1958) 35–92.

George, A. R. *The Babylonian Gilgamesh Epic*. Oxford UP, 2003.

———. *The Epic of Gilgamesh*. London: Penguin, 1999.

Grayson, A. K. *ARI*. Wiesbaden: Harrassowitz, 1976.

———. *The Royal Inscriptions of Mesopotamia, Assyrian Periods*. Volume 3. Toronto UP, 1996.

Greengus, S. "Law." In *ABD* IV: 242a–52a.

———. "Law." In the OT in *IBDSup*: 532b–37b.

Grohman, E. D. "Amaw." In *IBD* I: 104a.

Hamilton, V. P. *NICOT Genesis*. Grand Rapids: Eerdmans, 1990.

Heidel, A. *The Gilgamesh Epic and Old Testament Parallels*. Chicago UP, 1946.

Hoffmeier, J. K. *Israel in Egypt*. Oxford UP, 1997.

Hope Simpson, R. and J. F. Lazenby. *The Catalogue of Ships in Homer's Iliad*. Oxford: Clarendon, 1970.

Hulse, E. V. "The Nature of Biblical 'Leprosy' and the use of alternative medical terms in modern translations of the Bible." *PEQ* 107 (1975) 87–105.

Ilgen, K. D. *Die Urkunden des Jerusalemischen Tempelarchivs in ihrer Urgestalt*. 1798.

James, P. *Centuries of Darkness*. London: Cape, 1991.

Kidner, D. *TC Genesis*. London: IVP, 1967.

Kirk, G. S. *Cambridge History of Classical Literature*. Edited by Easterling, P. E. 1983.

Kitchen, K. A. *Ancient Orient and Old Testament*. London: IVP, 1966.

———. *The Arty-crafty Kaphtorim and the Old Testament* (unpublished).

———. *The Bible in its World*. Exeter: Paternoster, 1977.

———. "Egypt, Egyptians." In *DOTP*: 207a–14b.

———. *On the Reliability of the Old Testament*. Grand Rapids: Eerdmans, 2003.

———. "The Rise and Fall of Covenant, Law and Treaty." *Tyndale Bulletin* 40 (1989), 118–35.

———. "Sinuhe: Scholarly method versus trendy fashion." *Bulletin of the Australian Centre for Egyptology* 7 (1996) 55–61.

———. "Theban Topographical Lists, Old and New." *Orientalia* 34 (1965) 1–9.

———. In Bietak, M. *The Synchronisation of Civilisations in the Eastern Mediterranean in the Second Millennium BC*. Vienna, 2000.

Kitchen, K. A. and P. J. N. Lawrence. *Treaty Law and Covenant in the Ancient Near East*. Three volumes. Wiesbaden: Otto Harrassowitz, 2012.

Kline, M. G. *The Treaty of the Great King*. Grand Rapids: Eerdmans, 1963.

Korošec, V. *Hethitische Staatsverträge*. Leipzig: Weicher, 1931.

Lambert, W. G. and A. R. Millard. *Atrahasis: The Babylonian Story of the Flood*. Oxford UP, 1969.

Landfester, M and B. Egger. In *Dictionary of Ancient Greek and Latin Authors and Texts*.

Landsberger, B. "Die babylonische Termini für Gesetz und Recht." *Symbolae Paulo Koschaker*. Leiden: Brill, 1939.

Latacz, J. "Homerus." In *BEAWNP*: 450–63.

———. "The Homeric Question." In *BEAWNP Classical Tradition* 2: 967–79.

———. *Troy and Homer*. Oxford UP, 2004.

Lawrence, P. J. N. "Anachronism." In *The Dictionary of Bible Translation* (forthcoming), Edited by Noss, P.
———. "Authorship, Date and Bible Translation." In *The Dictionary of Bible Translation* (forthcoming), Edited by Noss, P.
———. *The Lion Atlas of Bible History*. Oxford: Lion Hudson, 2006.
———. "Oh no, he's still wearing his watch! – Avoiding Anachronism in Old Testament Translation." *BT* 59 (2008) 14–17.
Lemaire, A. and J-M. Durand. *Les Inscriptions Araméennes*. Geneva: Droz, 1984.
Levine, B. A. "Leviticus." In *ABD* IV, 312a.
Lewis, C. S. *Fern-seed and Elephants and Other Essays on Christianity*. Glasgow: Collins, 1975.
Lichtheim, M. "The Story of Sinuhe." In *Ancient Egyptian Literature A Book of Readings Volume 1*, 222–35. *The Old and Middle Kingdoms*. Berkley/Los Angeles: California UP, 1973.
Liddell, H. G. and R. Scott. *English-Greek Lexicon*. Oxford UP (1940 edition used).
Lloyd, S. *Ancient Turkey*. London: British Museum, 1989.
Luckenbill, D. D. *Ancient Records of Assyria and Babylonia*. Chicago UP, 1926.
Manley, G. T. *The Book of the Law*. London: Tyndale, 1957.
Marín, J. A. B. *Répertoire Géographique des Textes Cunéiformes* XII/2. Wiesbaden: Reichert, 2001.
Marshall, I. M. "Jewels." In *IllBD*: 781b–88b.
Mayes, A. D. H. *NCB Deuteronomy*. London: Marshall, Morgan and Scott, 1979.
McCarthy, D. J. *Treaty and Covenant*. 2nd ed. Analecta Biblica 21A. Rome: Pontifical Biblical Institute, 1981.
Meek, T. J. "The Code of Hammurabi." In *ANET*: 163b–80a.
Mendenhall, G. E. "Covenant Forms in Israelite Tradition." *BA* 17 (1954) 50–76.
Mendenhall, G. E. and G. A. Herion. "Covenant." In *ABD* I: 1179a–1202a.
Merkelbach, R. *Untersuchungen zur Odysee*. Munich: Beck, 1951.
Migne, J. P. *Patrologia Graeca* 9. Paris, 1890.
———. *Patrologia Graeca* 80. Paris, 1864.
Moore, J. M. *The Manuscript Tradition of Polybius*. Cambridge UP, 1965.
Moran, W. L. *The Amarna Letters*. Baltimore/London: Johns Hopkins UP, 1992.
Mountjoy, P. A. "The East Aegean – West Anatolian Interface in the Late Bronze Age: Mycenaeans and the Kingdom of Ahhiyawa." *AnSt* 48 (1998).
Muchiki, Y. *Egyptian Proper Names and Loanwords in North-West Semitic*. Atlanta: Society of Biblical Literature, 1999.
Niehaus, J. J. "Joshua and Ancient Near Eastern warfare." *JETS* 31 (1988) 45–50.
Norrback, A. *The Fatherless and the Widow in the Deuteronomic Covenant*. Abo Akademi UP, 2001.
Oppenheim, A. L. *Ancient Mesopotamia*. Chicago UP, 1977.
———. "Chaldeans." In *IBD* I: 550a.
Osborne, W. "Table of the Nations." In *DOTP*: 588b–96a.
Parkinson, R. B. *The Tale of Sinuhe and other Ancient Egyptian Poems 1940–1640 BC*. Oxford UP, 1998.
Parpola, S. and K. Watanabe. *Neo Assyrian Treaties and Loyalty Oaths* (State Archives of Assyria II). Helsinki, 1989.
Parry, A (ed.). *The making of Homeric Verse: The Collected Papers of Milman Parry*. Oxford: Clarendon, 1971.

Payton, R. "The Uluburun Writing-Board Set." *AnSt* 41 (1991) 99–106.
Peden, A. J. *Egyptian Historical Inscriptions of the 20th Dynasty*. Jonsered: Paul Åströms Förlag, 1994.
Powell, B. B. *Homer and the Origin of the Greek Alphabet*. Cambridge UP, 1991.
Rainey, A. J. *Canaanite in the Amarna Letters*. Vol. 1. Leiden/New York/Cologne: Brill, 1996.
Richardson, M. E. J. *Hammurabi's Laws*. Sheffield Academic, 2000.
Riemann, P. A. "Covenant, Mosaic." In *IntBDSup*: 192a–97a.
Roberts, C and K. Manchester. *The Archaeology of Disease*. 3rd ed. Ithaca: Cornell UP, 2005.
Rogers, C. "Moses: Meek or Miserable?" *JETS* 29 (1986) 257–63.
Rohl, D. M. *A Test of Time*. London: Century, 1995.
Roth, M. "The Laws of Hammurabi." In *CoS* 2: 335–53.
Sandars, N. K. *The Sea Peoples*. London: Thames & Hudson, 1978.
Schneidewind, W. M. *How the Bible Became a Book*. Cambridge, 2004.
Shanks, H. "On the Trail of Hazor's Royal Archive." *Biblical Archaeology Review* 36/6 (2010) 16.
Ska, J-L. *Introduction to Reading the Pentateuch*. Winona Lake: Eisenbrauns, 2006.
———. *"Our Fathers Have Told Us" Introduction to the Analysis of Hebrew Narratives*. 2nd ed. Subsidia Biblica 13. Rome: Pontifico Instituto Biblico, 2000.
Skinner, J. *ICC Genesis*. Edinburgh: T&T Clark, 1910.
Smend, R. *From Astruc to Zimmerli*. Tübingen: Mohr Sieback, 2007.
Speiser, E. A. *AB Genesis*. Garden City: Doubleday, 1964.
Stanford, W. B. *The Odyssey of Homer*. 1. London: Macmillan, 1947.
———. *The Odyssey of Homer*. 2. London: Macmillan, 1948.
Stubbings, F. H. "The Recession of Mycenaean Civilization." In *CAH II/2*: 338–58.
Taplin, O. "Homer." In *The Oxford History of the Classical World*, edited by J. Boardman, J. Griffin, and O. Murray. 50–77. Oxford UP, 1986.
Thompson, H. O. "Amaw." In *ABD* I: 183b.
Tigay, J. H. *Empirical Models for Biblical Criticism*. Philadelphia: University of Pennsylvania, 1985.
———. *The Evolution of the Gilgamesh Epic*. Philadelphia: University of Pennsylvania, 1982.
van Koppen, F. and K. Radner. "Der Hyksospalast bei Tell el-Dab'a, Zweite und Dritte Grabungskampagne." In *Ägypten und Levante* 19 (2009) 115–19.
Vermes, G. *The Complete Dead Sea Scrolls in English*. 2nd ed. London: Penguin, 2004.
von Rad, G. *OTL Genesis*. London: OTL, 1961.
Wachsmann, S. *Aegeans in the Theban Tombs*. OLA 20. Louvain: Peeters, 1987.
Walker, L. L. "Notes on Higher Criticism and the Dating of Biblical Hebrew." In *A tribute to Gleason Archer*, edited by W. C. Kaiser and R. F. Youngblood. 35–52. Chicago: Moody, 1986.
Weinfeld, M. "Covenant Making in Anatolia and Mesopotamia." *JANES* 22: 133–39.
———. *Deuteronomy and the Deuteronomic School*. Oxford: Clarendon, 1972.
———. "Traces of Assyrian treaty Formulae in Deuteronomy." *Biblica* 46 (1965) 417–27.
Wellhausen, J. *Die Composition des Hexateuchs*. 1877.
———. *Geschichte Israels*. 1894.
———. *Prolegomena zur Geschichte Israels*. 1878.
Wenham, G. J. *TC Numbers*. Leicester: IVP, 1981.

———. *WBC Genesis*. Waco: Word, 1987.
West, M. L. *The East Face of Helicon*. Oxford: Clarendon, 1997.
Westbrook, R. *Old Babylonian Marriage Law*. Horn: AfO Beiheft 23, 1998.
Westermann, C. *SPCK Genesis 1–11*. London, 1984.
de Wette, M. L. *Beiträge zur Einleiting in das Alte Testament*. 1806.
———. *Dissertatio critica qua a prioribus Deuteronomium Pentateuchi libris diversum alius cujiusdam recentioris auctoris opus esse monstratur*. 1805.
Wilson, J. A. "An Egyptian Letter." In *ANET*: 475a–79b.
———. "Egyptian Historical Texts." In *ANET*: 227a–64b.
———. "The Story of Sinuhe." In *ANET*: 18a–22b.
Wilson, W. *The Writings of Clement of Alexandria*. Edinburgh, 1867–9.
Wiseman, P. J. *Clues to Creation in Genesis*. London: Marshall, Morgan and Scott, 1977.
Whitman, C. H. *Homer and the Heroic Tradition*. Cambridge MA: Harvard UP, 1958.
Wolf, F. A. *Prolegomena ad Homerum*. 1795.
Wood, M. *In Search of the Trojan War*. London: BBC, 1985.
Würtwein, E. *The Text of the Old Testament*. Grand Rapids: Eerdmans, 1979.
Wyrick, J. *The Ascension of Authorship*. Cambridge MA: Harvard UP, 2004.
Young, I. M. In *Gilgameš and the World of Assyria*. Ancient Near Eastern Studies Supplement 21. Leuven (Louvain): Peeters, 2007.

# Index of Ancient Sources

The following ancient texts from outside the collection of Treaties and Law Collections are also cited in this work:

### AKKADIAN TEXTS

*Amarna Letter 286.5*
    96 n 4

*Annals of Shalmaneser III* 19, ii
35b–36a
    32 n 5

*Annals of Shalmaneser III* 51, i
40b–43a
    32 n 5

*Annals of Tiglath-pileser I*
1.62
    36 n 19

*Atrahasis* Rev.5:22–23
    86

*Black Obelisk of Shalmaneser III*
    36 n 20

*Epic of Gilgamesh*
1.10–11      110
11.9–196      107, 110
11.325–26      110

### EGYPTIAN TEXTS

*Ankhtifi's tomb-chapel at Mo'alla*
    86

*Great Harris Papyrus of Ramesses IV*
    27

*Ramesses III inscription from 8th year*
    27

### GREEK WRITERS

Aristotle *Physics*
1.4.188a.17–18      127 n 5

Aristotle *Posterior Analytics*
1.25.86a.33–35      127 n 5

Clement of Alexandria *Stromata (Miscellanies)*
5.6.76      14 n 53

Diogenes Laertius
1.57      115 n 43

Flavius Josephus *Antiquities of the Jews*
1.29      9

Herodotus *Histories*
2.53      111
7.73      28 n 35

## Index of Ancient Sources

**Homer** Iliad
| | |
|---|---|
| 2.108 | 115 |
| 2.484–62 | 115 |
| 2.546–56 | 115 n 43 |
| 2.558 | 115 n 43 |
| 2.569–80 | 115 |
| 2.816–77 | 115 |
| 3.16 | 67 n 7 |
| 6.168b–69 | 113 |
| 7.175–76 | 113 |
| 7.334–43 | 113 n 34 |
| 10.1–579 | 116 |
| 11.632–37 | 112 |

**Homer** Odyssey
| | |
|---|---|
| 8.62–82 | 112 n 24 |

**Hymn to Apollo**
| | |
|---|---|
| 169–173 | 112 n 24 |

**Linear B tablet from Knossos**
| | |
|---|---|
| [U 0478] | 34 n 12 |

**Linear B tablet from Pylos**
| | |
|---|---|
| [Vn 1191] | 34 n 12 |

**Lucian of Samosata** True Histories
| | |
|---|---|
| 2.20 | 112 n 25 |

**Pausanias** Guide to Greece
| | |
|---|---|
| 7.26 | 113 n 33 |

**Polybius** Histories
| | |
|---|---|
| 7.9.1–17 | 118 |

**Scholiast on Origen's** Hexapla
| | |
|---|---|
| | 14 n 53 |

**Stephanus Byzantius** Ethnika
| | |
|---|---|
| 554.5 | 67 n 7 |

**Theodoret of Cyrrhus** Questions on Exodus
| | |
|---|---|
| 15 | 14 n 53 |

### LATIN WRITERS

**Cicero** De Oratore
| | |
|---|---|
| 3.137 | 113 n 32 |

**Jerome (Sophronius Eusebius Hieronymus) on Dt.33:2**
| | |
|---|---|
| | 100 n 22 |

### HEBREW WRITERS

**Pirqê Abōt**
| | |
|---|---|
| 1.1 | 9 |

### SUMERIAN TEXTS

**Sumerian King List**
| | |
|---|---|
| 3.17 | 109 |

# Index of Scripture

*Genesis*

| | |
|---|---|
| 1:1–2:3 | 15, 31 |
| 1:1 | 31 n 3 |
| 1:5 | 9 |
| 2:4a | 30–31 |
| 2:4b–26 | 31 |
| 5:1 | 15, 30 |
| 6:1—9:19 | 13, 107 n 2 |
| 6:2, 4 | 15 |
| 6:9a | 30 |
| 8:1a | 13 n 50 |
| 9:8–17 | 42 |
| 9:26–27 | 15 |
| 10:1–32 | 35–36, 123 |
| 10:1 | 30 |
| 10:2 | 35–36 |
| 10:3 | 35 |
| 10:4 | 36 |
| 10:10 | 109 n 9 |
| 10:11 | 58 n 32 |
| 10:13 | 35 |
| 10:14 | 35 |
| 10:22 | 35 |
| 11:10a | 30 |
| 11:27 | 30 |
| 11:28 | 33, 45, 122 |
| 11:31 | 33, 45, 122 |
| 12:11–19 | 11 |
| 13:10 | 32, 45, 122 |
| 14:2 | 32 |
| 14:3 | 32 |
| 14:7 | 32 |
| 14:8 | 32 |
| 14:14 | 33, 38, 45, 122 |
| 14:17 | 32 |
| 15:7 | 13, 45, 122 |
| 15:7–21 | 42–44 |
| 16:14 | 32 |
| 19:4–8 | 12 |
| 20:2–5 | 11 |
| 21:23–24 | 40, 42, 121 |
| 21:29–33 | 40 |
| 21:32 | 33, 45, 122 |
| 21:34 | 33, 45, 122 |
| 22:14 | 34, 45, 122 |
| 23:2 | 32 |
| 23:19 | 32 |
| 25:7 | 30 n 2 |
| 25:12 | 30 |
| 25:19a | 30 |
| 26:1 | 33, 45, 122 |
| 26:8 | 33, 45, 122 |
| 26:14 | 33, 45, 122 |
| 26:15 | 33, 45, 122 |
| 26:18 | 33, 45, 122 |
| 26:21 | 33, 45, 122 |
| 26:28–31 | 40–41 |
| 26:33 | 34, 45, 122 |
| 31:44–54 | 41 |
| 32:32 | 34, 45, 122 |
| 35:20 | 34, 45, 122 |
| 36:1 | 30 |
| 36:9 | 30 |
| 36:28 | 30 n 2 |
| 36:31–43 | 35–38, 123 |
| 37:1–5 | 12 |
| 37:1 | 36 |
| 37:2a | 30–31 |

## Genesis (continued)

| | |
|---|---|
| 37:28 | 44, 46, 121 |
| 41:1 | 38 |
| 41:2 | 38 |
| 41:8 | 38 |
| 41:42 | 38 |
| 41:45 | 38 |
| 45:10 | 18 |
| 47:9 | 30 n 2 |
| 47:11 | 33, 45 |
| 47:11–26 | 21 |
| 50:22 | 30 n 2 |

## Exodus

| | |
|---|---|
| 1:11 | 6, 18 |
| 2:1–10 | 1 n 2 |
| 2:3 | 96, 100, 122 |
| 2:10 | 20 |
| 2:11—4:17 | 1 n 6 |
| 2:22 | 25 |
| 3:1—4:17 | 22 |
| 6:3 | 14 n 53 |
| 7:1 | 3 n 14 |
| 7:7 | 2 n 7, 7 n 29 |
| 12:40 | 18 |
| 14:5—15:21 | 2 n 10 |
| 16:15 | 96 |
| 16:31 | 96, 100 |
| 17:14 | 113 n 30 |
| 19:5 | 97, 100 |
| 20:1—23:19 | 8 |
| 20:1 | 48, 65 |
| 20:2 | 48–49 |
| 20:2–17 | 5, 71 |
| 20:12 | 8 |
| 20:17 | 71 |
| 20:18—23:19 | 49 |
| 21:2–6 | 71 |
| 21:16 | 102 |
| 21:28 | 103 |
| 21:29 | 104 |
| 21:31–32 | 103–4 |
| 21:32 | 44 |
| 21:35 | 103 |

| | |
|---|---|
| 24:12 | 113 n 30 |
| 28:17–20 | 21 n 7, 97–98, 100, 121 |
| 28:18 | 97–98 |
| 28:19 | 97–98 |
| 28:20 | 98 |
| 32:16 | 113 n 30 |
| 32:32 | 113 n 30 |
| 34:1 | 113 n 30 |
| 34:27 | 113 n 30 |
| 34:8 | 49 |
| 35:19 | 49 |

## Leviticus

| | |
|---|---|
| 19:23–25 | 105 |
| 26:18b | 87 |
| 26:19 | 82 |
| 26:21b | 87 |
| 26:24b | 87 |
| 26:28b | 87 |
| 26:46 | 49 |
| 27:1–33 | 49 |
| 27:34 | 49 |

## Numbers

| | |
|---|---|
| 1:1–46 | 95 |
| 5:11–31 | 70 n A, 96 |
| 5:23 | 113 n 30 |
| 6:24–26 | 4 |
| 12:3 | 99, 101, 123 |
| 13:1—14:45 | 95 |
| 13:22 | 98, 100, 122 |
| 16:1—17:12 | 95 |
| 17:2 | 113 n 20 |
| 17:3 | 113 n 20 |
| 20:1–13 | 95 |
| 22:5 | 98–100, 121 |
| 26:1–65 | 95 |
| 27:6–11 | 70 n A, 96 |
| 32:39–42 | 99, 101, 123 |
| 34:1–29 | 99 |
| 36:5–9 | 70 n A, 96 |

## Deuteronomy

| | |
|---|---|
| 1:1 | 65, 67 |
| 1:2 | 89 |

## Index of Scripture

| | | | |
|---|---|---|---|
| 1:6—3:9 | 48, 69, 121 | 28:16–19 | 77 |
| 2:10–12 | 89–90 | 28:23 | 82 |
| 2:14 | 7 n 29 | 28:24 | 86 |
| 2:20–23 | 90 | 28:25b | 86–87 |
| 2:22 | 90 | 28:26 | 83 |
| 3:9 | 90 | 28:27 | 83, 86 |
| 3:11 | 90 | 28:28a | 86 |
| 3:13b–14 | 90 | 28:28–29a | 83, 86 |
| 3:14a | 90 | 28:30a | 84 |
| 4:45a–49 | 90 | 28:33 | 84 |
| 5:2–6 | 90 | 28:37 | 86 |
| 5:6–21 | 5, 90 | 28:38 | 84 |
| 5:7 | 2 n 12 | 28:38–40 | 87 |
| 5:16 | 8 | 28:41 | 86 |
| 5:22–31 | 90 | 28:53–57 | 84 |
| 6:9 | 113 n 30 | 28:58 | 113 n 30 |
| 6:10–12 | 91 | 29:1—31:8 | 88 |
| 6:21–23 | 91 | 29:20 | 113 n 30 |
| 7:6 | 97, 100 | 29:21 | 113 n 30 |
| 7:18–19 | 91 | 29:27 | 113 n 30 |
| 8:2–4 | 91 | 30:10 | 113 n 30 |
| 8:14–16 | 91 | 31:10–11 | 75 |
| 9:7—10:11 | 91 | 31:19, 24 | 113 n 30 |
| 10:2 | 113 n 30 | 32:44–47 | 48 |
| 10:4 | 113 n 30 | 32:48–52 | 48 |
| 11:2–7 | 91 | 33:1–29 | 48 |
| 11:20 | 113 n 30 | 33:2 | 99–100 |
| 14:2 | 91 | 33:17 | 21 n 7 |
| 17:18 | 113 n 30 | 34:1–5 | 2 n 12 |
| 18:15 | 8 | 34:1–12 | 48 |
| 18:18 | 8 | 34:10–12 | 2 |
| 18:19 | 8 | | |
| 23:3–6 | 91 | *Joshua* | |
| 24:1 | 113 n 30 | 19:47 | 33 n 7 |
| 24:3 | 113 n 30 | 24:2 | 65 |
| 24:7 | 103 | 24:2c–13 | 69 n 10 |
| 24:9 | 91, 91 n 60 | 24:20b | 56 n 30 |
| 25:4 | 8 | | |
| 25:17–18 | 91 | *Judges* | |
| 26:5b–9 | 91 | 11:26 | 7 n 31 |
| 26:18 | 97, 100 | 18:29 | 33 |
| 27:3, 8 | 113 n 30 | 19:22–23 | 12 |
| 27:4–8 | 74 | | |
| 28:3–6 | 77 | *1 Kings* | |
| | | 6:1 | 7 n 31 |

## Index of Scripture

*1 Kings* (continued)
| | |
|---|---|
| 9:14 | 28 n 36 |
| 14:25 | 28 n 36 |

*2 Kings*
| | |
|---|---|
| 25:27–30 | 35 n 13 |

*1 Chronicles*
| | |
|---|---|
| 6:3–8 | 7 n 30 |

*2 Chronicles*
| | |
|---|---|
| 34:14 | 10 n 42 |

*Mark*
| | |
|---|---|
| 7:10 | 8 |

*Acts*
| | |
|---|---|
| 3:22–23 | 8 |
| 7:23 | 1 n 4 |
| 7:36 | 2 n 9 |
| 13:20 | 7 n 31 |

*1 Corinthians*
| | |
|---|---|
| 9:9 | 8 |

*Hebrews*
| | |
|---|---|
| 11:29 | 2 n 9 |

*Ecclesiasticus*
| | |
|---|---|
| 24:23 | 8 |

# Index of Subjects

A-anne-padda, ruler of Ur, 109 n 14
Aaron, brother of Moses, 7 n 30
Abba-An, king of Aleppo in Syria, 44
Abdi-Heba, king of Jerusalem in Amarna Letters, 96
Abiate, ruler of Qedar in Arabia, 58 n 35, 69 n 12, 92
Abimelech, king of Gerar in Canaan, 11, 40, 43, 55
Abiram, Israelite rebel, 91
Abraham, 11, 30, 34, 38, 40–44, 55, 89
Abram, earlier name of Abraham, 33, 38, 43
Abu Simbel, temple of Ramesses II in S Egypt, 20
Achaeans, name given to the Mycenaean Greeks in the writings of Homer, 28, 115–16, 119
Adad, Mesopotamian storm god, 62
Adad-guppi, mother of Nabonidus, king of Babylon, 131 n 4
Aeolic, Greek dialect, 112
Agamemnon, commander-in-chief of Achaeans (Greeks) at Troy, 115
agate, precious stone, 21, 98
Agga, King of Kish in S Mesopotamia (Iraq), 109 n 14
Ahhiyawa, Hittite equivalent of Achaeans, 28 n 34
Aias (Ajax), Greek hero, 113
Ain el-Qudeirat, place in Sinai peninsula (=Kadesh Barnea), 89 n 56

Akhenaten, king of Egypt, 19, 22
Akhetaten, capital of Akhenaten, king of Egypt (modern Tell el-Amarna in central Egypt) 19
Akkadian, the Semitic language of the Assyrians and Babylonians spoken in Mesopotamia, 16, 20, 22, 25, 52–53, 55 n 25, 63, 66–67, 76 n 31, 80 n 34, 83 n 44, 97–98, 109, 110 n 18
Alaksandus, king of Wilusa in Anatolia, 67, 67 n 7, 76, 76 n 28, 80
Alalakh, city in Syria, 43, 44, 52 n 6, 97, 99
Alasia, an ancient name of Cyprus, 23, 24, 27, 36, 52, 75
Aleppo, city in Syria, 43–44, 56, 58 n 31, 67, 72, 91, 99
Aleppo Codex of Hebrew Bible, 5 n 24
Alexander the Great, 91 n 60
Alexandria, capital of Ptolemaic Egypt, 113 n 32
Alexandros, name of a Trojan prince, = Priam's son Paris in Homer's *Iliad*, 67 n 7
Amarna Letters, archive of Akhenaten, king of Egypt, 22–23, 25, 36, 96, 100
Amaw, area in Syria, 99, 99 n 15, 100
Amenemhat I, king of Egypt, 108
Amenmesses, king of Egypt, 130 n 2
Amenophis II, king of Egypt, 99

## Index of Subjects

Amenophis III, king of Egypt, 21, 22, 24, 98
Amenophis IV, king of Egypt also known as Akhenaten, 19, 22–23
amethyst, precious stone, 21
Amman, capital of modern Jordan, 90 n 59
Ammisaduqa, king of Babylon, 23 n 15
Ammonites, people inhabiting Transjordan, 90
Amnisos, town in Crete, 24
Amurru, kingdom in Syria, 52, 56, 66–67, 76 n 31, 79, 92
Anakites, people inhabiting Transjordan, 89
Anatolia, modern Asiatic Turkey, 20, 20 n 3
Andarig, kingdom in Syria, 42
Ankhtifi, local Egyptian governor, 86
Antakya stela, of Assyrian governor Shamshi-ilu, 55 n 27
Apiru, nomadic inhabitants of ancient Canaan, 23 n 12
apodictic law, 71
Apum, kingdom on Turkish/Syrian border, 42
Aqaba, Gulf of, gulf between Sinai peninsula and Arabia, 25
Aqawasha, one of the Sea Peoples, 26, 28
Arabs, 92
Aramaeans, ancient inhabitants of Syria, 28
*Arithmoi*, Greek name for Old Testament book of Numbers, 3
Arcadia, area in Greece, 115
Argob, town in Bashan, 90
Argolis, area in Greece, 115
Argos, city in Greece, 115
Arinna, Hittite cultic centre in vicinity of Hattusas, location unknown, 74, 74 n 26, 75, 88
Aristarchean Vulgate of *Iliad*, 113, 117
Aristarchus of Samothrace, head of library at Alexandria, compiler of standard edition of Homer's *Iliad*, 113, 115 n 43
Aristeas, Letter of, 6 n 25
Aristotle, Greek philosopher, 113 n 32, 127 n 5
Armenians, people living in eastern Anatolia and Transcaucasus, 54 n 21
Arnuwandas I, king of the Hittites, 54, 66, 73, 78
Arpad, kingdom in Syria, 55, 55 n 27, 58, 68, 89
Arzawa, kingdom in W Anatolia, 23, 26–27
Asenath, wife of Joseph, 38
Ashurbanipal, king of Assyria, 58 n 35, 69, 69 n 12, 86 n 48, 92, 131 n 4
Ashur-uballit I, king of Assyria, 24
Asshur, Hebrew form of Assyria, 35
Assur, first capital of Assyria, 42, 58
Assyria, state in northern Mesopotamia (modern Iraq), 19, 23–24, 35, 68–69, 83, 88, 92
Assyrian King List, 24 n 18
Astruc, Jean, Old Testament scholar and critic, 9–10
Atamrum, king of Andarig in Syria, 42
Atar-sumki, king of Arpad in Syria, 55, 68
Aten, god (personification of sun disc) of Amenophis IV, king of Egypt, 19
Athens, 113
Atrahasis, Epic of, work of Mesopotamian literature, 86, 86 n 48, 110 n 18
Attica, area around Athens, 113
aurochs, wild-bull *Bos primigenius* (now extinct), 21 n 7
Authorized Version of the Bible, 100 n 22
Avaris, town in Egyptian Delta, 22 n 8

Avvites, ancient inhabitants of Canaan, 90
Awel-Marduk, king of Babylon, 35 n 13
Aziru, king of Amurru in Syria, 56, 76 n 31, 79
Azzi, region in Anatolia, 61

Baal, king of Tyre 68, 118 n 46
Babel, Tower of, 37 n 21
Babylon, capital of Babylonia in S Mesopotamia (modern Iraq), 23, 42, 60–61, 68, 86
Badakshan, area in NE Afghanistan, 98
Bakır Çayı, river in W Anatolia (=Kaikos) 67 n 6
Balaam, "false prophet" from near the Euphrates in Syria, 98
Bar-Gayah, king of KTK in Syria, 55, 58, 68, 72, 92
basket, of Moses, 1, 96, 122
Beer Lahai Roi, place in Canaan, 32
Beersheba, town in Canaan, 34, 40
Bela, place in Canaan (=Zoar) 32
Bellerophon, a Greek hero, whose story occurs in the *Iliad*, 113
Bentesina, king of Amurru in Syria, 56, 67
Bered, place in Canaan, 32
$b^e$-*rēšît* Hebrew name for book of Genesis meaning "In the beginning", 4
blessings in treaties and covenants, 76–81, 121
blindness, curse of, 83–84
Boğazköy, modern name for Hattusas, the capital of the Hittites, 24, 52
Bomberg edition of the Hebrew Bible, 100 n 21
Book of the Covenant, 8, 49, 53 n 14
*Bos primigenius* wild ox, 21 n 7
Briges, people who migrated into Anatolia, also known as Phrygians, 28 n 35
British Library Pentateuch, 5 n 24

bronze, 82, 85, 112
Bukān 88 n 52
Burnaburiash II, king of Babylon, 23
Büyük Nefesköy, a possible location for Arinna, south of Hattusas, 74 n 26

Calah, city in Assyria, modern Nimrud, 58 n 32
Canaan, conquest of, 7, 23
Canaanite, language, 22
cannibalism, curse of, 84–85
Caphtor, ancient name for Crete, 35, 90
Carchemish, satellite kingdom of the Hittites, centered around site of same name on Turkish-Syrian border, 27, 99
Carter, Howard, English Archaeologist who discovered tomb of Tutankhamun, 19
Carthage, ancient city in modern Tunisia, 118
casuistic law, 71
Catalogue of Ships, section of Homer's *Iliad Book Two*, 115, 115 n 43, 116, 119
Catalogue of the Trojan Allies, section of Homer's *Iliad Book Two*, 115, 115 n 44, 116, 119
cedar, 21
Chaldeans, Semitic people who migrated into S Mesopotamia (Iraq), 33, 42, 45, 112
chiasm, a literary device in which elements are picked up in inverted order, 13, 13 n 50
*chōrizontes* (Gk. separators) the name given to those who believe the *Iliad* and *Odyssey* were written by different authors, 114
Chronology, 2 n 4, 6–7, 7 n 31, 22 n 9, 23 n 15, 24 n 18, 129–31, 130 n 2, 131 n 3, 131 n 4

## Index of Subjects

Cicero, Marcus Tullius, Roman orator, 113, 113 n 32
Cilicia, area in S Anatolia (Turkey), 66 n 2
Clement of Alexandria, early church father, 14 n 53
colophon, note at end of a document detailing contents, 5 n 24, 30 n 3, 49-51, 58 n 36
Colophon, place in W Anatolia (Turkey), 112
Constantinople, capital of Byzantine Empire, modern Istanbul, 20 n 3, 113
Corinth, city in Greece, 115
covenant, definition of, 8 n 35
Crates of Mallos, librarian of Pergamum and Homeric scholar, 113 n 32
Crete, 24, 34, 35, 70, 90 n 57, 105
cuneiform, wedge-shaped writing system used by Assyrians, Babylonians and Hittites, 22, 25, 61, 113 n 31
cuneiform tablets, number of 16 n 57
curses, in treaties and covenants, 77-88, 121
Cyprus, 23-24, 27, 36, 52, 75

D (=Deuteronomist) source, 10-12
Dadusha, king of Eshnunna, 102 n 2
Dan, town in Canaan, 33
Danites, Israelite tribe, 33
Dardanelles, ancient Hellespont, strait separating Asia from Europe, 111 n 23
Darius I, king of Persia, 100
David, king of Israel, 34, 117
Dathan, Israelite rebel, 91
Dead Sea Scrolls 4-5, 117-18
Dead Sea Scrolls, date of, 4 n 21, 5 n 22
Deir-el-Bahri, temple of Queen Hatshepsut, W Thebes, S Egypt, 19

Demodocus, blind bard in Homer's *Odyssey*, 112 n 24
Demotic Laws from Hermopolis, central Egypt, 70, 105
Denyen, one of the "Sea Peoples", 27
Deposit of treaties and covenants, 48, 51, 57, 59, 72, 74-75, 93, 121
Deuteronomic style, 11 n 45
Deuteronomy (book of), 3, 5, 47-48
Deuteronomy, as a covenant document 48
Deuteronomy, compared with Exodus/Leviticus, 51
Deuteronomy, meaning of name, 3
Deuteronomy, vocabulary, 12 n 47
Dibon, place in Moab in modern Jordan, 14 n 53
Diogenes Laertius, Greek writer, 115 n 43
Diomedes, Greek warrior in *Iliad*, 116
Documentary Hypothesis, 9-15, 114, 123-127
Dolon, Trojan spy in *Iliad*, 116
Dophkah, site in Sinai peninsula, perhaps Serabit el-Khadim, 26
Dorian Greeks, 28
Duppi-Tesub, king of Amurru in Syria 66, 76 n 31, 79
Dur-Sharruken, Assyrian city, modern Khorsabad in N Iraq, 58

E or (Elohist) source, 10-12
Ea, Mesopotamian god of freshwater ocean, 62
Eannatum, king of Lagash, 16
Eannatum's Stele of the Vultures, 69, 71 n 17, 86
Ebal, Mount, mountain near Shechem in Palestine, 74
Eblaite language, 16
Ecclesiasticus, book of Apocrypha, 8
Edom, area south of Dead Sea, 35
Edom, List of Rulers of, 35-38

Egyptian language, 1 n 2, 11 n 45, 14 n 53, 16, 20–22, 24–26, 31 n 3, 38, 38 n 24, 52–53, 63, 68 n 9, 73, 80, 80 n 34, 96–97, 100, 108 n 7, 113 n 31, 122

Elam, kingdom in SW Iran, 23, 35

Elamite language, 16

Elisha, a Hebrew name for Cyprus = Alasia, 36

$^e$lōhîm Hebrew word for "God", 14

Emar, city in Syria (Tell Meskene), 109

emerald, precious stone, 98 n 12

Enanna, Sumerian goddess, 110, 110 n 15

Enkidu, friend of Gilgamesh, 110

En-me-baragesi, king of Kish in S Mesopotamia, 109 n 14

En Mishpat, place in Canaan = Kadesh, 32

*enuma eliš* Mesopotamian Creation Epic, 3 n 15

Epilogues in treaties and covenants, 48, 51, 57, 59–60, 88–89

*Erythra Thalassa* = Red Sea (Greek) 2 n 9

Esarhaddon, king of Assyria, 58–59, 68–69, 118 n 46

Esarhaddon, Succession Treaty of, 54 n 23, 58 n 36, 82–86, 82 n 37

Esau, brother of Jacob, 30, 89–90

Eshnunna, Law Collection of, 102–5

Eshnunna, site in Central Mesopotamia, 42, 102, 102 n 1

eunuch, 55 n 27

Evil-Merodach, king of Babylon, 35 n 13

execration (curse) texts, Egyptian, 38

exile, curse of, 86, 87 n D

Exodus (book), 3–5

Exodus (book), meaning of name, 3

Exodus/Leviticus, division not original, 50

Exodus, date of, 7, 7 n 31

Exodus/Leviticus, as a covenant document, compared with Deuteronomy 48–52

explanatory notes in cuneiform texts 32 n 5

Ezra, 10

feldspar, precious stone, 98

Flood Story, 13, 110, 110 n 18

fruit trees, law about, 105

Galeed, name given to a place in Syria, 41, 41 n B

Gaza, city in Canaan, 90

Gebel Barkal, town in Sudan, 25

Gediz, river in W Anatolia (=Hermos), 67 n 6

Genesis, 3–5, 29–46

Genesis, meaning of name, 3

Gershom, son of Moses, 25

Gezer, town in Canaan, 28 n 36

Gibeonites, a Canaanite people, 54 n 22

Gilgamesh, king of Uruk in Mesopotamia, 109

Gilgamesh, Epic of, 3 n 15, 109–11

Gomorrah, city in ancient Canaan, 32

goring ox, laws about, 103–105

Gortyn, town in Crete, 70

Gortyn, Laws from, 70, 70 n 14, 105

Goshen, area in N Egypt, 18, 98

Great Harris Papyrus of Ramesses IV, 27

Greek, language, 3, 3 n B, 4, 6, 8 n 33, 13 n 50, 16, 20 n 2, 24, 29, 67 n 7, 67 n 8, 112

Gürün, town in modern Turkey, 35

Hahhum, area in E Anatolia, 42

Ham, son of Noah, 30–31, 36

Hammurabi, king of Babylon, 23, 42, 60

Hammurabi, Law Collection, 44, 60–62, 69–70, 70 n B, 76, 86, 87 n D, 94, 97, 102–5

Hannibal, Carthaginian leader, 118

## Index of Subjects

Hansen's disease, 91 n 60
Hapalla, kingdom in W Anatolia, 52
haš-šēm (Hebrew) "the Name (of God)"
Hatshepsut, queen of Egypt, 19, 25
Hatti, the Hittites, 26–27, 61, 66–68, 68 n 9, 72, 74, 76, 80–81, 89
Hattusas, capital of the Hittites, modern Boğazköy, 20, 24, 28, 52–53, 61, 74 n 26, 109
Hattusil III, king of the Hittites, 20, 52 n 7, 53, 56, 67–68, 68 n 9, 73, 80
Hayasa, area in N Anatolia, 52, 54, 54 n 21, 56 n 30, 61, 66, 73, 91
Hazor, Laws from, 70, 70 n B
Hebron, town in Canaan, 32, 98
Hermon, mountain in Lebanon/Syria, 90
Hermopolis, Laws from, central Egypt, 70, 105
Hermos, river in W Anatolia (=Gediz) 67 n 6
Herodotus, Greek historian, 28 n 35, 111
hieratic, an Egyptian script, 20, 25, 38 n 23
hieroglyphics, a Hittite script, 113 n 31
hieroglyphics, an Egyptian script, 20, 25, 113 n 31
Hısarlık, modern name of the site of Troy, 111 n 23
Historical Flashback in treaties and covenants, 89–93
Historical Prologues in treaties and covenants, 48, 57, 69
Historical reminiscence, archaeological flashback = Historical Flashback, 89
Hittite, language, 16, 22, 28 n 34, 52, 54 n 19, 55 n 25, 63, 66, 76 n 31, 109, 111 n 23, 113 n 31
Hittite Laws, 70
Hittite treaties, 52–57, 60–61, 66–81, 91–92
Homer, Greek Epic poet, 17, 28, 111–17

Horeb, name of Mount Sinai, 12, 90
Humbaresh, vassal from among the Medes of Esarhaddon, king of Assyria, 54 n 23, 68
Huqqanas, ruler of Hayasa in E Anatolia, 54, 56 n 30, 60, 66, 73
Hurrian language, 22, 22 n 10, 98, 109
Hurrians, see also Mitanni, 72, 78, 98
Hurro-Akkadian dialect, 22
Hypostyle Hall of Temple of Amun, Thebes, S Egypt, 20

Ibal-pi-el, king of Eshnunna in Central Mesopotamia, 42
Idrimi, king of Alalakh in Syria, 52 n 6, 99
Ilgen, Karl David, Old Testament scholar and critic, 10
*Iliad*, Greek Epic poem attributed to Homer, 67 n 7, 111–17
Ilion, alternative name for Troy, 67 n 8, 111 n 23
India, 91 n 60
Indo-European, 24
Ionic, Greek dialect, 112
Ios, Greek island, 112
Ir-Adad, king of Tunip in Syria, 52 n 6, 97
iron, 82, 82 n 36, 85
Isaac, Hebrew patriarch, 29–31, 30 n 3, 40–41, 89
Ischia, Italian island, 112
Ischian jug, citing text of Homer's *Iliad*, 112, 117
Ishmael, son of Abraham, 30–31, 30 n 3
Ishmaelites, 44,
Ishtar, Babylonian goddess of sex and war, 89
Isin, city in S Mesopotamia, 60
Ismirika, area in E Anatolia, 52, 54, 66
Ithaca, Greek island, 112
Iyyar, Assyrian month (April-May), 58 n 36
Izmir, city in modern Turkey, 112

Index of Subjects   165

J or (Jahwist source), 9–10
Jacob, Hebrew patriarch, 29–30, 30 n 2, 30 n 3, 41, 89
Jacob ben Hayim, printer of Hebrew Bible, 101 n 21
Japheth, son of Noah, 30–31, 36
jasper, precious stone, 98
Jebel en-Neba (Mount Nebo), 2 n 11
Jebusites, people inhabiting Jerusalem before Israelite conquest, 43
JEDP Hypothesis (also see Documentary Hypothesis), 9–15, 111 n 22, 123–28
Jegar Sahadutha, name given to a place in Syria, 41, 41 n A
Jehoiachin, king of Judah, 35 n 13
Jehovah, form of YHWH personal name of God, 14 n 53
Jerome (Sophronius Eusebius Hieronymus), 100 n 22
Jerusalem, 4, 96
Jesus', view of Ten Commandments, 8
Jesus, son of Sirach, 8
Jordan, plain of, 32
Joseph, Hebrew patriarch, 29–30, 30 n 2, 33, 95, 122
Josephus, Flavius, Jewish historian writing in Greek, 9
Joshua, Israelite leader, 9, 54 n 22
Josiah, king of Judah, 10
Judah, son of Jacob, 37 n 22

Kadesh, place in Canaan, 32
Kadesh Barnea, place in Sinai peninsula, 89
Kahat, area in Syria, 42, 74
Kaikos, river in W Anatolia (Bakır Çayı), 67 n 6
Kanesh, site in Anatolia, modern Kültepe near Kayseri, 24, 35, 42
Karduniash, a name for Babylonia in Mesopotamia, 72, 72 n 18

Kaskeans, people living in N Anatolia 28, 52–54, 56 n 30, 73, 78
Kassites, name of people who ruled Babylon, 23, 52 n 10
Keftiu, Egyptian name for Crete, 24, 35
Ketef Hinnom amulets, 4, 6, 117
kidnapping, laws about, 102–3
King's Valley, place in Canaan, 32
Kings, books of, 34 n 13
Kiriath-Arba, town in Canaan = Hebron, 32
Kish, city in Central Mesopotamia, 109 n 14
Kizzuwatna, kingdom in S Anatolia, 52, 52 n 6, 55 n 25, 66
Knossos, city in Crete, 24, 34
Kode, classical Cilicia in Anatolia, 27
KTK, kingdom in Syria (pronunciation uncertain), 55, 55 n 27, 58, 68, 72, 92
Kuenen, Abraham, Old Testament scholar and critic, 10
Kültepe, modern name for Kanesh in central Anatolia, 24
Kupanta-Kurunta, king of Mira in W Anatolia, 66, 75
Kurda, place in Syria, 42
Kurunta, king of Hittite satellite kingdom of Tarhuntassa, 55, 67, 74, 81, 92
Kythera, Greek island, 24

Laban, uncle of Jacob, 41
Laish, town in Canaan, later called Dan, 33
lapis lazuli, precious stone, 98
Late Egyptian language, 21, 25, 108 n 7
Law Code, 60 n 38
Law Collection, 60, 60 n 38, 70, 76–77
Lebanon, 2 n 11, 21
"leprosy", 83, 83 n 44, 91, 91 n 60
Leviticus, Dead Sea Scroll, 4
Leviticus, meaning of name, 3, 3 n A
Libya, 27

## Index of Subjects

Linear B, early Greek syllabic script, 34, 113 n 31
Lipit-Ishtar, Law Collection of, king of Isin in S Mesopotamia, 60, 69–70
locusts, as a curse, 84, 84 n 46, 85, 88
LORD, the, 14, 14 n 53
Louvre, museum in Paris, 23
Lucian of Samosata, Greek writer in Roman period, 112 n 25
Lukku, one of the Sea Peoples, 26
Lycia, area in SW Anatolia, 28
Lyktos, town in Crete, 24

Madai, Hebrew name for the Medes, 36
Makir, son of Manasseh, Israelite warrior, 99, 101
malachite, mineral, 21
Mamre, place in Canaan, 32
Manapa-Tarhunta, king of Seha River Land in W Anatolia, 67
manna, 96
Mardin, town in modern Turkey, 24 n 17
Marduk-zakir-shumi, king of Babylon 61
Mari, city in Syria, 35, 42, 44
Maryas, Hittite courtier guilty of sexual indiscretion, 61, 91
Masoretes, Jewish scribes who preserved the text of the Hebrew Bible, 5–6
Masoretic Text 5, 117
Massanuzzi, sister of Muwattalis II, king of the Hittites, 92
Masturi, king of Seha River Land in W Anatolia, 92
Matiel, king of Arpad in Syria, 55, 58, 68, 89
Medes, 28, 36, 58, 68
Medinet Habu, temple of Ramesses III, W Thebes, S Egypt, 21, 27, 34
Megarians, inhabitants of Greek city of Megara, 115 n 43

Megiddo, city in Canaan, 109, 109 n 10
Menzaleh, Lake, salt water lake in N Egypt, 98
Merenptah, king of Egypt, 26
Mes-anne-padda, ruler of Ur in S Mesopotamia, 109 n 14
Meshech, Anatolian people = Mushki, 36
Middle Assyrian Laws, 70
Middle Babylonian language, 52 n 8
Middle Egyptian language, 20–21, 38 n 25, 108 n 7
Midian, area in NE Arabia, 1, 1 n 3, 1 n 4
Midianites, 44
Miletus, city in W Anatolia, 28 n 34
Minoans, name given by archaeologists to the pre-Greek civilization in Crete, 35 n 16
Miriam, sister of Moses, 91
Mira, kingdom in W Anatolia, 52, 66, 75
Mishnah, a codification of oral Jewish law, 8, 8 n 34
Misraim, name in Table of Nations = Egypt, 35
Mitanni, kingdom in eastern Anatolia and northern Syria, 19, 23–24, 24 n 17, 53 n 12, 56 n 29, 57, 66, 71–72, 74–75, 75 n 27, 78
Mizpah, name given to a place in Syria, 41
Mo'alla, place in S Egypt, 86
Moab, Plains of, 55, 95
Moabite Stone, 14 n 53
Moses, death of, 2, 2 n 12, 9, 17–18, 48
Moses, humility of, 99
Moses, name of, 1 n 1, 1 n 2
Motylos, possible echo in Greek of Muwattalis, 67 n 7
Mukish, an area in Syria, 26
Mursil I, king of the Hittites, 23
Mursil II, king of the Hittites, 55–56, 66–67, 68 n 9, 75, 76 n 31, 79, 92

Mursil III, king of the Hittites, 92 n 61
Mushki, Anatolian people = Meshech, 36
Muwatallis II, king of the Hittites, 20, 56, 67, 67 n 7, 76, 76 n 28, 80, 91
Mycenae, city in Greece, 24, 115
Mycenaean Greek language, 34
Mycenaean Greeks, 28, 34 n 28, 112, 117

Nabonidus, king of Babylon, 131 n 4
Nabu-apla-iddina, Babylonian ally of Assyrian king Sin-shar-ishkun, 69
Nabu-bel-usur, Assyrian eponym (official giving his name to the year), 58 n 36
Nahshimarti, town of the Medes in Iran, 54 n 23, 68
Nash Papyrus, liturgical version of Ten Commandments from Egypt, 5, 117
Nauplia, town in Greece, 24
Nebo, mount, site of Moses' death, mountain in Transjordan, overlooking the Promised Land of Canaan, 2, 2 n 11, 18, 48
Nefru, wife of Egyptian king Sesostris I, 108
Nehemiah, 10
Neo-Babylonian Laws, 70, 105
Nestor's cup, 112
"Night Expedition", title sometimes given to 10th book of Homer's *Iliad*, 116
Nimrud, an Assyrian city in N Iraq (ancient Calah), 58
Nineveh, Largest city in Assyria, near Mosul in N Iraq, 58, 86 n 48
Ninurta, Assyrian warrior god, 83
Ninurta-apil-ekur, king of Assyria, 24 n 18, 131 n 3
Niqmad II, king of Ugarit in Syria, 52 n 6, 55, 66

Niqmad III, king of Ugarit in Syria, 52 n 6, 52
Niqmepa, king of Ugarit in Syria, 52 n 6, 55, 66, 76 n 31, 79–80, 97
Noah, 13, 15, 30, 31, 36, 42
Nubia, modern N Sudan, 21, 97
Nuhasse, place in Syria, 66, 66 n 4, 72, 76 n 28, 78
Numbers (book of), meaning of name, 3, 3 n B, 95
Nuzi, site in mountains east of Mesopotamia, in modern Iraq 44

Ockham's razor, 127, 127 n 5
Odysseus, Greek warrior and hero of the *Odyssey*, 111, 116
*Odyssey*, epic poem attributed to Homer, 111–12, 114–15
Og, king of Bashan, 90
Old Assyrian Laws, 70
Origen's Hexapla, parallel text of the Old Testament in six columns (giving several Greek translations) compiled by the early church father Origen of Alexandria, 14 n 53
Orontes, river in Syria, 56 n 28

P for "the Priestly Writer", 10–13
Panathenaic Festival, four yearly festival at Athens, 113
Papyrus Anastasi I, 25 n 24
Paris, Trojan prince, 67 n 7
Parry, Milman, researcher into the oral composition of the Homeric Epics, 112, 115
parsimony, philosophical principle of, 127
Paul, view of Deuteronomy, 8
Pazarcık stela, of Assyrian governor, Shamshi-ilu, 55 n 27
Peisistratus, ruler of Athens 113, 113 n 32, 117

Peleset, one of the Sea Peoples, the Philistines of the Old Testament, 27
Pentatuech, meaning of name, 4
Pergamum, city in Anatolia, 67 n 6, 113 n 32
Persian language, 24, 100
Persians, 28, 100
Peter, view of Deuteronomy, 8
Phaeacians, people visited by Odysseus in the *Odyssey*, 111–12
Phaestos, town in Crete, 24
Philip V, king of Macedonia, 118
Philistines, 27, 33, 34, 122
Phoenicians, people living along the Mediterranean coast of Lebanon and Syria, 112
Phrygians, an Anatolian people, 28 n 35
Pilliya, king of Kizzuwatna in S Anatolia, 52 n 6
Pi-Ramesse, city in N Egypt, 18, 18 n 2
*Pirqê Abōt* (Hebrew) "Sayings of the Fathers", 9
Pithekoussai, Greek colony in bay of Naples, Italy, 112
Pithom, store city built by Israelites in N Egypt, 6, 18, 18 n 1
Polis, place on the Greek island of Ithaca, 112
Polybius, Greek historian, 118–19
Potiphera, priest of On (Heliopolis) in N Egypt, 38, 38 n 25
Priam, king of Troy, 67 n 7
Priestly style writing, 11 n 45
Ptolemy II, Greek king of Egypt, 6
Punt, E Sudan to the Red Sea and parts of Eritrea, 25
Pylos, city in Greece, 34

Qadesh, city in Syria (modern Tell Nebi Mend), 20
Qantir, modern name of Pi-Ramesse, in N Egypt, 18 n 2

Qedar, tribal people living in N Arabia, 58 n 35, 69 n 12, 92
Qen-Amun, an officer of Egyptian king Amenophis II, 99
Qumran, site near Dead Sea, 4 n 21

Rabbah, city now in modern Jordan, 90
Rachel, wife of Jacob 34
Rameses, store city built by Israelites in Egypt, 6, 6 n 27, 18, 33, 45
Ramesses I, king of Egypt 7 n 28, 68 n 9
Ramesses II, king of Egypt, 6, 18 n 2, 20, 20 n 4, 33, 52–53, 52 n 7, 67–68, 68 n 9, 73, 80
Ramesses III, king of Egypt, 21, 27–28, 33
Ramesses IV, king of Egypt 27
Ramesseum, memorial temple of Ramesses II at Thebes, S Egypt, 20, 20 n 4
rape, as a curse, 84–85
Reading the terms of treaties and covenants 75–76
Red Sea 2 n 9
Reed Sea, 2, 2 n 9
Rehoboam, king of Judah 28 n 36
Rephaites, a Canaanite people 43, 90
Rhesus, king of Thrace in *Iliad*, 116
Rhind Mathematical Papyrus, 20 n 6
Rhodes, Greek island, 28 n 34

Salamis, Greek island, 115 n 43
Salt Sea, another name for the Dead Sea, 32
Samaria, capital of northern kingdom of Israel, 87 n D
Samaritans, 14 n 53
Samothrace, Greek island, 113
San el-Hagar, modern name for Zoan (Tanis) in N Egypt 18 n 2
Sanskrit 24, 98 n 12
sapphire, precious stone, 98
Sarah, wife of Abraham 11, 30–31
Sardinia, 28

## Index of Subjects     169

Sarruma, Hittite god, 89
Saul, first king of Israel, 35
Sausga-muwa, king of Amurru in Syria, 67, 92
Schliemann, Heinrich, excavator of Troy 111 n 23
Sea Peoples, 26–28, 33, 58 n 33
Sefire, site in Syria, 58, 58 n 31, 63, 68, 87, 88 n 50, 88 n 51, 89, 92, 121 n B
Seha River Land, kingdom in W Anatolia, 52, 67, 67 n 6, 92
Seir, area south of Dead Sea, 30–31, 89
Sennacherib, king of Assyria, 68–69
Septuagint, Greek translation of Old Testament, 2 n 9, 6, 12 n 53
Serabit el-Khadim, site in Sinai peninsula, perhaps ancient Dophkah, 26
Sesostris I, king of Egypt, 108
Sethos I, king of Egypt, 68, 68 n 9
Shaduppum, ancient name of Tell Harmal in central Mesopotamia, 102 n 1
Shalmaneser III, king of Assyria, Annals of, 32 n 5
Shalmaneser III, king of Assyria, Black Obelisk of, 36 n 20
Shamash, Mesopotamian sun god 76 n 29, 84, 84 n 45
Shamash-shum-ukin, king of Babylon 58 n 34, 58 n 36, 68–69
Shamshi-Adad V, king of Assyria, 61–62
Shamshi-ilu, provincial governor of Assyria, 55 n 27
Shapira W.M and fake scroll of Deuteronomy 6 n 26
Shattiwaza, king of Mitanni 24, 24 n 20, 53 n 12, 56 n 29, 57, 66, 71–72, 74–75, 75 n 27, 78
Shaveh, place in Canaan 32
Sheba, ancient name for Yemen 35
Shechem, town in Canaan, 74

shekel, weight of approximately ten grams, 44, 104, 121
Sheklesh, one of the Sea Peoples, 26
Shem, son of Noah, 30–31, 36
Sherden, one of the Sea Peoples, 27
Shiba, alternative name of Beersheba 34
Shishak, king of Egypt, 28 n 36
Shoshenq I, king of Egypt, 28 n 36
Shubat-Enlil, ancient name for Tell Leilan in Syria, 42
Shutruk-nahhunte, king of Elam, 23, 133 n B
Siamun, king of Egypt, 28 n 36
Sicily 28
Siddim, place in Canaan, 32
Silifke, town in modern Turkey 26
"Simplicity is a sign of truth", 127
Sin, Mesopotamian moon god, 62, 83
Sinai, Mount, 9, 12, 47–49, 55, 89 n 55, 95
Sinai, peninsula / desert, 2, 21, 25–26, 89 n 56
Sin-leqi-unninni, scribe attributed with writing *Epic of Gilgamesh*, 109
Sin-shar-ishkun, king of Assyria, 69
Sinuhe, story of, work of Egyptian Literature, 108
Sippar, city in central Mesopotamia, 133 n B
Sirion, alternative name for Mount Hermon in Lebanon/Syria, 90
Siverek, town in modern Turkey, 54 n 20
slate palettes, Egyptian, 86
Smyrna, city in Anatolia, modern Izmir 112
Sodom, city in ancient Canaan, 32
"Sola scriptura" [Only scripture], 16
Solomon, king of Israel, 34, 117
"sons of God", 15
St. Mark's, Venice, 114
St. Petersburg Codex of Hebrew Bible, 5 n 24

Stephanus Byzantius, Greek writer 67 n 7
stylistic criteria in Documentary Hypothesis, 11–12
Suez, Gulf of 2 n 9
Sumerian King List, 109
Sumerian language, 16, 98, 109, 110 n 18
Sumerian Laws on exercise tablets, 70
Sunassura, king of Kizzuwatna in S Anatolia 55 n 25, 66
Suppiluliuma I, king of the Hittites, 24, 52 n 6, 53 n 12, 54–57, 55 n 25, 56 n 29, 60, 66, 71–75, 76 n 28, 76 n 31, 78–79, 91
Suppiluliuma II, king of the Hittites, 26, 52, 52 n 6, 75
Susa, capital of Elam in SW Iran, 23, 133 n B

Taanach, city in Canaan 38
*Tabarna*, title of Hittite king 66–67
tabernacle, 49
Tabernacles, Feast of, 75
Table of the Nations, 35–37, 116, 123
Talayim, town belonging to kingdom of KTK in Syria, 92
Talmi-sarruma, king of Aleppo in Syria 56, 67, 91
Tamar, daughter-in-law of Judah, 37 n 22
tamarisk, a tree *Tamarix syriaca*, 40
Tanis, city in N Egypt, Hebrew Zoan, 18 n 2, 98
Tarhuntassa, Hittite satellite kingdom in S Anatolia, 27, 27 n 30, 52, 55, 67, 73–75, 81, 88, 92
Tegea, town in Greece, 24 n 21
Tell Asmar, site in central Mesopotamia, ancient Eshnunna, 102 n 1,
Tell el-Amarna, city in central Egypt, ancient Akhetaten, capital of Akhenaten, king of Egypt 22

Tell el-Retaba, city in N Egypt, ancient Pithom, store city built by Israelites in Egypt, 18 n 1
Tell Fekheriyeh, probably ancient Washukkanni, capital of Mitanni, in Syria, 24, 88 n 52
Tell Haddad, site in central Mesopotamia, 133 n A
Tell Harmal, ancient Shuduppum in central Mesopotamia, 102 n 1
Tell Leilan, ancient Shubat-Enlil, in Syria, 42
Tell Meskene, ancient Emar, in Syria 109
Tell Nebi Mend, ancient Qadesh, in Syria, 20
Tello, ancient Girsu, in S Mesopotamia 86
Ten Commandments, 5, 8, 48–49, 71
Tette, king of Nuhasse in Syria, 66, 72, 76 n 28, 76 n 31, 78–79
Thebes, city in S Egypt, 19, 20, 20 n 4, 21, 24, 27, 34, 52–53, 68 n 9, 73
Thebes, Greek city, 24
Theodoret of Cyrrhus, early church father, 14 n 53
"*These are the generations of*" formula, 30–32
Tiglath-pileser I, king of Assyria, 11 n 45, 36, 36 n 19
Tigranes, name for Homer, 112 n 25
Till-Abnu, king of Apum in Syria, 42
Timna, site in Sinai peninsula, N of Gulf of Aqaba, 25
Titles in treaties and covenants, 65–69
Tjekker, one of the Sea Peoples, 27
"*to this day*" 9 n 36, 34, 90, 122
Togarmah, area in central Anatolia, 35
topaz, precious stone, 98 n 12
treaties
  suzerainty, 53
  parity, 53
  vassal, 53
Treaties in Genesis, 39–44

Trojan War, 67 n 7, 111, 115
Troy, ancient city in NW Turkey, 111, 111 n 23
Tubal, place in central Anatolia, 35
Tudkhalia II, king of the Hittites, 55 n 25, 66
Tudkhalia III, king of the Hittites, 55 n 25, 56 n 30
Tudkhalia IV, king of the Hittites, 55, 67, 73–74, 81, 88, 92
Tukulti-Ninurta I, king of Assyria, 11 n 45
Tunip, city in Syria, 52 n 6, 97
Turks 20 n 3
turquoise, precious stone, 21, 97
*turtānu* Assyrian official, army commander, 55 n 27
Tushratta, king of Mitanni, 24 n 17, 66, 98
Tutankhamun, king of Egypt, 19, 22, 22 n 9
Tuthmosis III, king of Egypt, 19, 21

Ugarit, Syrian sea-port city, 11 n 45, 26, 28, 36, 44, 52, 52 n 6, 55, 66, 76 n 31, 79, 109
Ugaritic language, 12 n 46, 16, 52, 63
Ulmi-Tesub, king of Hittite satellite kingdom of Tarhuntassa 55, 73, 75, 81, 88
Uluburun, site of shipwreck off S coast of Turkey, 113 n 31
Ur, of the Chaldeans, birthplace of Abraham in Mesopotamia, 33, 42, 109 n 14, 122
Ur, Standard of, 98
Ura, place in S Anatolia (modern Silifke) 26
Urartian, language, 11 n 45, 22 n 10
Urhi-Tesub, king of the Hittites, also known as Mursil III, 92, 92 n 61
Ur-Nammu, Laws of, king of Ur, 69, 70, 85

Ur-shanabi, the ferryman of Utnapishtim, (the hero of the Flood Story), in *Epic of Gilgamesh*, 110, 110 n 16
Uruk, city in S Mesopotamia, 109, 109 n 9, 110

Valley of the Kings, W Thebes, S Egypt, 19
Vaticanus Urbinas Graecus 102; 118
Venetus Marcianus 822; 114
Venus, planet, 23 n 15, 84
vocabulary preferences in Documentary Hypothesis, 11–12
Vulgate, Latin translation of Bible by Jerome, 100 n 22

Wadi el-Hol, site in S Egypt, 26
Warka, modern name for Uruk in S Mesopotamia, 109 n 9
Washukkanni, capital of Kingdom of Mitanni in Syria 24
Wellhausen, Julius, Old Testament scholar and critic, 10, 10 n 43, 127 n 4
Weshwesh, one of the Sea Peoples, 27
de Wette, Wilhelm Martin Leberecht, Old Testament scholar and critic, 10
William of Ockham, medieval philosopher, 127 n 5
Wilusa, kingdom in NW Anatolia, 52, 67, 67 n 8, 76, 76 n 28, 80, 111 n 23
writing in Homer's *Iliad*, 113
writing in the Pentateuch, 113 n 30

Yahwa, form of YHWH the personal name of God, 14 n 53
Yahweh, the personal name of God 14 n 53
*yam sūp* (Hebrew) Reed Sea 2 n 9
Yamsi-Hadnu, ruler of Kahat in Syria, 42

Yarim-Lim, king of Alalakh in Syria, 43–44
Yauta, rebel of Arabian tribe of Qedar, 92–93
Yemen, 35
YHWH, the personal name of God, 14, 14 n 53

Zababa, Mesopotamian warrior god, 60
Zadok, Israelite High Priest, 7 n 30
Zakutu, queen of Assyria, 58 n 34, 68–69
Zaphenath-Parnea, Egyptian name of Joseph, 38
Zimri-Lim, king of Mari in Syria, 42
Zoan, place in N Egypt, Greek Tanis, 18 n 2, 98, 100, 122
Zoar, place in Canaan, 32

www.ingramcontent.com/pod-product-compliance
Lightning Source LLC
Chambersburg PA
CBHW071515150426
43191CB00009B/1537